GET OUT THE VOTE

GET OUT

HOW TO INCREASE VOTER TURNOUT

THE VOTE

SECOND EDITION

Donald P. Green
Alan S. Gerber

Brookings Institution Press
Washington, D.C.

Copyright © 2008
THE BROOKINGS INSTITUTION
1775 Massachusetts Avenue, N.W., Washington, D.C. 20036
www.brookings.edu

Library of Congress Cataloging-in-Publication data
Green, Donald P., 1961–
Get out the vote : how to increase voter turnout / Donald P. Green and Alan S. Gerber. — 2nd ed.
    p. cm.
Summary: "Expanded and updated edition incorporates data from more than 100 new studies, shedding light on the cost-effectiveness and efficiency of various campaign tactics, including door-to-door canvassing, e-mail, direct mail, and telephone calls. Two new chapters focus on the effectiveness of mass media campaigns and candidate forums and Election Day festivals"— Provided by publisher.
    Includes bibliographical references and index.
    ISBN-13: 978-0-8157-3267-9 (pbk. : alk. paper)
1. Political campaigns—United States. 2. Campaign management—United States. 3. Voting—United States. I. Gerber, Alan S. II. Title.
JK2281.G74 2008
324.70973—dc22   2007048074

9 8 7 6 5 4 3 2 1

The paper used in this publication meets minimum requirements of the American National Standard for Information Sciences—Permanence of Paper for Printed Library Materials: ANSI Z39.48-1992.

Typeset in Life and Univers Condensed

Composition by Cynthia Stock
Silver Spring, Maryland

Printed by R. R. Donnelley
Harrisonburg, Virginia

Contents

Preface

What are the most cost-effective ways to increase voter turnout? Whether the ambition is to win elections, promote civic engagement in a community, or bolster the legitimacy of democratic institutions, this question is of enormous practical significance. Until recently, however, discussions of how best to mobilize voters have been rather unsystematic and short on reliable evidence. Most books on campaign strategy mention the importance of mobilizing voters but focus primarily on how to persuade voters. Training guides for nonpartisan groups tend to walk through a variety of get-out-the-vote techniques without marshaling convincing evidence about their effectiveness.

This book presents a practical guide to managing get-out-the-vote drives, while at the same time pulling together all of the scientific evidence about the cost-effectiveness of face-to-face canvassing, leafleting, direct mail, phone calls, and other tactics. In the decade since our initial field experiment in New Haven in 1998, which compared the effects of nonpartisan face-to-face canvassing, phone calls, and mailings, experimental research on voter mobilization has grown rapidly. Ten election cycles during the period 1998–2007 have furnished a wealth of studies that encompass municipal, state, and federal contests; campaigns run by Democrats, Republicans, interest groups, and nonpartisan coalitions; campaigns targeting populations living in urban, rural, and suburban neighborhoods; and voter mobilization efforts directed at African Americans, Latinos, and Asian Americans. Although many questions remain unanswered, these studies have brought new scientific rigor to the study of campaigns. Unfortunately, most have been published in technical, academic journals, and several scientific reports have never been published at all. This book aims to bring this research to the attention of a broader audience.

We are deeply grateful to the many researchers, candidates, consultants, organizations, and campaign workers who made this line of research possible. Some of the studies reported here were conducted under our direction, but with each passing year, the network of scholars and groups who conduct this type of research grows larger and more diverse. Whereas the first edition of *Get Out The Vote* described a few dozen experiments, this edition summarizes well over 100.

We are indebted to researchers from various universities and organizations, who graciously shared their results with us: Elizabeth Addonizio (Yale University), Kevin Arceneaux (Temple University), Julia Azari (Marquette University), Lisa García Bedolla (University of California, Irvine), Elizabeth Bennion (University of Indiana, South Bend), Daniel Bergan (Michigan State University), Emily Cardy (Yale University), Allison Dale (University of Michigan), Tiffany Davenport (Yale University), Valerie Frey (Yale University), Andra Gillespie (Emory University), James Gimpel (University of Maryland), Jim Glaser (Tufts University), Mark Grebner (Practical Political Consulting), Shang Ha (Yale University), Dean Karlan (Yale University), Robin Kolodny (Temple University), Jon Krasno (Binghamton University), Chris Larimer (University of Northern Iowa), Carrie LeVan (California State University, Bakersfield), Hal Malchow (MSHC Partners), Chris Mann (MSHC Partners), Maggie McConnell (California Institute of Technology), John McNulty (Binghamton University), Melissa Michelson (California State University, East Bay), Joel Middleton (Yale University), Gregg R. Murray (University of Texas, Brownsville), Costas Panagopoulos (Fordham University), Ricardo Ramírez (University of Southern California), Hope Rippeon (State Leagues of Conservation Voters), Daron Shaw (University of Texas, Austin), Betsy Sinclair (University of Chicago), Heather Smith (Rock the Vote), Alissa Stollwerk (Yale University), Aaron Strauss (Princeton University), Santiago Suárez (Yale University), Neema Trivedi (Harvard Law School), Lynn Vavreck (University of California, Los Angeles), Ebonya Washington (Yale University), and Janelle Wong (University of Southern California). We are especially indebted to David Nickerson (University of Notre Dame), who has played such a central role in the growth and development of field experimental studies of voter turnout.

Special thanks go to the campaigns and organizations that allowed us to study their voter mobilization efforts. Organizations such as the Association of Community Organizations for Reform Now (ACORN), the League of Conservation Voters, the National Association of Latino Elected Officials (NALEO), the National Voter Fund of the National Association for the Advancement of Colored People, the New Voters Project, People for the American Way, the Public Interest Research Group, Rock the Vote, Strategic Concepts in Organizing and Policy Education (SCOPE), Southwest Voter Registration and Education Project, Votes For Students, the Youth Vote Coalition, Texans for Rick Perry, and several partisan campaigns that asked to remain anonymous deserve the gratitude of all those who will learn from their experiences.

Generous financial support for our research and research conducted jointly with our collaborators has come from a variety of sources. The Smith Richardson Foundation funded our first studies in 1998. The Pew Charitable Trusts invited us to evaluate the Youth Vote campaign in 2000 and the New Voters Project in 2004. A grant from CIRCLE at the University of Maryland made possible our 2001 and 2002 studies of Youth Vote and Votes For Students. The Carnegie Foundation funded research we conducted with Lynn Vavreck on the effects of Rock the Vote's 2004 television campaign. In 2006 and 2007 the James Irvine Foundation sponsored field experiments associated with its California Votes Initiative that Melissa Michelson and Lisa García Bedolla conducted with Donald Green. Working Assets funded a series of experiments that Donald Green conducted with Elizabeth Addonizio, James Glaser, and Costas Panagopoulos in 2006 assessing the effects of Election Day festivals and radio advertisements publicizing mayoral and congressional elections. In 2006 the JEHT Foundation funded the creation of a website that provides a clearinghouse for randomized experiments on voter turnout, a resource that proved invaluable as we assembled the material for this book. We wish to thank Mark Steinmeyer (Smith Richardson), Tobi Walker (Pew), Peter Levine and Mark López (Center for Information and Research on Civic Learning and Engagement, CIRCLE), Geri Mannion (Carnegie), Latonya Slack and Amy Domínguez-Arms (James Irvine), Kristin Engberg (JEHT), and Becky Bond, Sarah Clusen Buecher, and Michael Kieschnick (Working Assets) for their support and encouragement. We are grateful as well to the Institution for Social and Policy Studies at Yale University, which provided research funding, a home for our sprawling projects, and a superb administrative staff. None of these funders, of course, bears any responsibility for the conclusions we draw.

Finally, we wish to express our gratitude to Tiffany Davenport, Beth Weinberger, Shang Ha, and Terence Leong. Tiffany assembled and organized the burgeoning experimental literature reviewed in this book and conducted a series of meta analyses that guide its conclusions. Beth, who played such an important role in crafting and editing the first edition, contributed enormously to the new chapters and updated material. Shang and Terence played a valuable role in analyzing data and checking results. The new edition reflects the skill and devotion that they brought to this project.

The first edition of *Get Out The Vote* earned a spot on the bookshelves of people from across the political spectrum. From our frequent correspondence with readers, we know that this book is read closely and that important decisions are informed by its conclusions. We take very seriously the charge of evaluating the experimental literature and presenting it in an accessible and accurate manner. Although many of the conclusions of the first edition are bolstered by the addition of dozens of new experiments, some need revision. Certain topics about which the first edition could only speculate are now addressed with hard evidence. The second edition of *Get Out The Vote* features two new chapters. The first deals with campaign events such as festivals, debates, and instructional seminars. The second discusses the effectiveness of mass media campaigns. The final chapter expands its description of how to conduct your own experiment, in light of the many in-house experiments that readers of the first edition have conducted. The mission of this book—to put the understanding of voter mobilization on firmer scientific footing—is best realized when campaigns understand the experimental method and how it can be used to address the practical decisions they confront.

GET OUT THE VOTE

CHAPTER ONE

Introduction:
Why Voter Mobilization Matters

The United States has the busiest election calendar on earth. Thanks to the many layers of federal, state, and local government, Americans have more opportunities to vote each decade than Britons, Germans, or Japanese have in their lifetime. Thousands of Americans seek elective office each year, running for legislative, judicial, and administrative posts.

Given the frequency with which elections occur and the mundane quality of most of the contests, those who write about elections tend to focus exclusively on the high-visibility contests for president, senator, or governor. This focus gives a distorted impression of how election battles are typically waged. First, high-profile races often involve professionalized campaigns, staffed by a coterie of media consultants, pollsters, speechwriters, and event coordinators. Second, in order to reach large and geographically dispersed populations, these campaigns often place enormous emphasis on mass communications, such as television advertising. Third, the importance of these races calls press attention to the issues at stake and the attributes of the candidates.

The typical election, by contrast, tends to be waged on a smaller scale and at a more personal level. Few candidates for state representative or probate judge have access to the financial resources needed to produce and air television commercials. Even long-standing incumbents in state and municipal posts are often unknown to a majority of their constituents. The challenge that confronts candidates in low-salience elections is to target potential supporters and get them to the polls, while living within the constraints of a tight campaign budget.

A similar challenge confronts political and nonpartisan organizations that seek to mobilize voters for state and local elections. Making scarce campaign dollars go as far as possible requires those who manage these campaigns to think hard about the trade-offs. Is it best to assemble a local phone bank? Hire a telemarketing firm? Field a team of canvassers to contact voters door-to-door? Send direct mail and, if so, how many pieces of direct mail?

This book offers a guide for campaigns and organizations that seek to formulate cost-effective strategies for mobilizing voters. For each form of voter mobilization, we pose two basic questions: (1) What steps are needed to put it into place, and (2) How many votes will be produced for each dollar spent? After summarizing the "how to do it" aspects of each get-out-the-vote (GOTV) tactic, we provide an impartial, scientifically rigorous assessment of whether it has been shown to produce votes in a cost-effective manner. We discuss some high-tech campaign tactics, such as voter mobilization through e-mail, some low-tech tactics, such as old-fashioned Election Day festivals, and some high-priced tactics, such as television, radio, and newspaper advertising. The concluding chapter discusses the uncharted frontiers of GOTV research and guides readers through the process of conducting their own experiments to evaluate the effectiveness of their campaigns.

Does Voter Mobilization Matter?

The sleepy quality of many state and local elections often conceals what is at stake politically. Take, for example, the 1998 Kansas State Board of Education election that created a six-to-four conservative majority. This election featured a well-organized campaign that used personal contact with voters to mobilize hundreds of churchgoers in low-turnout Republican primaries. This victory at the polls culminated a year later in a dramatic change in policy. In August 1999, the Kansas State Board of Education voted six to four to drop evolution from science education standards, letting localities decide whether to teach creationism in addition to or instead of evolution. The story of hard-fought campaigns for the Board of Education does not end there. In 2000 moderates regained the majority and reinstated evolution into the science education standards. The 2002 election resulted in a five-five split between moderates and conservatives, and 2004 put conservatives back in control of the

Board of Education. The conservative majority approved the teaching of intelligent design as an alternative to evolution (which could now be taught as a theory but not a scientific fact). Power switched once again in 2006, and moderates repealed science guidelines questioning evolution.

These elections and their policy implications attracted national attention and renewed debates about science curricula and religious conviction. But what occurred in Kansas is a story not only about clashing ideologies but also about how campaigns work to get voters to the polls. We suspect that very few Kansans changed their mind about the merits of evolution and creationism over the course of these election cycles. What changed in 1998—and in each of the following elections, as mobilization and countermobilization campaigns caused conservatives and then moderates to lose their majority—was who showed up to vote.

Although Americans often take a cynical view of state and local elections, supposing that who fills a given office makes no difference, the Kansas example is not as exceptional as it may seem. During the 1960s, the U.S. Supreme Court struck down many states' system of legislative representation as inconsistent with the principle of "one man, one vote." Before the Supreme Court's rulings, several states assigned equal representation to all counties, which meant that rural voters were heavily overrepresented in proportion to their share of the population. Once state legislatures were reorganized according to the "one man, one vote" principle, the share of government funds flowing to rural counties dropped dramatically.[1] Voting power matters. When groups such as conservative Christians or elderly Americans vote in large numbers, policymakers have an incentive to take their concerns seriously. By the same token, elected officials can afford to disregard groups who vote at low rates, such as southern blacks before the Voting Rights Act in 1965. Largely excluded from the electorate by racially biased voter registration practices, southern blacks saw their needs for schooling, transportation, and jobs go unheeded by state and local government.

The Kansas State Board of Education elections also illustrate the power of small numbers in elections where turnout is low. The ability to mobilize a few hundred supporters can prove decisive when only a few thousand votes are cast. Given that five congressional elections were decided by fewer than a thousand votes in 2006, knowing what it takes to generate votes can be extremely valuable. It can be valuable not only for a specific candidate conducting the voter mobilization campaign but also for all of the candidates who share similar party labels. Mobilizing

500 Republicans to support the GOP nominee in a state assembly race furnishes votes for Republican candidates up and down the ticket.

Even when turnout is high, as in presidential elections, the capacity to mobilize large numbers of voters can be decisive. The 2004 election marked a turning point in presidential campaign strategy. Before 2004, presidential contenders sought to persuade undecided voters. In 2004 both major candidates' campaigns, sensing that the electorate had largely made up its mind, poured unprecedented resources into voter mobilization in so-called "battleground" states. Roving armies of canvassers went door-to-door, while vast numbers of callers implored battleground residents to come out to vote in support of a candidate. According to the National Election Study survey, voters in battleground states were more likely to report having been visited or called by the campaigns in 2004 than in any previous national election going back to 1948. Although the impact of this activity on the ground is hard to measure precisely, it appears to have contributed significantly to the dramatic surge in voter turnout in battleground states that occurred between 2000 and 2004.[2]

Getting Advice on Getting Out the Vote

Campaigns vary enormously in their goals: some are partisan, some nonpartisan; some focus on name recognition, some on persuasion, and some on mobilizing their base of loyal voters. Some campaigns seek to educate citizens, some to register citizens, and some to motivate citizens. But varied as they are, campaigns have important and obvious commonalities. As Election Day approaches and campaigns move into GOTV mode, their aims become quite similar and their purposes very narrow. By the week before the election, they are all homing in on one simple task: to get their people to the polls. Each campaign struggles with the same basic challenge: how to allocate remaining resources in order to turn out the largest number of targeted voters.

Ask around and you will receive plenty of advice on the best way to mobilize voters in those final days or weeks. You may hear that it is one part mailings to three parts phone calls for an incumbent race. You may hear that, regardless of the office, you should build your campaign around phone calls and, if you can afford it, buy radio airtime. You may even hear that, for a nonpartisan GOTV campaign, you should try door-to-door canvassing, but fall back on leafleting if you run short on campaign workers. Almost all this advice is based on conjecture—conjecture' drawn from experience perhaps, but conjecture nonetheless (see box 1-1).

Box 1-1. Dubious Evidence

Many campaign services can be purchased from private vendors. These vendors often present evidence about the effectiveness of their products in the form of testimonials. Here is one example from the website of a leading commercial phone bank:

> On June 5, Election Day in Los Angeles, at 5 p.m. EST, [our phone bank] received a telephone call from the James Hahn for Mayor campaign. Voter turnout was heavy in precincts of his opponent, and the Hahn campaign had to get out more of his voters.
>
> In one hour, [our phone bank] had perfected a script, manipulated voter data to match phone numbers, and programmed the calls. By the time the polls closed, our firm had placed 30,000 live GOTV calls and reached 10,000 targeted voters.
>
> James Hahn was elected mayor with almost 54 percent of the vote.

For all we know, this phone bank did a splendid job of mobilizing voters. And, in fairness, this firm does not claim credit for Hahn's 54 percent share of the vote; the fact is simply allowed to speak for itself.

When reading this type of testimonial, it is important to bear in mind that *there is no control group.* How many votes would Hahn have won had his campaign not conducted this eleventh-hour calling campaign?

It is also useful to keep things in proportion. This phone bank spoke with 10,000 voters, but Hahn won the election by a margin of 38,782 votes.

What sets this book apart from the existing "how to win an election" canon is a decade of rigorous scientific research. The studies reported in this book use a *randomized experimental design,* which is a research methodology that produces a reliable way to gauge effects—in this case, the effects of GOTV interventions. In a nutshell, the experiments we describe divide lists of registered voters into a group that receives the intervention in question and a group that does not. After the election is over, researchers examine public records to see who voted and then tabulate the results in order to determine whether those assigned to receive the GOTV treatment voted at higher rates than those assigned to the control group. Although these field experiments still leave room for interpretation, they go a long way toward replacing speculation with evidence (see box 1-2).

Another aspect of our work that contributes to our objectivity is that we are not in the business of selling campaign services. In the past, scanning for truth about the effectiveness of various GOTV strategies was like having to consult with salespeople about whether or not to purchase the items they are selling. Many campaign consultants have financial interests in direct mail companies, phone banks, or media consultancy services. In this book, we make a concerted effort to incorporate the results of *every* experimental study, not just the ones that are congenial to a particular campaign's style.

Two constraints of this work must be acknowledged at the outset. First, high-profile campaigns, such as U.S. Senate races or presidential races, have rarely conducted experiments. Although we believe that the findings discussed here are relevant to such large-scale campaigns insofar as they rely on GOTV tactics such as phone banks or direct mail, we have only recently begun to conduct experiments that speak directly to the effectiveness of mass media, on which these large-scale campaigns rely heavily.[3]

Second, although they are of obvious importance, GOTV strategies are not the only factors at play in an election. When we speak of the effectiveness of GOTV techniques, we have in mind the percentage *increase* in voter turnout that can be attributed to professional phone callers or direct mail, for instance. Using the most effective get-out-the-vote strategy will not guarantee victory. All the other factors that shape the electoral fortunes of a candidate—persona, platform, party, and campaign management—are relevant as well. A spectacularly successful GOTV campaign might lift an overmatched candidate from 28 to 38 percent or a competitive candidate from 48 to 58 percent. Often, winning elections is possible only when voter mobilization strategies are combined with messages that persuade voters to vote in a particular way (see box 1-3).

GOTV Research and Larger Questions about Why People Do Not Vote

Political observers often turn to broad-gauge explanations for why so few Americans vote: alienation from public life, the lack of a proportional representation system, the failings of civic education, the geographic

Box 1-2. Dubious Analysis

One enticing but misleading way to analyze cost-effectiveness is to compute the rate of spending per vote. A recent article in *Campaigns & Elections* magazine illustrates this style of analysis:[1]

> For George W. Bush and John Kerry in 2004, for example, just spending a few extra cents per voter paid off. Kerry averaged $5.56 per vote and lost. Bush spent $5.92 for each of his 62,040,606 votes and now calls Camp David a family vacation spot.

This calculation mistakenly assumes that the candidates would have received no votes had they not spent any money and that their expenditures caused them to win all of the votes they eventually received. This is obviously absurd. In order to estimate the effects of spending "a few extra cents per voter," one must first conduct some kind of controlled comparison—such as an experiment—that measures outcomes for similar electorates that were treated with different amounts of campaign spending.

1. Brittney Pescatore, "Hey Big Spender: Here's What It Costs to Buy Those Votes," *Campaigns & Elections* (September 2007): 13.

mobility of the population. We might call these long-term—very long-term—GOTV considerations. Many books written by academics focus exclusively on these explanations.

This book, in contrast, is concerned with GOTV considerations in the short term. We do not discuss the ways in which political participation is shaped by fundamental features of our political, social, and economic system, although we agree that structural and psychological barriers to voting are worthy of study and that certain large-scale reforms might raise turnout. In the concluding chapter, we describe research that might be useful to those interested in learning more about how voter turnout relates to these broader features of society. The focus of this book is quite different. Our aim is to look closely at how GOTV campaigns are structured and to figure out how various GOTV tactics affect voter participation. This close-to-the-ground approach is designed to provide campaigns with useful information about the effectiveness of common

Box 1-3. Generating Votes: Mobilization versus Persuasion

In order to see how GOTV fits into campaign strategy, imagine that you are a Republican candidate running for local office. There are 8,000 registered voters, and Election Day is approaching. The 2,000 registered Republicans favor you 80 versus 20 percent, but ordinarily only half of them vote. The remaining 6,000 people in the electorate favor your opponent 67.5 versus 32.5 percent; one-third of them can be expected to vote. So, with 800 votes from registered Republicans and 650 from the rest of the electorate, you are in danger of losing 1,450 to 1,550:

	Voters		Nonvoters	
Intent	Registered Republicans	Others	Registered Republicans	Others
Intend to vote for you	800	650	800	1,300
Intend to vote for your opponent	200	1,350	200	2,700

Thinking about how to win in this situation is really a matter of thinking about where to find at least 100 *additional* votes. All the factors that got you those 1,450 votes—your good looks, your record in office, and so forth—are important in shaping the eventual outcome of the election, but the strategic decisions from this point forward must focus on what you will do now to change the expected outcome.

A GOTV strategy aims to transform nonvoters into voters. If you can identify the 2,100 abstainers who would vote for you, try to get at least 100 of them to the polls. Voter identification (ID) programs use brief polls to identify these potential supporters, who will later be targeted for mobilization.

Voter ID programs require planning and money, however. A simpler approach is to focus GOTV attention solely on Republicans. Bear in mind that if you attempt to mobilize some of the 1,000 Republicans who otherwise would not vote, you will need to get at least 167 to the polls because you only gain sixty net votes for every 100 Republicans you mobilize.

Conversely, a demobilization strategy strives to transform voters into nonvoters. You could accomplish this by scaring or demoralizing some of the 1,550 people who would otherwise cast votes for your opponent.

Finally, a persuasion strategy attempts to convert some of these 1,550 voters into your supporters. Conversions rapidly close the margin of votes between you and your opponent. Just fifty successes would make the race a dead heat. It is also possible to blend persuasion and mobilization strategies, for example, by appealing to the 2,000 Republicans in ways that both mobilize and persuade them. By focusing solely on voter mobilization, this book understates the number of net votes generated by tactics that simultaneously mobilize and persuade.

GOTV techniques. With six weeks until an election, even the most dedicated campaign team will not be able to reshape the country's culture and basic constitutional framework. What a campaign can do, however, is make informed choices about its GOTV plans, ensuring that its resources are being used efficiently to produce votes.

Evidence versus War Stories

Before delving into the research findings, we want to call attention to a cluster of assumptions that often hinder informed GOTV decisionmaking. One is the belief that the experts know what works. People who have worked with a lot of campaigns are assumed to know which tactics work and which do not. On the other end of the spectrum is the assumption that no one really knows what works because no one can adequately measure what works. There is no way to rerun an election using different GOTV methods, no parallel universe in which to watch the very same campaign focusing its efforts on mass mailings, then on phone banks, and then on television ads. The final assumption is that if everybody is doing it, it must be useful: 5,000 campaigners can't be wrong about prerecorded calls!

The following chapters respond to these misguided assumptions. In short,

✔ Experts, be they consultants, seasoned campaigners, or purveyors of GOTV technology, rarely measure effectiveness. Hal Malchow, one of the few consultants to embrace experimentation, reports that his calls for rigorous evaluation often go unheeded. Notwithstanding the large quantities of money at stake, Malchow observes, "No one really knows how much difference mail and phone GOTV programs make."[4]

✔ Experts may report speculations in the guise of "findings," but without a rigorous research design, those "findings" are suspect. People who manage campaigns and sell campaign services have a wealth of experience in deploying campaign resources, formulating campaign messages, and supervising campaign staff. But lacking a background in research design or statistical inference, they frequently misrepresent (innocently in many cases) correlation as causation. They might claim, for instance, that a radio GOTV campaign is responsible for increasing the Latino vote in a particular media market. In support of this assertion, they might point to the lack of change in the Latino vote in a neighboring media market. Because it is difficult to know whether the two media markets are truly comparable, this form of proof-by-anecdote is dubious and potentially quite misleading.

✔ There *is* an accurate way to measure the effectiveness of GOTV techniques, namely, through experimental research. Randomly assigning a set of precincts or media markets to different campaign tactics makes meaningful causal inferences possible.

✔ Lastly, our results may surprise you. Just because everybody is doing it does not necessarily mean that it works. It appears that large sums of money are routinely wasted on ineffective GOTV tactics.

We will count ourselves successful if you not only learn from the experimental results we report but also become more discerning when evaluating claims that rest on anecdotes and other nonexperimental evidence. The recurrent theme of this book is the importance of adopting a scientific attitude when evaluating campaign tactics.

Preview of Our Findings

The Kansas State Board of Education election mentioned at the outset of this chapter illustrates the central finding of voter turnout research: *A personal approach to mobilizing voters is usually more successful than an impersonal approach.* That is, the more personal the interaction between campaign and potential voter, the more it raises a person's chances of voting. Door-to-door canvassing by friends and neighbors is the gold-standard mobilization tactic; chatty, unhurried phone calls seem to work well, too. Automatically dialed, prerecorded GOTV phone calls, by contrast, are utterly impersonal and, evidently, wholly ineffective at getting people to vote.

Here is the trade-off confronting those who manage campaigns: the more personal the interaction, the harder it is to reproduce on a large scale. Canvassing door-to-door is therefore not the answer for every GOTV campaign. That is why we consider this book to be a "shoppers' guide." No candidate or campaign manager can read this book and, without considering his or her own circumstances, find the answer. The key is to assess your resources, goals, and political situation and then form a judgment about what tactics will produce the most votes at the lowest cost. What we do is provide a synopsis of scientifically rigorous evidence about what has worked in other campaigns.

Structure of the Book

We begin the book by explaining why experimental evidence warrants special attention. Chapter 2 discusses the nuts and bolts of how randomized experiments are conducted and why they are better than other approaches to studying the effectiveness of GOTV tactics. Chapters 3 through 9 present our evaluations of GOTV mobilization techniques: door-to-door canvassing, leaflets, mail, phone calls, e-mail, campaign events, and communication through the mass media. These chapters discuss the practical challenges of conducting these campaigns and provide a cost-benefit analysis of each GOTV tactic. Chapter 10 wraps up by discussing some of the many unanswered questions in GOTV research. In the interest of helping you to customize research for your own purposes, the concluding chapter also gives some pointers about how to conduct experimental studies of voter turnout. The experimental study of voter mobilization is not some special form of sorcery known only to Yale professors. Anyone can do it, and several innovative experiments have been conducted by readers of the first edition of this book. We close by discussing the role that scientifically rigorous GOTV research may play in encouraging voter participation.

CHAPTER TWO

Evidence versus Received Wisdom

I t is not hard to find advice about how to run an effective get-out-the-vote campaign. The Democratic National Committee recommends, "If your GOTV resources allow you to do only one thing, do telephones. Telephones offer the greatest coverage with the smallest expenditure of resources."[1] In a rare show of bipartisan agreement, the Republican National Committee concurs that "Election Day phoning can often mean the difference between victory and defeat" but also explains to its organizers that "tried and true methods of street campaigning where candidates 'press the flesh' in door-to-door activity, voter blitzes, business tours, in-home receptions, and the like are especially effective in state legislative and local campaigns."[2] A local chapter of the Green Party emphasizes a rather different GOTV strategy: "Depending on your budget, mailers are often one of the best ways to help get out the vote." More specifically it suggests, "One or two mailers are generally adequate, with the final one coming in the mail two or three days before the election."[3] The litany of advice can easily be expanded to include prerecorded messages delivered by phone (so-called robotic, or robo, calls), leafleting (lit drops), and e-mail, as well as special combinations of phone and mail that are said to have synergistic effects.

Direct mail, phone calls, and precinct walking all sound like good campaign tactics, and a campaign with an infinite supply of time and money would use them all. But here on planet earth campaigns face budget constraints. So the question is not, What are some helpful campaign tactics? but rather, What are the most cost-effective campaign tactics?

Box 2-1. Thinking about Cost-Effectiveness

When thinking about the cost-effectiveness of a get-out-the-vote tactic, it is helpful to ask, How many dollars will it take to produce one additional vote? This yardstick will help you to compare the cost-effectiveness of various types of GOTV tactics. One tactic might produce votes at a rate of $40 per vote; another, at $75 per vote.

Keep three things in mind as you read our assessments of cost-effectiveness. First, some tactics, such as robotic calls, generate votes cheaply insofar as they give a tiny nudge to vast numbers of people. If your constituency does not have vast numbers of people, these tactics might be useless to you—even if they were free! Second, the costs and benefits we report in the chapters that follow are calculated based on the experiences of particular campaigns. A campaign that goes door-to-door to mobilize voters might successfully contact every fourth person and generate votes at a rate of $29 per vote. This finding says something about the efficiency of that type of campaign, but it might not provide an accurate assessment of what would happen if your canvassers returned repeatedly to each house in an effort to contact three out of four voters. The cost of returning to each house might prove prohibitive, but the harvest of additional votes might offset the cost. It is hard to say. Be cautious when extrapolating to campaigns that are very different from the ones we have studied. Finally, special considerations sometimes come into play when assessing campaign costs. Depending on the specific campaign finance laws under which you are operating, you might have special financial incentives to spend dollars on one campaign tactic rather than another. Or you might know someone in the printing or telemarketing business willing to offer you a great deal. It is important to read the fine print of how we are calculating our cost-efficiency estimates so that you can tailor them to your particular situation.

In order to know whether a campaign tactic is cost-effective, it is necessary to determine how many votes are produced for each dollar spent (see box 2-1). Most firms and organizations that offer campaign services or recommend campaign tactics have a fairly clear idea about the costs involved. Those experienced in running campaigns know the approximate unit cost of each mailer or phone call, the hourly rates of canvassers and supervisors, and the setup costs of producing literature and supervising these campaign operations. Indeed, one of the reasons that campaign professionals are valuable is that they possess an immense amount of knowledge about what it takes to execute a campaign. Seasoned campaign veterans know a great deal about the *inputs,* but they seldom possess reliable information about the *outputs*: the number of votes that these tactics produce.

Campaign professionals and candidates frequently tell war stories about the mailers that Candidate X distributed before winning a big upset victory or how Candidate Y squandered her big lead in the polls by failing to mobilize her base. These anecdotes do not enable you to isolate the influence of any particular input. They simply encourage you to imagine a world in which the campaign behaved differently, while everything else about the campaign remained the same. The skeptic might well wonder, Was Candidate X's victory really due to mailers? Might something about Candidate Y have caused her campaign to run into trouble other than her alleged problems in mobilizing her core supporters?

The problem of drawing sound conclusions from anecdotes persists even when campaign veterans are equipped with many, many war stories and perhaps even a statistical analysis to boot. It is sometimes quipped that the word "data" is plural for "anecdote." Suppose that voter turnout rates tend to be higher in districts where campaigns spend unusually large sums on professional phone banks. What would this say about the influence of phone banks on voter turnout? Not a whole lot. It could be that the same forces that bring a lot of money into campaigns—such as a tight race for an important office—are the very things that attract voter interest. We might observe a correlation between turnout and expenditures on professional phone banks even if calls from phone banks have no effect whatsoever on voter turnout.

Even fancy statistical analysis of survey data or historical voting patterns cannot overcome the basic principle that correlation is not causation. Suppose that you ask survey respondents to describe whether they were called by a campaign and whether they voted. The correlation between these two reports may be quite misleading. First, to put it politely, respondents may "inaccurately recall" whether they were contacted and whether they voted. Those who wish to present themselves as politically involved may be more likely to indicate both that they were contacted and that they voted. Second, campaigns often target likely voters. Even if canvassing had no effect, your survey would still reveal higher voting rates among the folks who were contacted. That is *why* they were contacted. Statistical fixes cannot resolve these problems without relying on untestable assumptions about response error and the targeting strategies used by campaigns. Complex statistical analysis creates a fog that is too often regarded as authoritative. When confronted with reams of impressive sounding numbers, it is easy to lose sight of the weak research design that produced them.

The situation is no better when scholars assemble historical data on voter turnout and attempt to tease out the effects of campaign tactics by "holding constant" various background factors. Suppose that voter turnout rates were unusually high in areas canvassed by labor unions. Does this pattern mean that canvassing increased turnout or that labor unions deployed their canvassers in areas with unusually high turnout?

The rigorous scientific study of voter mobilization requires something more than trends and correlations. It requires a method for making valid comparisons between instances where a campaign tactic was or was not used. It requires a method for establishing that the people who were canvassed, phoned, or mailed were just like those who were left alone. Only one procedure ensures a fair comparison, and that is random assignment. Flip a coin to decide whether each person will be exposed to some form of "treatment" or instead assigned to a control group. Since every person has the same chance of getting into the treatment group, there will be no systematic tendency for the treatment group to contain a disproportionate number of frequent voters. As the number of people in the study increases, chance differences in the composition of the treatment and control groups will tend to disappear. When thousands of people are randomly assigned to treatment and control groups, experiments enable researchers to form a precise assessment of a treatment's impact.

What sets this book apart is that its conclusions about which campaign tactics work are based on evidence from randomized experiments. The remainder of this chapter provides an overview of how and where these experiments were conducted. If you are eager to hear about the conclusions of these studies, you may wish to skip this chapter and move on to chapter 3, but we encourage you to acquire at least some passing familiarity with experimental research. The more you understand about these studies, the easier it will be for you to recognize the strengths and limitations of the results when applying them to your own situation. Who knows? You may even be inspired to launch your own experiment.

Randomized Experiments

Randomized experimentation is the tool often used in medical research to gauge the effectiveness of new medications or treatment protocols.

The reason is simple: in medical research, the stakes are enormous. Lives hang in the balance and so do billions of dollars in pharmaceutical sales. In order to prevent profit-driven companies from exaggerating the claims of their products, the Food and Drug Administration maintains a very high standard of scientific rigor when evaluating new treatments.

Compared with the world of pharmaceuticals, the world of elections is free-wheeling and unregulated. No government agency demands that consultants furnish proof to back up their claims about the effectiveness of campaign tactics. Randomized experiments are therefore about as rare in politics as successful third-party candidates.

Recognizing the importance of obtaining reliable evidence about how to increase voter turnout, we have made extensive use of randomized experimentation since 1998, and our work has inspired others to conduct experiments of their own. In all, more than 100 experiments have been conducted at various points in the electoral calendar: presidential elections, federal midterm elections, state off-year elections, municipal elections, runoff elections, and party primaries. Some of these studies have taken place in states with traditional voting systems (such as New York), while others have occurred in early-voting states (Colorado) or in vote-by-mail-only states (Oregon). These get-out-the-vote campaigns have taken place in areas as different as Detroit, Eugene, Houston, and the rural outskirts of Fresno. (Recently, in fact, GOTV experiments have been conducted in China, England, India, Japan, and Poland.) Many of these experiments have involved nonpartisan efforts to get people to the polls; some, however, have studied attempts by partisan campaigns to both mobilize and persuade voters.

Despite these differences, the randomized studies of voter turnout discussed in this volume have a common structure, which consists of six components.

✔ A population of observations is defined. This population includes all the people or geographically defined groups whose actions will be measured (whether they are exposed to a GOTV intervention or not). Most studies draw their sample from lists of registered voters, although a few studies draw samples from lists of streets or precincts or media markets.

✔ The observations are *randomly* divided into a treatment and a control group. Random assignment has a very specific meaning in this context. It does not refer to haphazard or arbitrary assignment. Special care is taken to ensure that every observation has the same chance of being assigned to the treatment group. In its most basic form, random assignment can be accomplished by flipping a coin for each individual, and assigning all those who receive "heads" to the treatment group. In practice, random assignment is performed using a computerized random number generator.

✔ An intervention is applied to persons in the treatment group. For example, members of the treatment group may be sent mail encouraging them to vote.

✔ The outcome variable is measured for those in each group. In the studies we discuss, voting is measured by examining public records, *not* by asking people whether they voted. The percentage of people in the treatment group who voted is then compared to the percentage in the control group who voted.

✔ The difference in voting rates is subjected to statistical analysis. The aim is to determine how much uncertainty remains about the true effect of the intervention. The larger the study (that is, the greater the number of observations assigned to treatment and control groups), the less uncertainty will remain after the experiment is analyzed. Statistical analysis also takes into account one of the annoying facts about both campaigning and experimenting: sometimes it is not possible to reach the people being targeted. If researchers know the rate at which people were contacted, they can calculate how much influence the experimental intervention had on those who were contacted. Both facts are needed to gauge how effective this intervention is likely to be when used in the future.

✔ The experiment is replicated in other times and places. A single experiment can establish that a GOTV tactic works in a particular setting; a series of experiments is necessary to show that the experimental hypothesis holds when the political, economic, or demographic conditions are different. Replicating experiments also enables researchers to figure out whether variations in the way a treatment is administered affect the results.

Conducting studies of this kind requires campaign management skills—in two senses. First, many of the experiments were the product of campaigns that the researchers themselves developed or helped to coordinate. The original 1998 studies in New Haven and West Haven, Connecticut, involved door-to-door canvassing, direct mail, and professional phone banks. Our research team plotted out canvassing routes, oversaw dozens of precinct walkers, worked with direct mail vendors to create and distribute nine different mailers, devised phone scripts, and monitored the calls from the phone bank. (The fact that we, as novices, were able to pull this off with only a few glitches should hearten those of you about to embark on your first campaign.) Our study harkens back to a randomized field experiment conducted in the 1950s by Sam Eldersveld, a University of Michigan political scientist whose campaign skills later catapulted him to the position of mayor of Ann Arbor.

The second sense in which we use the term "campaign management" refers to the fact that many of the experiments we report have grown out of collaborations with actual campaigns. We never turn down an opportunity to study campaigns experimentally and are proud to have worked with candidates and groups across the ideological spectrum: Republican gubernatorial and congressional campaigns, Democratic campaigns for state assembly and mayor, interest group campaigns designed to mobilize African Americans, women, and environmentalists, and nonpartisan campaigns designed to mobilize Latinos, Asians, and voters between the ages of eighteen and twenty-five. For these groups, mobilizing votes is understandably a higher priority than conducting research. Nevertheless, amid the time pressures of an impending election, these campaigns assigned a random portion of their target lists to a control group. Collaboration with actual campaigns has greatly enhanced our understanding of how various mobilization tactics work under a range of real-world conditions.

Many things can go awry in the conduct of these experiments. If canvassers are allowed to choose which houses to visit, they may inadvertently administer the treatment to subjects in the control group. We take pains, therefore, to make sure that these experiments are carried out according to the randomized experimental protocols that we have devised. We have orchestrated dozens of successful experiments but also several fiascos that had to be discarded because the experimental plan was not followed.

One final point bears emphasis. Although we have conducted a great many experiments and evaluations, we do not work as campaign consultants. When hired to evaluate voter mobilization campaigns, we present our results after the election has passed. When asked to maintain the anonymity of names and places, we have done so, but all of the experiments we conduct are arranged with the clear understanding that the results will be made public in a form that permits the accumulation of knowledge.

The Studies Described in This Book

This book reports the results of experiments conducted each year from 1998 through 2007. The following section offers a brief chronology of the studies that we and others conducted during this period.

Federal Midterm Elections, 1998

Our first foray into the world of randomized field experiments was conducted in our own backyard. In an attempt to get away from students, however, we excluded the Yale ward from our study of New Haven. Under the auspices of the League of Women Voters, we created a nonpartisan campaign called "Vote '98" and conducted three experiments. We designed and managed a door-to-door canvassing effort that spoke with more than 1,600 people across all parts of the city. Direct mail was sent to more than 11,000 households. Leftover copies of these 8.5" x 11" direct mail postcards were distributed as leaflets to randomly selected streets in the nearby town of Hamden during the final weekend before Election Day. In New Haven and the neighboring city of West Haven, a commercial phone bank contacted more than 4,800 people.

State and Municipal Elections, 1999

We returned to New Haven for a reprise of the direct mail campaign used a year earlier. Whereas in 1998 we randomly assigned households to receive no, one, two, or three mailings, in 1999 we raised the maximum number of mailings to eight in an effort to locate the point at which additional mailings would be fruitless. These mailings were again nonpartisan, although we experimented with different content in order to determine whether the messages we used affected voter turnout. Again, leftover postcards were distributed as leaflets in certain neighborhoods of New Haven. In a departure from nonpartisan mobilization drives, Alan Gerber collaborated with three Democratic candidates, one running for mayor of a small city and two running for state legislative seats in New Jersey. By randomly extracting a control group from their mailing lists, he was able to gauge the effects of partisan direct mail on voter turnout.

Presidential Elections, 2000

This year featured a wide array of experimental studies. Partisan direct mail was randomized in another state legislative campaign, this time on behalf of a Democratic candidate in Connecticut. A randomized evaluation was conducted of the National Association for the Advancement of Colored People (NAACP) National Voter Fund's multi-million-dollar direct mail and phone bank campaign, which, in conjunction with a media campaign and door-to-door efforts, was designed to mobilize African Americans in more than a dozen states. Although not explicitly partisan in character, the NAACP National Voter Fund's phone and direct mail campaign messages argued vehemently that then-governor George W. Bush was not the candidate who would best serve black interests. On the nonpartisan front, we performed randomized evaluations of Youth Vote 2000's efforts to mobilize young voters through volunteer phone calls and door-to-door canvassing. Finally, Youth Vote launched a pilot study designed to assess whether e-mail is successful in mobilizing young voters.

Municipal Elections, 2001

In the interest of corroborating our earlier findings about nonpartisan face-to-face canvassing across a variety of urban settings, we collaborated with a coalition of nonpartisan groups urging voter participation in municipal elections in Bridgeport, Columbus, Detroit, Minneapolis, Raleigh, and St. Paul. Moving this line of research outside of urban settings, Melissa Michelson conducted a door-to-door mobilization campaign in the rural and largely Latino community of Dos Palos. In Boston and Seattle, a series of phone bank experiments were conducted by David Nickerson, one of which used prerecorded calls from the local registrar of voters to remind residents to vote on Election Day.

Federal Midterm Elections, 2002

This election cycle saw a number of studies examining the effects of partisan campaign efforts. Alan Gerber conducted a randomized direct mail experiment in collaboration with a Republican congressional incumbent before the primary and general elections. David Nickerson, who oversaw the Youth Vote 2000 studies, teamed up with Ryan Friedrichs and David King to conduct a randomized evaluation of a campaign by the Michigan Democratic Party to mobilize young voters. David Nickerson also conducted a series of door-to-door and phone bank experiments as part of an evaluation of the Youth Vote 2002 campaign. John McNulty gauged the effects of a campaign's attempt to mobilize voters in opposition to a municipal ballot proposition in San Francisco.

Nonpartisan mobilization studies also grew increasingly refined in 2002. Melissa Michelson tested whether Anglo and Latino canvassers are differentially effective in mobilizing Anglo and Latino voters. Janelle

Wong examined whether various Asian ethnic groups in Los Angeles— Chinese, Indian, Japanese, Korean, Filipino—are stimulated to vote by direct mail and phone calls. Ricardo Ramírez evaluated the phone canvassing and direct mail efforts of the National Association of Latino Elected Officials, a nonpartisan group that sought to mobilize Latino voters in four states using local phone banks, direct mail, and robo calls. The Michelson, Wong, and Ramírez studies all involved appeals that were communicated in English and other languages. Elizabeth Bennion examined the effects of door-to-door canvassing in the context of a hotly contested congressional election. Applying the experimental method to the study of e-mail, David Nickerson and Donald Green conducted an evaluation of the nonpartisan organization Votes For Students, which attempted to mobilize more than 300,000 college students via e-mail. Finally, David Nickerson launched a highly imaginative series of experiments to test whether canvassing one member of a household boosts the turnout of others living at the same address.

Municipal Elections, 2003

Several experiments were conducted in 2003 by groups seeking to hone their GOTV tactics with an eye toward the 2004 presidential election. In the New Jersey state legislative elections, the Public Interest Research Group conducted a phone bank experiment designed to assess the value added by a follow-up phone call on Election Day. In Kansas City and Phoenix, the Association of Community Organizations for Reform Now (ACORN) conducted two issue-based canvassing drives, one aimed at raising the local sales tax in order to preserve bus service in poor neighborhoods and the other aimed at preventing the closure of a local hospital. Local elections were the setting for a pair of e-mail experiments that David Nickerson conducted in collaboration with Youth Vote. Lynn Vavreck launched the first of a series of path-breaking experiments on the effects of televised public service announcements. Another innovative line of research commenced as Elizabeth Addonizio conducted a series of experiments designed to test the effects of seminars teaching high school seniors how to register and vote.

Presidential Elections, 2004

Given the extraordinary emphasis on voter mobilization tactics during the 2004 election and growing attention to scientific evaluation of voter mobilization campaigns, 2004 was a notable year for both turnout and research. Turnout increased from 107 million in 2000 to 123 million in 2004—fortunately for us, as we would have looked silly had turnout remained flat amid massive door-to-door canvassing and volunteer phone bank efforts. In terms of research, Kevin Arceneaux conducted the first study involving a candidate going door-to-door and also conducted a get-out-the-vote campaign in which canvassers sought to garner voters' support for a ballot proposition. Lynn Vavreck studied the effects of Rock the Vote's televised advertisements. David Nickerson studied Working Assets' efforts to register and mobilize voters via e-mail. Dean Karlan conducted the first experiment that randomly varied the quality of GOTV phone calls, targeting voters in North Carolina and Missouri; he also conducted a robo-call experiment comparing "election protection" messages with more conventional GOTV messages.[4] Various experiments, some in collaboration with interest groups, sought to test the effects of leaflets and live calls from commercial phone banks. Door-to-door canvassing studies were conducted by Carrie Levan in low-turnout precincts in California, by Joel Middleton in heavily African American precincts in several battleground states, and by Gregg Murray and Richard Matland in heavily Latino precincts in Brownsville, Texas.

Municipal and State Elections, 2005

Several innovative lines of research emerged during the 2005 election cycle. Elizabeth Addonizio, Donald Green, and James Glaser collaborated on a series of experiments designed to measure the effects of Election Day festivals at polling locations. Costas Panagopoulos and Donald Green conducted the first randomized experiment to gauge the effects of radio and newspaper ads on voter turnout in municipal elections. Costas Panagopoulos also tested whether the effects of a live call from a commercial phone bank has a greater effect depending on whether the script is partisan or nonpartisan. Mark Grebner, a campaign consultant specializing in direct mail, conducted the first in a series of experiments designed to test whether turnout increases when people are told whether they and their neighbors voted in recent elections. Alan Gerber, Dean Karlan, and Daniel Bergan randomly assigned newspaper subscriptions to households not receiving a daily paper, enabling them to test whether those who receive a paper in the weeks leading up to a statewide election are more likely to vote. Alissa Stollwerk conducted an e-mail experiment in conjunction with the Democratic National Committee encouraging its regular e-mail recipients to vote in support of the Democratic nominee in the New York City mayoral election.

Federal Midterm Elections, 2006

Many of the studies conducted in 2006 were extensions and refinements of previous research. Costas Panagopoulos and Donald Green replicated their radio study in mayoral elections and extended their research to congressional elections, this time targeting Spanish language audiences. Elizabeth Addonizio and James Glaser collaborated with a team of people at Working Assets to conduct Election Day festivals at sites around the country, mostly in the context of primary elections. David Nickerson conducted a phone bank and door-knocking experiment with Clean Water Action and a door-knocking experiment with Jobs for Justice. Mark Grebner teamed up with Christopher Larimer and us to conduct a large-scale test of whether mailing people information about their own and their neighbors' vote history increases turnout. One of the new research initiatives in 2006 involved a Republican gubernatorial campaign in Texas. This study, conducted in collaboration with James Gimpel and Daron Shaw, tested the effectiveness of robotic phone calls designed to increase turnout on behalf of a supreme court justice running in a tight reelection battle in a primary. No less novel was David Nickerson's study of the Candidates Gone Wild event, a light-hearted evening at which local candidates shared their views and talents. A broad-ranging experimental initiative got under way in California under the direction of Melissa Michelson, Lisa García Bedolla, and Donald Green. In the primary and general elections, groups associated with the California Votes Initiative conducted dozens of experiments with ethnic and religious groups targeting low-propensity voters. Valerie Frey and Santiago Suárez conducted a leafleting experiment to test whether providing polling place information boosts turnout. Allison Dale and Aaron Strauss conducted the first large-scale study examining the mobilizing effects of text messaging. Jason Barabas, Charles Barrilleaux, and Daniel Scheller conducted a pair of direct mail experiments designed to assess whether priming voters to think about ballot measures increases voter turnout. Julia Gray and Philip Potter conducted an experiment in collaboration with a Republican candidate for local office in which they distributed pens or pencils in conjunction with door-to-door canvassing.

GOTV Shoppers' Guide

As you make your way through this book, consider the applicability of these studies to your particular circumstances and goals. Think about whether the tactics that we reveal to be successful are feasible for you. For example, you may not have access to large numbers of canvassers or to the money needed to send out six pieces of direct mail. You may also want to think about whether you can tweak a strategy we discuss to fit your circumstances. If you cannot mount a door-to-door campaign, perhaps you can make face-to-face contact with voters in retirement homes, shopping centers, night schools, or religious centers. We have not studied these tactics directly, so there is more uncertainty about whether they work. Use your judgment when making the leap from our research findings to analogous situations that your campaign may encounter.

In order to help you to keep track of the uncertainty surrounding each of the lessons learned from the experimental studies, we have created a simple rating system.

★★★ A three-star rating indicates that the finding is based on experiments involving large numbers of voters and that the GOTV tactic has been tested by different groups in a variety of sites.

★★ A two-star rating indicates that the finding is based on a small number of experiments. We have a reasonable level of confidence in the results but harbor some reservations because they have not been replicated across a wide array of political, demographic, or geographic conditions.

★ A one-star rating indicates that the finding is suggested by experimental evidence but not demonstrated conclusively in one or more studies.

For example, we have a rather clear impression of how well commercial phone banks mobilize voters when callers read a brief script. Several truly massive experiments have estimated this effect with a great deal of precision based on studies of both partisan and nonpartisan campaigns. The results warrant three stars. Experiments gauging the effectiveness of Election Day festivals, by comparison, are much fewer in number, and taken as a whole they provide less precise estimates than the typical phone bank experiment. Conclusions drawn from these studies therefore warrant two stars. Conclusions about the mobilizing effects of radio advertising warrant one star because the results to date remain statistically inconclusive. In general, we assign one star to what might be called "post hoc hypotheses," that is, interpretations that are suggested by experimental results but which await a fresh round of tests.

Keep in mind that experimental evaluation of campaign tactics is a rapidly accelerating scientific enterprise. As this book goes to press, more studies are getting under way. The growing collaboration between scholars and practitioners promises to refine our current stock of knowledge and to broaden the range of campaign techniques that we have subjected to rigorous inquiry. Our research—like all research—is provisional and incomplete. Nevertheless, the findings reported here can help you to form realistic expectations about your GOTV campaign. How many votes would you realistically expect to generate as a result of 200,000 robo calls? How about 26,000 nonpartisan mailers? Or 2,800 conversations at voters' doorsteps? By the time you finish this book, you will understand why the answer is approximately 200.

CHAPTER THREE

Door-to-Door Canvassing:
Shoe Leather Politics

D oor-to-door canvassing was once the bread and butter of party mobilization, particularly in urban areas. Ward leaders made special
efforts to canvass their neighborhoods, occasionally calling in favors or
offering small financial incentives to ensure that their constituents delivered their votes on Election Day. Petty corruption was rife, but turnout
rates were high, even in relatively poor neighborhoods.

With the decline of patronage politics and the rise of technologies that
sharply reduced the cost of phone calls and mass mailings, shoe leather
politics gradually faded away. The shift away from door-to-door canvassing occurred not because this type of mobilization was discovered to be
ineffective, but rather because the economic and political incentives facing parties, candidates, and campaign professionals changed over time.

Although local parties still tend to favor face-to-face mobilization,
national parties typically prefer campaign tactics that afford them centralized control over the deployment of campaign resources. The decentralized network of local ward heelers was replaced by phone banks and
direct mail firms, whose messages could be standardized and whose
operations could be started with very short lead time and deployed virtually anywhere on an enormous scale. National parties and their allied
organizations have invested more resources in "ground operations" in
recent years, but these activities still account for a relatively small share
of total campaign outlays.

Candidates, too, gradually drifted away from door-to-door canvassing,
lured by the short lead times and minimal start-up costs of impersonal

campaigning. Furthermore, the ability to translate campaign funds directly into voter mobilization activities through private vendors selling direct mail and phone bank services meant that candidates were less beholden to local party activists. Candidates with money but without much affection for or experience with their party could run credible campaigns without many supporters, even in large jurisdictions.

Finally, a class of professional campaign consultants emerged to take advantage of the profits that could be made brokering direct mail, phone banks, and mass media. Less money was to be made from door-to-door canvassing, and campaign professionals had little incentive to invest in the on-the-ground infrastructure of local volunteers because there was no guarantee that they would be hired back to work in the same area.

You should therefore expect to get conflicting advice about the value of door-to-door canvassing. Campaign professionals, for example, sometimes belittle this type of campaign, because it is associated with candidates who must watch their budget and therefore make unattractive customers. Local party officials often swear by it, but because they are in a tug-of-war with their national party for resources, local activists have an incentive to tout these activities.

In this chapter, we discuss the practical challenges of organizing a door-to-door campaign and review the results from more than three dozen experimental studies. The evidence leaves little doubt that door-to-door canvassing by campaign workers can increase turnout substantially, but the studies also show that mounting a canvassing campaign has its drawbacks. Successful campaigns require planning, motivated canvassers, and access to large numbers of residences. As you review the evidence, think about whether your campaign or organization has the ingredients for a successful and cost-efficient door-to-door campaign.

Organizing and Conducting a Door-to-Door Canvassing Campaign

Door-to-door canvassing encompasses a variety of activities that involve making direct contact with citizens. In partisan campaigns, for example, canvassing may be performed by candidates themselves, their campaign workers, or allied groups. Canvassers may both talk with voters and distribute literature, absentee ballot applications, lawn signs, or other campaign paraphernalia. On Election Day, canvassers may be equipped with cell phones to enable them to coordinate rides to the polls. Lastly, canvassing should be thought of not only as a means of getting out votes but also as a vehicle for recruiting campaign volunteers and improving the public visibility of a campaign.

Canvassing on a scale sufficient to reach thousands of voters over the span of three or four weeks requires a great deal of planning and organization. But even a small-scale canvassing effort requires a fair amount of preparation. When planning, it is often helpful to break the canvassing operation into a set of discrete tasks: targeting, recruiting, scheduling, training, and supervising.

Targeting

As with any get-out-the-vote effort, canvassing begins with a target population, that is, a set of potential voters whom you think it worthwhile to mobilize. For instance, your target voters might be all registered Republicans who voted in the last general election or all registered Latinos or Christian conservatives. It is important to think about what you need to do to find your target group. Can you just canvass certain neighborhoods, or do you need to identify the specific individuals or households that fit your target?

If the latter, you will need to begin by creating or purchasing an accurate list of potential voters (see boxes 3-1, 3-2, and 3-3 on obtaining, updating, and refining lists). Ideally, your list should be accurate in two

---

Box 3-1. How to Get Lists

In most jurisdictions, lists of registered voters are accessible to the public and generally are available from local registrars, county clerks, and secretaries of state. The costs of these lists vary wildly across jurisdictions. You may pay $5 or $500. Depending on your needs and resources, you may also want to hire a private list vendor or work with a political party or organization that maintains lists. Lists of registered voters always contain addresses and sometimes contain other information that could be useful to a canvassing effort such as voter history (whether an individual has voted in the last one, two, or more elections), party registration, sex, and birth date. In some jurisdictions, these records also include phone number, although this information is often out of date. In states covered by the Voting Rights Act, registration lists indicate the race of each voter.

Box 3-2. Adding Extra Information to Lists

For a fee, list vendors usually can provide two additional pieces of information that can be useful to door-to-door campaigns: four-digit zip code extensions (which identify addresses in small clusters) and mail carrier route numbers (which can be used to create geographically compact walk lists). When requesting or purchasing any list, it is important to find out when it was last updated. Whenever possible, get the list in electronic form so that you can manipulate and update the data easily.

Box 3-3. Refining the List

There are three ways to pare down a list to include only the subgroup you would like to canvass. Information on a particular ethnic or socioeconomic sector of the voting population is available from the U.S. Census Bureau at its website: www.census.gov. Although you cannot get information about individual households, you can get information about census blocks, the smallest geographic area delineated by the census. This will allow you to determine, for instance, which neighborhoods in a particular district have a high concentration of, say, homeowners or Asians or people living below the poverty line. You can then pull the names of registrants from those neighborhoods for your canvassing effort or just canvass those neighborhoods in their entirety, if you have reason to believe that doing so would be efficient.

List vendors can also help with ethnic targeting, for a price. Private firms have name-matching software that allows them to pull names that tend to be associated with a particular ethnicity or nationality. A firm may be able to provide a list of registered voters in a given district whose last names are typically Latino or Chinese, for example. If all else fails, you can team up with ethnic or religious groups that maintain mailing lists of individuals who might serve as targets for your campaign. Since those lists do not indicate whether the individuals are registered, you will need to match them against the registration files.

Although the voter file does not say how a person voted, it often contains information about each person's party registration and record of voting in previous elections. Voting in closed primaries usually provides good clues about a person's partisan leanings. These clues can be useful when developing a targeted GOTV campaign.

ways. It should accurately reflect the pool of individuals you want to contact, and it should provide accurate contact information for those individuals. Maintaining an updated voter list is invaluable. You should enter the list into your computer and adjust it as information comes in. Suppose your candidate is running as a Democrat. Some people listed as Democrats may no longer consider themselves Democrats. Some people, when canvassed, may indicate that they do not support your candidate. If you have the capacity to recontact people after your initial canvass, you should take the time to update your list.

The task of meeting people at their doorstep poses a variety of challenges. How accessible are the people on your target list? There is no sense wasting time cursing locked security apartments. When are the residents likely to be home? If most registered voters in the neighborhood work, your canvassers will have to wait until evenings or weekends to make efficient use of their time.

If you plan to canvass in the evenings, consider the safety of your canvassers. By late October it may be getting dark before 7:00 p.m., and residents may react poorly to an evening visit from a stranger. You do not want to frighten or offend the potential voter you are trying to engage. You should instruct your canvassers to step back from the door after ringing the bell so that they seem less threatening to apprehensive residents. It is sometimes argued that people are more willing to open their door to female canvassers; it turns out, however, that the gender composition of a canvassing team is a poor predictor of the rate at which voters are contacted. Well-trained teams with two males, a male and a female, or two females tend, on average, to have about the same success in reaching voters.

Because there are so many contingencies, and so many details that can throw a wrench into your plans, it might make sense to prioritize your walk lists. This entails choosing the most essential neighborhoods and making sure that they get covered. You may want to get to them first, in order to ensure that they have been reached, or you may want to visit them right before the election, in order to ensure that your message is fresh in voters' minds on Election Day.

Recruiting Activists and Paid Volunteers

Unlike professional phone banks and direct mail, canvassing is almost entirely dependent on labor that, one way or another, you will have to produce. High schools and colleges are good sources of labor, particularly when students know the neighborhoods in which they will be working. Other sources of labor include churches, civic groups, unions, and interest groups such as the Sierra Club or National Rifle Association.

There are, of course, advantages and disadvantages to forging an alliance with a social or political group that supports your candidate or shares a common political goal with your campaign. Any organization that becomes an ally has its own agenda. By collaborating on a GOTV partnership, you may be tacitly endorsing your ally's politics, and the canvassers it supplies may have difficulty staying on message for you. In addition, if the partnership is seen as a personal favor, then a favor may be expected in return. The decision to collaborate may hinge on whether your ally will supply enough canvassing labor to make an alliance worthwhile.

Scheduling

The number of canvassers your campaign needs depends on how many contacts they will make per hour. This number may be difficult to predict. An experienced canvasser working in an area with accessible apartments or other densely packed housing may be able to speak with members of eight households per hour. This rate may drop by a factor of two when it is difficult, dangerous, or time-consuming to reach voters' doors. Splitting the difference, we assume for purposes of making some rough calculations that canvassers on average speak with voters at six households each hour.[1]

Using your best guess about your canvassers and the conditions they are likely to face, use the rate of contact to calculate how many hours of labor you will need for the campaign. Simply divide the number of contacts desired by the average number of contacts per hour. The resulting quotient is the number of volunteer hours required. Then divide the number of total canvassing hours into the number of weeks over which the canvassing will take place to obtain an average number of canvassing hours per week. The number of available canvassing hours in a week varies from region to region, but most campaigns conduct their canvassing efforts from 5:00 to 7:00 p.m. on weeknights and from 10:00 a.m. to 5:00 p.m. on Saturdays. Sunday afternoon canvassing depends entirely on the region and population but seldom takes place outside the hours of 1:00 to 5:00 p.m.

Safety

Unlike more impersonal GOTV tactics, door-to-door canvassing can place volunteers at some personal risk. However, you can minimize risk and increase the effectiveness of the campaign in several ways. First, you can send canvassers out in pairs. Each canvasser should go to separate doors, but they can do this while remaining near enough to each other (by working opposite sides of the street or visiting alternating addresses) that they can see or hear if the other encounters a problem. Sending workers out in pairs has the added benefit of providing some assurance that the canvassers are actually doing what they are supposed to, especially if you pair trusted canvassers with newcomers.

Second, you should provide canvassers with maps of their assigned areas so they do not get lost. Third, you should provide canvassers with an emergency number so that they can call you in the event they encounter a problem. Each canvasser should be equipped with a cell phone. Fourth, whenever possible, you should assign canvassers to neighborhoods with which they are familiar. Not only are canvassers less likely to face a problem in a familiar neighborhood, but familiarity also should strengthen their personal connection to the voters—something that may prove beneficial in getting those who are contacted to vote. Fifth, you should give canvassers something to identify them as canvassers and not marauders (whom they may sometimes resemble). For example, it is helpful for canvassers to wear a campaign T-shirt or campaign button. They also can put a campaign bumper sticker on the back of their clipboard, so that residents see it when they peek out their door. Finally, you should require all canvassers to reconvene at a predetermined time and location so that you can count heads. Reconvening all canvassers at the conclusion of the shift also allows you to collect the walk lists and verify their work.

Weather sometimes presents safety and efficiency concerns of its own. Getting stuck in a downpour or an unexpected snow squall can leave canvassers demoralized, not to mention cold and wet. It is useful to discuss ahead of time the contingency plans that will go into effect in case of bad weather. In principle, poor weather presents a good opportunity for canvassing, since more people can be found at home, but the success of the operation hinges on whether canvassers have umbrellas and plastic sheets to protect their walk list.

Training

Door-to-door canvassing is a simple technique that anyone willing to knock on a stranger's door can be taught to do. Interestingly enough, experiments have shown that experienced canvassers tend to be only slightly more effective than newcomers. The power of canvassing stems from the personal connection that face-to-face communication provides. Training of volunteer canvassers does not need to be extensive. A half-hour session should include the following:

✔ An explanation of the purpose of the canvass,

✔ Precise instruction on what to say and do at each door,

✔ Division of volunteers into pairs and the assignment of a canvassing area to each pair,

✔ An opportunity for canvassers to practice the script with their partner, preferably under the supervision of someone who coaches them not to recite the script in a canned fashion,

✔ Distribution of all necessary materials, such as clipboards, walk lists, maps, and pens,

✔ Explanation of what information canvassers should record after visiting an address,

✔ At least one phone number to call in the event of an emergency, and

✔ Designation of a time and location at which all canvassers will meet up at the end of the shift.

The message given in door-to-door canvassing should be consistent with the message of the overall campaign. The written pitch provided to volunteers should be treated more as a rough guideline than as a script to be read verbatim (see box 3-4). As we show in the chapter on phone banks, an informal style of communicating with potential voters works best. Scripts are necessary to provide guidance and confidence for inexperienced personnel, but the goal is not to create an army of automatons mindlessly parroting the same words. Encourage canvassers to make their presentations in words that are compatible with their own informal speaking style. This will help them to convey their message in a manner that increases the listener's motivation to vote.

When done properly, canvassing opens a conversation with voters. Prepare your canvassers to field some basic questions that voters might

---

**Box 3-4. Script of a Message
Directed toward Latino Voters**

A door-to-door campaign in Fresno, California, included some messages directed specifically toward Latino voters:

> Hi. My name is [your name], and I'm a student at Fresno State. I want to talk to you a few minutes about the upcoming elections on Tuesday, November 5. [Canvassers were then asked to talk briefly about the following points]:
>
> ✔ Voting gives the Latino community a voice.
>
> ✔ Your vote helps your family and neighbors by increasing Latino political power.
>
> ✔ Voting tells politicians to pay attention to the Latino community.

Canvassers closed their conversation by asking voters whether they could be counted on to vote on Tuesday.

---

throw at them. The more comfortable canvassers feel conversing with voters, the better. In the context of a campaign in support of a candidate or an issue, canvassers may be asked to explain a candidate or interest group's position. Unless you have an unusually savvy group of canvassers, it is probably best to instruct them to invite voters to call campaign headquarters. To the extent that canvassers answer questions, they should focus on why they personally support the campaign.[2]

Supervising

Once the canvassers take to the streets, problems may range from bashfulness to drunkenness. Campaign managers have developed a number of tactics for monitoring the progress of canvassers, particularly those who are working for hourly wages. First, have them fill out the names of the people they meet at each door they visit. Since this report conceivably could be faked (claims to have contacted an unusually large number of people should raise a red flag), another useful tactic is to send canvassers out with lawn signs or placards advertising the campaign. The goal is to convince residents to plant the sign in their yard or put the poster in their window; seeing who can plant the most signs can be a useful source of friendly competition among canvassers. This visible indicator of success makes it easy for a supervisor to see where canvassers have been and to gauge how they are doing.

Nowadays, cell phones are sufficiently cheap and plentiful to enable every canvasser to have one. Although it is unwise for their phones to be turned on—lest canvassers spend their day gabbing with friends—you should instruct them to call in at scheduled times and in case of trouble or questions. If canvassers depend on you for a ride to the canvassing area, cell phones can help you to coordinate pickup times and locations.

Payment for services is best done on a weekly rather than an on-the-spot basis. First, weekly payment schedules encourage canvassers to think of this activity as an ongoing commitment. Second, it gives you a chance to discuss their performance with them after a day on the job, while they are still thinking about the payment that they expect to receive in the future.

Finally, you must take responsibility for dealing with unexpected events. The most common problem, at least in some parts of the country, is bad weather. Along with clipboards containing maps and address lists, canvassers should carry plastic covers in case of rain. A backup supply of umbrellas will keep the canvassing campaign from dissolving in a downpour. Besides weather problems, you should expect to field an occasional follow-up call from a resident, building manager, or local politician wondering what your campaign is up to. Think of canvassing as a big walk through town, a meet-and-greet with thousands of strangers. The outcomes are generally positive, but anything can happen.

Experimental Research on Door-to-Door Canvassing

More than three dozen door-to-door canvassing experiments have been conducted since 1998. Although the nature and scope of these campaigns varied from place to place, they shared many common elements. Registered voters in targeted neighborhoods were placed randomly into treatment and control groups. Canvassers, who usually were paid volunteers working under the supervision of campaign staff, were put through roughly an hour of training, given a list of target names and addresses, and instructed to speak only to voters on their target list. The particular GOTV pitches used by the canvassers varied from experiment to experiment (we discuss these variations momentarily), but the communication was designed to be informal and personal. In some cases, canvassers also distributed campaign material, voter guides, or information about polling locations.

The canvassing experiments can be grouped into four broad categories. The first encompasses nonpartisan canvassing efforts that were orchestrated by college professors. Such studies occurred in Dos Palos (a farm community in central California),[3] Fresno,[4] New Haven,[5] South Bend,[6] and Brownsville (a largely Latino city on the Texas and Mexico border).[7] The second category includes door-to-door campaigns that were organized and conducted by nonpartisan groups such as Youth Vote[8] and issue advocacy groups such as ACORN (Association of Community Organizations for Reform Now),[9] SCOPE (Strategic Concepts in Organizing and Policy Education),[10] Southwest Voter Registration and Education Project, and PIRG (Public Interest Research Group).[11] Researchers helped to randomize the walk lists used by these canvassers but otherwise played a minor role. This type of canvassing occurred in Boulder, Bridgeport, Columbus, Detroit,[12] Eugene,[13] Minneapolis, Phoenix,[14] Raleigh, and St. Paul, as well as in several California sites (Bakersfield, Colusa, Los Angeles, Orange County, Riverside, and San Bernardino).[15] The third category includes precinct walking conducted by partisan campaigns. Here we have four studies: a 2002 GOTV effort funded by the Michigan Democratic Party,[16] which targeted young voters in approximately a dozen assembly districts, a 2004 Election Day mobilization effort targeting several inner cities within battleground states,[17] a 2005 GOTV campaign coordinated by the Young Democrats of America[18] targeting voters under thirty-six years of age, and a Republican candidate for local election in Kentucky.[19] The final category includes one instance in which candidates, rather than volunteers, canvassed voters. Kevin Arceneaux conducted an innovative study in the context of a 2004 New Mexico primary election.[20] Precincts were randomly assigned to three experimental groups: one to be walked by the candidate, one to be walked by campaign volunteers, and a control group.

As this list of sites makes apparent, these experiments were conducted in a wide array of political and demographic settings. The precincts canvassed in Detroit were largely African American, whereas canvassers in Columbus and Eugene rarely encountered nonwhites. Bridgeport, Brownsville, and Fresno contained large Latino populations, and the areas canvassed in Los Angeles, Minneapolis, and St. Paul were multiethnic. The suburban areas of Raleigh and the rural precincts of Dos Palos stood in marked contrast to the urban environments of Detroit or

St. Paul. The political climate also varied across sites. Bridgeport, Columbus, and Dos Palos were canvassed amid uncompetitive municipal elections. Somewhat more competitive were elections in Minneapolis and New Haven, where at least some of the races featured credible challengers. By contrast, South Bend and Virginia were canvassed amid a hotly contested congressional campaign, which saw both parties engaging in door-to-door campaigning. Detroit, Raleigh, and St. Paul were also canvassed during the last two weeks of closely contested mayoral elections. When it comes to competitiveness, nothing tops the 2004 Election Day canvassing efforts in the inner cities of battleground states, which were visited repeatedly by Democrats and their allied organizations.

Lessons Learned

The lessons emerging from these studies are rated according to the system detailed in chapter 2: three stars are for findings that have received solid confirmation from several experiments, two stars are for more equivocal findings based on one or two experiments, and one star is for findings that are suggestive but not conclusive.

★★★ *Contacting eligible voters can be difficult.* If your campaign is trying to reach a target group that frequently changes address—young voters living off campus, for example—expect to reach roughly one in six of the people you are looking for on each pass through the neighborhood. Typically, higher-propensity voters (elderly voters, for example) have stable addresses and are easier to find at home, but don't expect to contact more than half of your targets. The Dos Palos study gives a sense of the maximum rate of contact that a GOTV campaign can expect to achieve. After combing the town for two weeks, making multiple attempts to contact each name on the target list, this campaign met up with three out of four voters it sought to target.

★★★ *When canvassers are able to reach voters, canvassing generates votes.* In thirty-six of forty-five experiments, canvassing was found to increase turnout. (The odds of obtaining such a lopsided distribution of experimental results purely by chance are less than one in 1,000.) Putting all of the evidence together suggests that, as a rule of thumb, one additional vote is produced for every fourteen people who are successfully contacted by canvassers.

★★★ *The effectiveness of canvassing varies depending on the type of election and type of voter.* The one-vote-per-fourteen-contacts rule is a good guide for most canvassing operations, but keep in mind that this figure assumes that the targeted voters would, in the absence of canvassing, turn out at a rate of around 50 percent. If you are trying to mobilize voters who would otherwise turn out at rates of 80 percent (for instance, regular voters in a presidential election) or 20 percent (infrequent voters in a municipal election), the rate of vote production drops to one vote for every nineteen contacts. As figure A-1 in appendix A illustrates, when canvassing very high- or very low-propensity voters, the number of contacts required to produce one vote increases.

Notice what this means for cost-efficient targeting of canvassing efforts. In a low-salience election, canvassing has the biggest impact on high-propensity voters, whereas in high-salience elections, canvassing has the biggest effect on low-propensity voters.[21] A few words of caution are in order, however. If you are walking a precinct in a low-salience election, it may not pay to bypass a door simply because infrequent voters live there. You have already paid the setup cost of the canvassing operation; the extra costs of contacting infrequent voters might still pay off, particularly if you think your campaign is especially effective in reaching out to the infrequent voter. Remember, too, that cost-efficiency is not everything. If your group or campaign is dedicated to mobilizing infrequent voters, your task is challenging, but certainly not impossible.

★★★ *Canvassing is effective both in competitive and in uncompetitive electoral settings.* Experimenters found big canvassing effects in landslide elections in Bridgeport, where little was at stake and many candidates ran unopposed. Experiments also found large canvassing effects in the closely contested mayoral elections that were held in Detroit and St. Paul. It appears that canvassers can successfully motivate citizens to participate in the voting process even when the election seems to have few policy repercussions. The fact that canvassing attracts voters to the polls regardless of the stakes provides an important insight into how and why canvassing works. Canvassing evidently makes voters feel that the election matters and that their civic participation is valued.

★ *A GOTV canvassing effort may be less effective if conducted in areas that are being canvassed by other campaigns.* One caveat to the principle that canvassing can increase voter turnout in competitive races is that some races are so hot that your canvassing campaign duplicates the efforts of others. This explanation may account for the failure of the non-partisan canvassing campaign in South Bend before the 2002 elections. Battling over a contested congressional seat, both parties apparently canvassed the same turf chosen by the nonpartisan campaign, which may have caused voters to become saturated with GOTV appeals. The burned-over turf problem may also explain the apparent failure of an Election Day canvassing effort in several inner cities during the 2004 election. The target sites in this experiment were all located in battleground states and therefore were saturated by months of canvassing by pro-Democratic campaigns. As a result, the treatment group may have received about as much canvassing as the control group.

★ *If possible, canvass close to Election Day.* Three experimental studies randomized the timing and frequency of canvassing attempts. The two largest studies found canvassing during the last week of the campaign to be more effective than canvassing earlier. The smallest of the three studies found no added value of an additional contact during the weekend before Election Day. This result is surprising because some of the most successful GOTV canvassing efforts begin with a voter ID campaign, during which voters are surveyed about their voting preferences, followed by a GOTV campaign targeting voters who earlier expressed sympathy for a given issue or candidate. The two larger studies seem to trump the smaller study, but more investigation of this question is needed because the financial stakes are quite high. The 2004 presidential contest saw enormous canvassing operations get under way as early as September; one wonders whether these efforts had a lasting impact on turnout or candidate preference.

★ *The messenger matters.* It remains unclear whether canvassers who "match" the ethnic profile of the neighborhood tend to have more success than those who do not. One canvassing campaign noteworthy for its ineffectiveness at mobilizing voters occurred in Raleigh, North Carolina, where black and white canvassers attempted to canvass a predominantly white suburban neighborhood. Some white residents refused to open their door to black canvassers. Two black canvassers were accosted by white residents and told to leave the neighborhood. A coincidental and concurrent canvassing effort by white supremacists seeking to deport Arabs raised residents' general level of hostility to canvassers, and local police stopped and questioned some of the white canvassers, thinking they were part of the white supremacist effort.

Other studies provide mixed support for the notion that canvassers who ethnically match their targets have better success. In Dos Palos, a team of Latino Democratic canvassers were randomly assigned to canvass Anglo or Latino registered voters. The effects of canvassing were greater when these canvassers talked to Latino Democrats than to Latino non-Democrats or to non-Latinos. In contrast, the Fresno experiment in 2002, which involved both Latino and non-Latino canvassers and a target population of voters eighteen to twenty-five years of age, showed no consistent pattern. Obviously, it makes little sense to canvass in areas where language barriers disrupt communication, but the role of race and ethnicity per se remains unclear.

Putting ethnicity aside, there seems to be growing evidence that local canvassers are more effective than canvassers from outside the turf they are canvassing. Researchers studying a large-scale canvassing effort in Los Angeles found that canvassers working in the same zip code in which they live are significantly more effective in mobilizing voters than those canvassing outside their home turf.[22] This finding may help to make sense of some of the variation in canvassing results across experiments. Groups who canvass close to their home base seem to be more effective, and when they spread out to other areas, their effectiveness diminishes. This hypothesis needs further testing, but the evidence as it stands suggests that local volunteers may be the key to conducting an especially effective canvassing effort.

★★ *The message does not seem to matter much.* Experimenters have tried many variations on the door-to-door canvassing theme. Canvassers have distributed voter guides, polling place information, and pens bearing a candidate's name. Canvassing scripts have emphasized neighborhood solidarity, ethnic solidarity, civic duty, and the closeness of the election. Sometimes the scripts have focused on the candidates, sometimes on the parties.[23] Although we cannot rule out the possibility that these variations in message and presentation make some difference, the effects seem to be so small that none of the studies was able to detect them reliably. And when we look across the dozens of canvassing experiments, the campaigns that were strictly nonpartisan were neither more nor less effective on average than the campaigns that organized around an issue or a candidate. We do not doubt—even without the benefit of experimental data!—that running door-to-door in a chicken suit or mentioning your support for outlandish political causes would undermine your effectiveness, but within the range of reasonable behaviors, we do not see much evidence that what you communicate matters.

Although we have concluded that the message does not matter very much, the data do suggest that some tactics might bump up turnout by an additional percentage point. One tactic is to ask citizens whether they can be counted on to vote. Another is to provide citizens with the location of their polling place. These effects are small, and researchers cannot claim to have isolated them with any precision, but they seem worth incorporating into most canvassing campaigns. Asking people whether they can be counted on to vote is virtually costless. Locating polling places requires a bit of effort, but not a whole lot. In general, we find that canvassers feel more comfortable conversing with people if they have information to convey and campaign paraphernalia to distribute, so nuances like providing polling information and asking for a commitment to vote may increase the effectiveness of canvassing simply by changing the tenor and length of the conversation on the doorstep. Speculating a bit, the reason local canvassers are more effective may be that it is easier for them to develop rapport with voters.

★★ *Door-to-door canvassing allows a campaign to influence people incidentally and indirectly.* One attractive feature of knocking on doors is that it provides an opportunity to converse with multiple voters living at the same address. The canvasser first talks to the person who answers the door and then asks to speak to the targeted voter. Everyone is told the purpose of the visit: the importance of the upcoming election.

In part, elevated turnout rates among nontargeted people reflect the fact that canvassers give their GOTV message to everyone who comes to the door, but that is not the only thing that is going on. Using a clever experiment, David Nickerson demonstrated that voters living at the same address also mobilize one another.[24] Nickerson led a canvassing effort that knocked on doors and gave a message only to the person who answered the door. Half of the messages were get-out-the-vote appeals; the other half, reminders to recycle. No messages were delivered to others in the household, yet other registered voters in households receiving the GOTV appeal voted at higher rates. Evidently, those who received the GOTV message communicated something about the upcoming election to others in their household. In light of this experiment and other evidence suggesting that canvassing affects both the intended targets and other voters in the household, the usual one-for-fourteen rule probably understates the effectiveness of door-to-door canvassing because about 60 percent of the direct impact of canvassing appears to be transmitted to voters' housemates.

All in all, we see strong evidence that canvassing generates votes. Canvassing seems particularly effective when aimed at frequent voters who otherwise might skip a low-turnout election. Extra bells and whistles, such as providing polling place information or inviting people to make a verbal commitment to vote, may enhance slightly the effectiveness of door-to-door campaigns, although this conclusion remains tentative. Finally, canvassing campaigns seem to encourage people to talk about the upcoming election with their housemates, thereby extending the influence of a canvassing campaign beyond those who are contacted directly.

Cost-Effectiveness

When you are evaluating the costs and benefits of canvassing, here are a few things to keep in mind. First, canvassing involves start-up costs. It takes time to plot out walking routes. If you intend to target specific individuals (as opposed to conducting a blanket GOTV campaign of all the residents living on certain streets), you need to obtain a voter registration list. You may want to hire a supervisor to recruit and coordinate canvassers. You may wish to send out your team of canvassers wearing the campaign's T-shirts and armed with maps, clipboards, printed material, buttons, or refrigerator magnets, all of which require some up-front investment. High-tech walking campaigns nowadays use small handheld computers to record and transmit data about every canvassing target.

Second, what counts as a "benefit" depends on your goals. The accounting we perform in this section considers only one goal: getting out votes. Using canvassers to persuade voters to vote in a certain way may generate extra benefits as well. Indeed, canvassing potentially provides all sorts of collateral benefits: canvassers receive useful feedback from voters about issues and candidates; the lawn signs and campaign buttons that canvassers distribute may help to publicize the campaign and communicate its message; canvassers can help to clean up an outdated target list of voters, weeding out the names of people who have moved; as canvassers go door-to-door, they can register new voters; and, by conversing with people about the campaign, canvassers can help to create databases of residents who are sympathetic to a given candidate and therefore warrant special GOTV efforts on Election Day. We have not attempted to quantify these extra returns to canvassing. The cost-benefit analysis that follows is admittedly narrow in focus.

The number of votes produced per dollar is a function of labor costs, the number of people contacted per hour, and the effectiveness with which a canvasser mobilizes the people contacted. According to Susan Burnside, a consultant who specializes in canvassing campaigns, the usual wage rate for canvassers varies from $10 to $16. In order to err on the side of caution, let's assume $16. If your canvasser speaks with voters at six households per hour, and each household contains an average of 1.5 voters, you are in effect getting six direct contacts and three indirect contacts per hour. Applying the one-for-fourteen rule for the direct contacts and Nickerson's one-for-twenty-three rule for the indirect contacts implies that it takes $29 worth of labor to produce one additional vote. You may cut labor costs dramatically by convincing a team of canvassers to work all afternoon in exchange for a dinner of pizza and beer (depending on how much they eat and drink). Similarly, an unusually energetic and persuasive group of canvassers may increase the number of voters per dollar, just as a hard-to-canvass neighborhood may decrease it. Nevertheless, training, supervision, and infrastructure drive costs up, so your campaign might encounter substantially higher costs per vote.

If you are canvassing by yourself or are using unpaid volunteers, you may find it helpful to look at the efficiency problem in terms of the number of hours required to produce one vote. Contacting six households per hour produces one additional vote every 107 minutes. Generating a serious number of votes requires a serious investment of canvassing hours.

Assessment and Conclusions

When we first began our experimental studies of voter turnout in 1998, we were eager to assess the effects of door-to-door canvassing. This campaign tactic has an almost mythic reputation. Talk to any veteran of local politics and you will hear a story about an overmatched challenger who used door-to-door canvassing to upset a complacent incumbent. Even campaign professionals who recognize the difficulty of mounting a canvassing campaign nonetheless advise, "If your program is well targeted, going door-to-door is the surest way to win votes."[25] We were at the time skeptical that a conversation at one's doorstep with a stranger would be sufficient to raise voters' probability of going to the polls. Our first experiment showed canvassing to have a surprisingly powerful effect.

Now that dozens of experiments have weighed in on the effects of canvassing, there no longer is any doubt that face-to-face contact with voters raises turnout.

Although canvassing has received a great deal of experimental attention, much remains to be learned. Just one study has attempted to measure the effects of candidates themselves going door-to-door. The effects were positive, but this study was unable to tell whether a local candidate, who in this case canvassed only a handful of precincts, was more effective at the door than her volunteers. Given the many demands on a candidate's time and the inherent constraints on how many households can be visited, it seems strange that the payoff from a candidate's door-knocking efforts has so seldom been the subject of experimental inquiry. Also uncertain are the benefits of multiple visits with voters and the optimal timing of those visits. These questions, which are of enormous practical importance to campaigns, can only be answered by means of a very large-scale experiment. Finally, there remains the unsettled question of whether certain kinds of canvassers are more effective than others. One persistent question about the 2004 presidential election is whether Republican canvassers were unusually effective because they were often drawn from the local community. Existing experimental evidence is suggestive but not definitive; a large-scale study is needed to gauge the relative effectiveness of canvassers drawn from inside and outside the targeted area.

Eventually, experiments will provide a more comprehensive and detailed account of which kinds of canvassing tactics do the best job of mobilizing voters. But even when best practices become clear, contacting voters at their doorstep will still present practical challenges. Precinct walking can be difficult and even dangerous. Anyone who has butted heads with managers of security apartments knows that some neighborhoods are inaccessible to political campaigns, notwithstanding court decisions that distinguish canvassing from commercial solicitation. Rural areas are often more hospitable, but the distance between houses undercuts the campaign's cost-efficiency.

Perhaps the biggest challenge is bringing a door-to-door campaign "to scale." It is one thing to canvass 3,600 voters; quite another to canvass 36,000 or 360,000. It is rare for a campaign to inspire (or hire) a work force sufficient to canvass a significant portion of a U.S. congressional district. A million dollars is not a particularly large sum by the standards of federal elections; media campaigns gobble up this amount in the production and distribution of a single ad. But a million dollars will hire an army of canvassers for GOTV work during the final weeks of a campaign. Even if your campaign wins only your canvassers' affections and no one else's, the number of votes produced would be considerable. The massive ground efforts by the political parties and allied organizations during the 2004 presidential elections represent an important turning point insofar as they demonstrated that large-scale precinct work is possible. If present trends continue, the parties will be competing to make their large-scale recruitment, training, and deployment efforts more efficient and effective.

The demonstrated effects of door-to-door canvassing suggest that other face-to-face tactics may stimulate voter turnout: shaking hands at a local supermarket, meeting voters at house parties, conversing with congregants at a church bingo night. We do not have direct evidence about the effectiveness of these time-honored campaign tactics, but they share much in common with conversations on a voter's doorstep. Face-to-face interaction makes politics come to life and helps voters to establish a personal connection with the electoral process. The canvasser's willingness to devote time and energy signals the importance of participation in the electoral process. Many nonvoters need just a nudge to motivate them to vote. A personal invitation sometimes makes all the difference.

CHAPTER FOUR

Leaflets: Walk, Don't Talk

L eafleting is a get-out-the-vote tactic that shares much in common with door-to-door canvassing. Teams of canvassers comb neighborhoods, dropping literature at the doorstep (or inside the screen door) of targeted households. Like door-to-door canvassing, leafleting requires you to recruit and manage a pool of canvassers and to deal with the vagaries of bad weather, confusing street maps, and menacing dogs. But leafleting is easier, faster, and considerably less demanding than door-to-door canvassing. Just about anyone can do it, even those too shy to knock on doors. Leaflets can be distributed at just about any time of day, which vastly increases the number of hours that can be devoted to this activity during the final stages of a campaign.

Unfortunately, finding a leaflet at one's door is less memorable than having a face-to-face conversation with a canvasser. So the question of whether to distribute leaflets comes down to a matter of cost-efficiency. Does the extra coverage that a campaign gets from a leafleting campaign offset its limited effectiveness? This chapter strives to answer that question.

Organizing a Leaflet Campaign

Although leafleting campaigns require less preparation than door-to-door canvassing efforts, planning is still an essential ingredient for success. Designing an effective leaflet, organizing walk lists, and assembling a corps of leafleteers require time and energy. If you wait until the last moment, the quality and distribution of your literature will suffer. Here are some things to consider as you craft your leafleting campaign.

Leaflet Design

A leaflet campaign starts with the leaflet itself. Unless you have something worthwhile to distribute, there is little point in recruiting, deploying, and supervising a team of leafleteers. Most professional designers strive for the following attributes when crafting a leaflet:

✔ Use a visually engaging layout to encourage recipients to glance at the leaflet before throwing it away.

✔ Convey a simple, clear message in large print so that the gist of your message is apparent at a glance.

✔ Give the message credibility by including more detailed information for interested readers, perhaps directing them to a phone number or website.

A conventional leaflet is not much more than a printed sheet of paper, something that in principle could be produced by a desktop publisher. Bear in mind, however, that leaflets found lying on the ground in front of the doormat are less likely to attract attention than so-called door hangers. Door hangers, as the name suggests, have a perforated hole in the top that allows them to be hung on a doorknob. Printing door hangers on this kind of card stock may require some professional assistance.

The lead time required to produce a leaflet depends on its sophistication. The easiest approach is to produce a generic leaflet for distribution to everyone. On the other end of the spectrum are leaflets customized for the recipients, perhaps listing their polling place or making a voting appeal tailored to their demographic profile. Somewhere in the middle are leaflets tailored to voting precincts; these might provide polling place information but not a message aimed at an individual recipient. This last approach is easy for even a low-tech campaign to pull off; just use adhesive labels or rubber stamps to put polling place information on each leaflet.[1]

Voter Lists

Not all leafleting campaigns require target lists. Some campaigns are content to drop their literature at every household, regardless of whether it contains registered voters. Sometimes these "blind canvassing" efforts are used because they serve other purposes, such as encouraging voter registration or publicizing an event or organization. Sometimes they are used by necessity, because canvassers are too young or unreliable to follow a walk list. Blind canvassing speeds up the process of visiting addresses because canvassers need only check which street they are on. For neighborhoods with high registration rates, blind canvassing is often an efficient way to go. In areas with low registration rates, such as urban apartment complexes, blind canvassing may waste quite a bit of time and paper.

More sophisticated leafleting campaigns that target particular households require database management. Printing customized leaflets, for example, requires a current voter registration list (see chapter 3 on how to obtain and prepare such lists). Even if you plan to use a generic leaflet for everyone in your target population, you need to obtain a registration list and sort it by street or carrier route. Assign each canvasser a set of contiguous carrier routes. As leafleteers return from each day's work, you should update these computer records to indicate where canvassers have visited.

The decision whether to canvass by street or by individual address in part depends on the purpose of the leafleting campaign. Some partisan leaflets are designed to mobilize loyal voters, in which case it makes little sense to leave them at the doorstep of people registered in the opposing party. Other leaflets are intended to build a candidate's name recognition and communicate positive information about him or her. Unless you fear that these messages will produce a backlash among voters registered in the opposing party, you may distribute these leaflets blindly. If you are unsure about the likely effect of your partisan leaflets, it is probably safer to focus on people who either are registered in your party or are undeclared. That means targeting specific addresses.

Canvassers

Distributing leaflets is a low-skill activity and one that is often assigned to teenagers. You do not need to train canvassers to deliver a script, but you should provide instructions about what to say if they encounter someone as they proceed from address to address. A bit of guidance should be given about where and how to position the leaflet on someone's property. It is a bad idea to place leaflets in mailboxes, which legally are the special domain of the postal service. In general, leaflets should be placed in ways that prevent them from blowing around and becoming litter. (They teeter on the edge of litter even under optimal conditions.) The great virtue of door hangers is that they stay put right where the voter is likely to see them.

Many of the same safety principles discussed in the previous chapter apply here. One further issue warrants mention. Leafleteers occasionally have the opportunity to sabotage other leafleting campaigns. On the day before the election, a leafleteer might encounter a stack of competing leaflets on a resident's doorstep. To prevent unpleasant confrontations with other campaigns, you ought to discourage your canvassers from discarding or destroying these competing messages, urging them instead to place your message at the top of the stack.

Assessing the Effectiveness of Leaflets

Eleven experimental leafleting campaigns—one by a partisan campaign that urged support for candidates, two by interest groups seeking to mobilize supporters of a presidential candidate, and eight by strictly nonpartisan campaigns—have assessed whether leaflets boost voter turnout.

During the final days of the 1998 campaign, we conducted a nonpartisan experiment in the suburban town of Hamden, Connecticut.[2] Streets in the town were randomly assigned to treatment and control groups, and leafleteers distributed 8.5" x 11" postcards to every house on a treatment group street. Since this procedure was tantamount to a blind canvass, efficiency was compromised a bit, but in these neighborhoods a very high percentage of households contained registered voters. The leaflets featured a large picture of a patriotic symbol, such as the Constitution or American soldiers hoisting the flag, described voting as a civic duty, gave the date of the upcoming election, and encouraged voters to participate. Leaflets did not list the polling location. This experiment involved 2,021 registered voters, which makes it much smaller than some of the studies we discuss below. A year later, in the context of an uncompetitive mayoral election in New Haven, we replicated this leafleting experiment, again distributing large postcards to randomly assigned streets. This study, too, was small, encompassing 3,011 voters living on seventy-six streets.

In 2002 a much larger partisan leafleting study was crafted by David Nickerson, Ryan Friedrichs, and David King.[3] In this campaign, the Michigan Democratic Party targeted young voters in thirteen Michigan assembly districts during the weeks leading up to the general elections. This study involved a very large number of registered voters, roughly 2,500 in each assembly district. Because Michigan's registration system no longer includes a declaration of party, the canvassing campaign targeted voters eighteen to thirty-five, focused on predominantly Democratic neighborhoods, and excluded voters who had registered as Republicans under the previous registration system. The Michigan experiment used a door hanger that conveyed a partisan message, encouraged voter turnout, and listed the polling place for residents of a given ward (see box 4-1). Thus the leaflet was customized for each precinct, but not each individual. Canvassers were instructed to deposit their door hangers only at specified addresses.

Two studies, described by Julia Azari and Ebonya Washington, examined the effects of leafleting in a battleground state.[4] During the closing days of the 2004 presidential election, an interest group supporting Democratic candidates conducted two leafleting experiments in Florida, one in Dade County and the other in Duvall County. In both cases, the targeted precincts were predominantly African American. The leaflets conveyed an "election protection" message, encouraging voters to go to the polls and to report any problems they might encounter to a hotline designed to provide assistance. This theme was prominent among Democratic supporters in 2004, still chafing over what they perceived to be voter intimidation tactics in the 2000 election.

During 2006, several groups embarked on nonpartisan leafleting experiments. Valerie Frey and Santiago Suárez coordinated a leafleting experiment in Philadelphia.[5] The setting for the experiment was a special election to fill a vacancy in the state legislature. In order to test alternative messages, the researchers divided the target population of 15,550 voters by street into three groups: a control group, a group receiving a standard GOTV leaflet, and a group receiving a leaflet that encouraged voting and pointed out that bilingual ballots would be available at the polls. In California's June primary elections, two groups affiliated with church-based civic outreach campaigns leafleted neighborhoods in Orange County and Long Beach. The Orange County leaflets listed polling place locations, while the Long Beach leaflets provided voters with a voter guide that reported how candidates vying for local office responded to questions about various issues confronting the city. In the days leading up to the November elections, church-based groups again conducted leafleting in Fresno and Long Beach, this time without providing voter guides or polling places. Each of the five California studies reported by Melissa Michelson, Lisa García Bedolla, and Donald Green was relatively small in scope; combined, the five sites encompassed 7,655 registered voters.[6]

Box 4-1. Sample Door Hanger

This door hanger was printed in three colors by the Michigan Democratic State Central Committee. It encourages both voting and support for Democratic candidates. Each door hanger indicates the voter's polling location and supplies a web address for further information.

Lessons Learned

The four lessons emerging from these studies are rated according to the system detailed in chapter 2: three stars are for findings that have received solid confirmation from several experiments, two stars are for more equivocal findings, and one star is for findings that are suggestive but not conclusive.

★★★ *Leaflets and door hangers typically have weak effects on voter turnout.* A weighted average of all eleven studies suggests that for every 189 registered voters whose doors receive hangers, one additional vote is produced. Although based on more than 65,000 registered voters, the results fall short of statistical significance, because there is about an 11 percent chance that we would observe an effect this large simply due to chance. The statistical evidence, however, is strong enough to rule out the idea that leafleting on average produces big effects. The upper bound for the effectiveness of an average leafleting campaign appears to be one vote per seventy-two people who receive leaflets.

★ *Partisan door hangers appear to have a slight edge in effectiveness over nonpartisan leaflets, but the difference is not statistically reliable.* In the Michigan experiment, for every seventy-eight registered voters whose doors received hangers, one additional vote was produced. However, the Florida leafleting campaigns, which had a less overt partisan message and did not include polling place information, failed to increase turnout. Combining Michigan's and Florida's results suggests that one vote is produced for each 127 people who receive leaflets. The corresponding number for the strictly nonpartisan leaflets is more than 500 contacts. In the absence of an experiment that pits partisan and nonpartisan messages head-to-head, we remain skeptical that the partisan content of the leaflet affects its ability to mobilize voters, particularly in light of the findings from the chapter on direct mail, which show few messaging effects and no superiority of partisan mailings.

★ *Nonpartisan leaflets seem to be equally (in)effective for different segments of the electorate.* After the initial 1998 nonpartisan experiment, it was thought that leaflets might have different effects depending on the recipients' party affiliation. Because undeclared voters receive less communication from campaigns, it seemed possible that leaflets might have greater salience for them. Consistent with this hypothesis, which was hinted at in the nonpartisan study, the Michigan experiment found fairly strong effects among young voters, who are usually ignored by campaigns. However, subsequent leafleting experiments failed to support this hypothesis. It now appears that recipients are about equally (un)responsive to leaflets, regardless of party or past rates of voter participation.

★ *Door hangers that provide information about polling locations and local candidates may be more effective than standard leaflets.* Although the statistical results remain tentative, the most successful campaigns to date were the partisan effort in Michigan, which provided polling locations, and the nonpartisan effort in Long Beach, which provided local voter guides. Election protection messages and information about the availability of bilingual ballots do not appear to enhance the effectiveness of leafleting.

Cost-Effectiveness

Once a campaign has secured a target list, leafleting involves two principal costs: the up-front cost of printing and the hourly cost of distribution. Assume that you are producing a partisan door hanger that tells each resident where to vote. The printing costs depend on the print volume, card size, paper stock, and number of colors. Suppose that you are planning to spend $0.10 on each leaflet (which is what the Michigan Democrats paid to print 100,000 door hangers, converted to 2008 dollars).

Leafleteers are generally cheaper per hour than canvassers. Suppose you pay them $12 per hour with the expectation that they will drop leaflets at forty-five addresses per hour. Assuming that addresses contain an average of 1.5 voters, your leaflets reach 67.5 voters every hour. For every 189 voters contacted, one additional vote is generated. The labor costs of leafleting therefore come to approximately $34 per vote. The printing costs of the literature needed to produce one vote bring the total cost to approximately $46. The cost goes up still further if you print a voter guide instead of or in addition to a door hanger.

Leafleting thus appears to be less cost-effective than canvassing in terms of dollars per vote. However, the efficiency advantages of face-to-face canvassing may be offset by the greater supervisory costs associated with training and recruiting canvassers. One other consideration worth noting is that leafleting campaigns are easier to manage than face-to-face campaigns. Door-to-door canvassing requires the right type of people and a modicum of training; almost anyone can leaflet, so dealing with an unexpected shortfall of labor is less problematic for a leafleting campaign. There is an upper limit to what a leafleting campaign can accomplish, but it makes fewer organizational demands.

Assessment and Conclusions

Leafleting operates on the principle that votes can be produced efficiently if leaflets have even a small impact on a large number of people.

If your target population is large, leafleting could be a cost-effective means of increasing turnout. However, if your jurisdiction is small enough to allow you to canvass the entire target population face-to-face, you should do so, because that will generate the most votes. Leafleting becomes an attractive option when vast numbers of voters otherwise would receive no contact from a face-to-face canvassing campaign.

Although leafleting experiments are relatively easy to conduct, they rarely have been conducted on a scale sufficient to produce informative results. The form and content of the leaflet have only begun to receive experimental attention. Do door hangers increase turnout regardless of whether they instruct people about their polling location, endorse candidates, or provide sample ballot information? Are door hangers better than other forms of leaflets?

More generally, does it matter how people receive GOTV literature? Are leaflets different from direct mail in terms of their effects on voters? Do recipients take notice of the manner in which they receive a given piece of printed material? Or are leaflets just direct mail delivered by volunteers? As experimental evidence about the effects of leaflets and direct mail has accumulated, their apparent effects have converged, but the definitive experiments on leafleting have yet to be conducted.

CHAPTER FIVE

Direct Mail:
Postal Service as Campaign Staff

Just as commercial direct mail enables vendors of all sizes to distribute advertising to large numbers of households, political direct mail permits a campaign of any size to contact large numbers of registered voters with a small investment of time and staff. Direct mail requires no recruiting of volunteers and no battles with inclement weather. With direct mail, much of the work can be done well in advance of the election, and a few paid professionals can be employed to design, print, and distribute the mailings.

Although the administrative burdens of direct mail are minimal, the cost of preparation, printing, and postage can be considerable. At the high end of the market are direct mailings that are personalized for each voter. For example, in states that permit it political campaigns send forms to voters enabling them to request an absentee ballot.[1] These forms have all of the necessary personal information already filled in; the addressee only needs to sign and mail the form. Another variation on this theme is direct mail that reminds the recipient of his or her polling location, perhaps even personalizing the campaign appeal based on the individual's demographic profile and place of residence. At the low end of the market are postcards with few colors, printed on relatively inexpensive paper stock. Regardless of the cost of preparing the mailer, postage must be paid for each piece of mail; for large mailings postage represents about half of the final cost. A typical direct mail campaign will cost somewhere between $0.50 and $0.75 per piece. If you were to mail 25,000 households three pieces of mail apiece, the final cost would be somewhere between $37,500 and $56,250. Cost per mailer drops when mailings are printed on a much larger scale or on small cardstock. And bear in mind, political parties receive a special discount on postage.

Is direct mail worth the cost? Most campaign managers seem to think so. Direct mail enables a campaign to tell its side of the story, in print and often with vivid images. Enthusiasm for direct mail has, if anything, grown over time as campaigns use so-called "microtargeting" databases that enable them to tailor mailings to match the ostensible political viewpoints of different segments of the electorate.[2] Microtargeting mail might direct one set of mailings to voters who feel strongly about abortion and a different set of mailings to those who feel strongly about immigration.

Another line of argument on behalf of direct mail is that it reinforces the effectiveness of other campaign tactics, such as the use of phone banks. This was the strategy behind the NAACP National Voter Fund campaign in 2000.[3] Given the overwhelmingly Democratic proclivities of African American voters, the campaign aimed to mobilize, not persuade. And to do this, a series of direct mailings dealing with issues such as racial profiling and hate crime were timed to coincide with televised advertisements and phone calls emphasizing similar themes. Even strictly nonpartisan efforts, such as the 2002 campaign of the National Association of Latino Elected Officials (NALEO) to mobilize Latino voters, sometimes combine direct mail with other GOTV tactics, such as live and prerecorded phone calls.[4]

Skeptics question whether direct mail works (a view sometimes volunteered by consultants selling other sorts of campaign services, such as robo calls). They argue that voters are inundated with junk mail and that at best they glance at campaign mail momentarily before putting it in the trash. The fact that these glances cost $0.50 apiece or more is cause for concern.

After summarizing the practical aspects of how a direct mail campaign is put together, this chapter attempts to determine whether direct mail raises voter turnout rates. Three broad types of direct mail are considered: strictly nonpartisan mail that seeks only to mobilize voters, advocacy mail that implicitly urges recipients to support a particular candidate or ballot measure, and partisan mail that openly endorses a particular candidate or ballot measure. We then discuss two further subcategories of mail: mail designed to exert social pressure on recipients by revealing whether or not they voted and mail encouraging absentee voting.

The bottom line is that strictly nonpartisan mail has, on average, a small positive effect on voter turnout, whereas advocacy and partisan mail appear to have no effect. Over the past ten years, twenty-eight studies comprising seventy-five distinct experiments have measured the effects of mail. Exactly half of these studies have found positive effects on turnout. Mail sometimes succeeds in getting people to register or sign up for an absentee ballot, but, interestingly enough, these efforts do not appear to increase voter turnout. With the exception of one instructive experiment that found large effects on voter turnout, the experimental literature as a whole indicates that direct mail is usually more costly than other methods of producing votes. Mail may serve the GOTV aims of campaigns that seek to reach a large and geographically dispersed audience whose phone numbers are unlisted or unreliable, but its effects on turnout are typically small.

Organizing and Conducting a Direct Mail Campaign

When designing and implementing a GOTV direct mail program, keep the following rules of thumb in mind: plan ahead, get an accurate list of voters, make your mailings readable and clear, line up your vendors, and learn the mechanics of sending bulk mail.

Plan Ahead

Carefully plan the format and content of your mailing, determine your targeted voters, and set a production schedule. Almost invariably, you will encounter a holdup somewhere along the line—a delay at the printer, a direct mail company that is behind schedule, or a post office that sits on your mail. Several extra days or, better, a week should be built into the schedule to account for the unexpected.

Get an Accurate List of Voters

As discussed in previous chapters, you can obtain voter lists from a number of sources (see also box 5-1). Whatever source you choose, take time to check out its reputation for reliability and accuracy and make sure that the list it provides is as up-to-date as possible. Ask your list vendor to group voters by household rather than listing each voter individually. Addressing each mailer to all of the voters who are registered at a given address will save you the cost of sending multiple pieces of mail to one home.

Box 5-1. Obtaining Mailing Lists

Registrars of voters, fortunately, keep fairly accurate records of current mailing addresses. If you get the most current list available prior to the election, expect less than 5 percent of mail sent to registered voters to be returned as undeliverable. If your target list comes from an interest group, such as a membership list, find out how recently the addresses were updated. One way to freshen a list is to pay a list vendor to check it against the national change of address registry. Some campaigns send a postcard to everyone on the mailing list, as an inexpensive way to determine which addresses are no longer valid. Others restrict their target list to voters who have recently shown some sign of life, either by voting or by registering.

Make Your GOTV Mail Readable

Some examples of successful nonpartisan mail use evocative language and images to emphasize the importance of voting. For example, the mail used in a New Haven campaign featured images of Iwo Jima and reminded recipients that soldiers sacrificed their lives to preserve the right to vote. Partisan mail should try to communicate in words and images one or two simple take-home messages. Resist the temptation to put a lot of prose on your mailer, particularly on the outside. Bear in mind that most recipients will glance at the piece only momentarily en route to the trash can, so make sure that this book can be judged by its cover.

As for graphics and print quality, there are two schools of thought. One is that eye-grabbing graphics will catch voters' attention and encourage them to read the mailer before discarding it. Perhaps this is true, but the experiments presented below include many instances of stylish but ineffective direct mail. The other school of thought holds that homely mail gets more attention because it looks like something from a local organization or neighborhood group. One of the most effective pieces of mail tested was nothing more than plain text on a folded sheet of light blue paper.

Although our experimental results suggest that a variety of reasonable direct mail appeals can be equally effective in mobilizing voters, those results apply to mailings that achieve a minimum threshold of professional competence. As noted above, mail can be extremely simple, but if it appears sloppy or inaccurate, anything can happen, so take pains to ensure that your mailings do not become an embarrassment. This means checking for spelling and punctuation errors, out-of-focus photos, and factual mistakes.

To avoid incurring unexpected costs, check with the post office to make sure that the piece envisioned is the proper size, weight, and format. Standard formats, with various folds, are 8.25" x 11" (one-fold card or postcard), 11" x 17", 11" x 22", or 5.5" x 8. 5" (postcard).[5]

Line up Your Vendors

If possible, check out references on both the printer and the direct mail firm that you plan to hire. Be sure that they have the capability to handle a job of the size envisioned and that they enjoy a reputation for producing quality work and delivering it on schedule. The printer needs to understand the scope of the print job, including piece specifications, number of copies of each piece, type of paper stock, number of colors, and turnaround time. The direct mail firm also needs to receive a detailed outline of the artwork specifications, the number of pieces to be mailed, and mail or drop dates. Be sure to get written price quotes from any firm with which you do business.

Learn the Mechanics of Bulk Mail

Except for the occasional first-class letter, all of your pieces probably will be classified as bulk mail and sent through a bulk mail facility. Sending mail in bulk, as opposed to first class, will save at least 30 percent on postage costs. A direct mail firm will handle the bulk mail arrangements for you and almost certainly will include the bulk mail facility's service charges in its fee. If you do not hire a direct mail firm, you will have to handle all of the arrangements yourself. This means, first, obtaining a bulk mail permit, which you can do at the bulk mail division of your local post office. The post office will give you a permit number, and you should verify the exact wording and size for the bulk mail indicia that must be printed on each piece (the indicia typically reads "U.S. postage paid, city name, state, permit number"). The post office also will require you to fill out a form for each mailing that you send.

A direct mail firm will handle the details of delivering your pieces to the appropriate bulk mail facility. If you do not have a direct mail firm, you will have to do this yourself. You should ask the local post office how it wants the mail to be sorted. The mailbags should be red tagged to indicate that they contain political direct mail. By law, the post office is required to make political direct mail a priority over other direct mail. From there, the direct mail facility will sort and deliver the pieces of your mailing to the appropriate post offices. Mail carriers will then deliver them to voters' homes.

The length of the process will vary. Some mail will move through the bulk mail facility and the post offices in one day and arrive at voters' homes within two to three days of its arrival at the bulk mail facility. Some post offices, however, move more slowly than others. And some post offices and bulk mail facilities get jammed with political mail during the days leading up to an election.

Try to determine the efficiency of the bulk mail facilities and post offices in your community. Be prepared to track your mail by establishing a relationship with a supervisor in the bulk mail facility and pushing to get the mail out in a timely manner. If your schedule is tight, visit the bulk mail facility in person when the mail arrives there. Following through can ensure that the mail is processed and distributed as quickly as possible. From there, you may need to contact each of the post offices that deliver to your targeted voters. For additional advice on designing and carrying out your mail campaign, you might look at Catherine Shaw's *The Campaign Manager*[6] or Judge Lawrence Grey's *How to Win a Local Election.*[7] Grey discusses a twist on conventional campaign mail. He proposes personalizing mail, explaining, "For the large campaign, bulk mail may be the only route, but for a small campaign without a lot of money, nothing is as effective as the personal letter. By a personal letter I mean a real letter with a stamp on it, written by a real, live person using a pen. This kind of letter gets read!"[8]

Experimental Research on Direct Mail

Political scientists began studying the effects of direct mail on voter turnout during the 1920s. Harold Gosnell tested the effectiveness of nonpartisan GOTV appeals by mailing letters to Chicago residents encouraging them to vote.[9] He found that turnout increased 1 percentage point in the presidential election of 1924 and 9 percentage points in the municipal election of 1925. Of course, Gosnell's experiments were conducted in the days before computerized mailing lists made direct mail commonplace. One could well imagine that Chicagoans of the 1920s, who received mail only occasionally, might read Gosnell's missives with a level of curiosity that would be rare nowadays.

Since 1998, many experiments have sought to bring Gosnell's findings up to date. What follows is a brief chronology of these studies and a description of the electoral context in which they took place.

Nonpartisan Mail, 1998

During Connecticut's 1998 statewide election, we conducted a nonpartisan direct mail campaign in the city of New Haven.[10] We sought to learn three things about this direct mail campaign. First, how did the number of campaign mailings sent to voters affect their likelihood of showing up at the polls? Second, were the mobilizing effects of mail amplified when mail was used in conjunction with other mobilization tactics, such as phone calls? Lastly, did the content of these mailings affect voter turnout?

We began with a sample of 31,098 registered voters, of whom 5,064 received one mailing, 5,321 received two, and 5,200 received three. The control group of 15,513 received no mailings. The nonpartisan mailings were developed by professionals and contained one of three messages: (1) it is one's civic duty to vote, (2) voting is important because politicians pay special attention to the needs of neighborhoods that vote at high rates, and (3) the election is close, and every vote counts. Mailings were sent out at three intervals—fifteen days, thirteen days, and eight days before the election.

In this experiment, some of the recipients of direct mail also received encouragement to vote from door-to-door canvassers and commercial phone banks. This experimental design enabled us to assess whether mail amplified the effects of other voter mobilization techniques.

Nonpartisan Mail, 1999

Before the November 1999 municipal election we performed a follow-up experiment designed to measure the effect of sending a larger number of mailers.[11] In 1999, households were again randomly assigned either to a control group or to a treatment group receiving two, four, six, or eight pieces of nonpartisan mail. Mailings were sent approximately every two days, up until four days prior to the election (the groups receiving eight mailings were sent the first mailing eighteen days before the election, the groups receiving six mailings were sent the first mailing fourteen days before the election, and so forth).

Each of the treatment groups was randomly subdivided into two sub-groups, with one group receiving mailings that emphasized the closeness of the election and the other receiving mailings that emphasized civic duty. The point of this experiment was to test the proposition that messages have to be relevant in some way to the election at hand. There was nothing "close" about the 1999 mayoral election, which featured a Democratic incumbent running against a weak challenger in an overwhelmingly Democratic city. Would the "close election" appeal still work in this context?

Partisan Mail, 1999

Alan Gerber conducted a series of studies that assessed the effectiveness of campaign mail. His study of a 1999 mayoral campaign in a small Connecticut city involved 9,900 registered voters.[12] The direct mail campaign is of special interest because of its negative tone and the quantity of mail sent to targeted households. The 1999 mayoral election was expected to be relatively close and was, by far, the most important and active contest on the ballot.

The Democratic challenger targeted households that had at least one of the following: (a) a registered Democrat, (b) a registered "unaffiliated voter" who had voted in a recent election, or (c) a resident who had registered after November 1998. Three weeks before the election, the challenger's campaign began sending a series of nine pieces of mail to households chosen by the campaign on the basis of party affiliation and turnout history. The campaign also sent a single postcard to all households with at least one registered voter approximately one week before the election. We tested the effectiveness of the nine-piece campaign, not the postcard. From the Democrat's target list for the nine mailings, we randomly selected a control group, which received none of these mailings.

The Republican incumbent also sent direct mail, so registered voters received five Republican mailings in addition to the Democratic mailings. In effect, this experiment tested whether a dose of nine mailings affected turnout, given that recipients also received a postcard and five competing mailings.

The Democratic challenger waged what was considered to be a negative campaign. He attacked the incumbent as an incompetent, wasteful manager who was looking out for special interests. As is common in such campaigns, the negative mailings were sandwiched between more positive mailings. The first and last pieces provided upbeat assessments of the sponsoring candidate, presumably with the intention of restoring good feelings about the candidate and inspiring support.

Another partisan mail experiment took place in New Jersey, which held state legislative elections in 1999.[13] New Jersey elects two state assembly members from each district. In this partisan campaign, an incumbent New Jersey state legislator ran what amounted to a joint campaign with another incumbent from the same district and party.

The assembly campaign targeted three groups with somewhat different mail campaigns. Households containing frequently voting Democrats, or "prime Democrats," received four mailings. Other Democrats and Independents received six pieces of mail. The Republicans and infrequently voting Independents received either four or six mailings. From each group, a randomly selected control group received no mailings from this campaign. Taken together, the New Jersey partisan mail experiments assigned approximately 30,000 voters to the treatment group and 5,000 to the control group. This protocol allowed us to evaluate whether certain potential voting groups were more influenced by direct mail than others.

Issue Advocacy, 2000

Before the 2000 elections, Donald Green conducted an experiment evaluating the direct mail campaign conducted by the NAACP National Voter Fund, which targeted African Americans and, where individuals' race could not be ascertained from the voter files, voters living in predominantly African American neighborhoods.[14] Before the experiment began, about one-third of the mailing list was sent a preliminary postcard to verify their address and two mailings dealing with the issue of hate crime. After these mailings went out, we randomized the distribution of subsequent mailings.

The GOTV mail that was the subject of this experimental analysis focused on the issue of discrimination. One mailer, for example, depicted a black motorist stopped by a white police officer brandishing a nightstick. The text surrounding the photo read, "Stopped again? Start voting." The text on the reverse side read:

Getting stopped for "Driving While Black" is swerving out of control. We all know someone. Or we've had to deal with the frustration of it. And racial profiling hasn't just stopped there. Now's the time to do something about it. Vote. Let's start pulling the ballot

lever and stop getting pulled over. Stop the madness. Vote. And get
in the real driver's seat. Vote on Election Day, Tuesday, November 7.

In certain states, voters who had not received an earlier mailing on
hate crime were sent a different version of this mailing, which again
implored them to "Stop the madness. Write Governor George W. Bush
and tell him that we need hate crime legislation." Depending on the state
being targeted, households were sent two or three pieces of GOTV mail.
A parallel phone bank campaign struck similar themes, and mail and
phone calls were timed to reinforce each other.

Partisan Mail, 2000

Alan Gerber evaluated the use of mail by a Democratic state assembly
incumbent in 2000. The campaign targeted Democrats and Independents and sent a random subset three mailings; a small group of Republicans also received the mailings as part of the experiment. The mailings
were positive and downplayed the incumbent's partisan affiliation. There
was no mention of the opponent's name. Two of the mailings emphasized
the candidate's efforts to improve education and health care. The third
mailing presented the candidate as a fiscally responsible legislator who
"knows that you work hard for your money . . . and believes that you
should keep more of it."[15]

Nonpartisan Mail, 2002

Two nonpartisan mobilization campaigns targeting ethnic minorities
tested the effects of direct mail in 2002.[16] Janelle Wong assessed the
effects of a single mailing aimed at Los Angeles County voters with Chinese, Indian, Japanese, Korean, and Filipino surnames. A total of 3,232
voters were sent mail, with 8,726 assigned to a control group. The mailing sent to Chinese Americans was bilingual; all other recipients received
English-language mail.

In collaboration with NALEO, Ricardo Ramírez conducted the first
large-scale experiment testing the effects of direct mail on Latino voter
turnout.[17] The multi-state study used high-quality bilingual mailings
designed by several professional mail firms. Depending on the site,
between two and four mailings were sent during the two weeks preced-
ing the November elections. The target population was low-propensity

voters with putatively Latino surnames whose rates of turnout varied from 3 percent to more than 40 percent across sites. This experiment was very large: roughly 300,000 voters were sent mail, and another 60,000 were relegated to a control group. Furthermore, the experiment examined whether the effectiveness of mail varied depending on whether it was paired with live or prerecorded phone calls.

Partisan Mail, 2002

In collaboration with a Republican congressional candidate, Alan Gerber conducted a series of experiments in the primary and then general campaign. The primary featured a credible challenger; the general election was won decisively. Randomization was performed at the precinct level. In the Republican primary election, 239 precincts were targeted for a two-piece direct mail campaign, and 5 were placed in a control group that received no mail. The general election campaign excluded households in which all members were Democrats who voted in primaries. The remaining households were categorized as prime Republicans, nonprime Republicans, and others, depending on party registration and the number of times they had voted in primary elections. The three groups were sent one, two, and three mailings, respectively.

In the same year, an experiment described by Emily Cardy tested the effect of mail from an abortion-rights interest group, which backed a pro-choice candidate in a gubernatorial primary campaign.[18] The group targeted strongly pro-choice voters who had been identified through phone calls. The experiment consisted of three treatment groups: phone only, mail only, and phone plus mail. There were between 1,940 and 2,022 voters in each treatment group and the control group, totaling 9,980 voters. The mail was printed in full color on glossy paper. It was sent five times between nineteen and six days before the election.

Partisan Mail, 2003

David Niven conducted a field experiment in the context of a West Palm Beach mayoral election in 2003.[19] Up to three negative mailings about the incumbent were sent on behalf of the challenger. Although this race was nominally "nonpartisan" because it did not involve party labels, we classify this experiment as a study in partisan mail because it attempted to persuade voters to support a candidate.

Nonpartisan Mail, 2004

Neema Trivedi conducted the first direct mail experiment involving citizens of South Asian ancestry.[20] Studying residents of Queens, New York, with Indian surnames, she sent three different kinds of messages designed to encourage turnout in the presidential election. Mailings were similar in form, although the photographs displayed varied. In addition, the messages varied, reflecting the identification they were intended to elicit. One group of voters received mail aimed at their identification as U.S. citizens, with text that emphasized their duty as citizens to participate in the election. The next mailing was intended to tap individuals' dual identification as both U.S. citizens and persons of color. The third group of voters received mail that addressed them as Indian Americans in the text. Each individual in the household was sent one mailing.

Richard Matland and Gregg Murray conducted a nonpartisan mail campaign in the largely Latino town of Brownsville, Texas.[21] Households were randomly assigned a postcard with one of two messages. One emphasized increased power for Latinos if they became more politically active and voted. The other emphasized civic duty and the closeness of the election as the reasons recipients should go to the polls and vote.

Partisan Mail, 2004

A second Texas experiment in 2004 was conducted in collaboration with a partisan campaign with an interesting ethnic dimension. James Gimpel, Daron Shaw, and Wendy Tam Cho worked with a Republican state legislative campaign in a district with a large Asian American population.[22] The campaign created three groups of bilingual mailings: Korean, Vietnamese, and Chinese. They randomly assigned up to five pieces of mail encouraging support for the incumbent, an Anglo candidate running against a Vietnamese opponent. One mailing warned that not voting would hurt the neighborhood's interests. Two of the mailings emphasized that voting as an ethnic bloc would help to ensure that the group's interests would be considered—these mailings either were specific to the country of origin (targeting Vietnamese Americans, for instance) or mentioned Asian American interests. One mailing conveyed a civic duty message, and one encouraged voters to look out for their interests in health care, education, and other areas.

A Republican state legislator in a northern state conducted a study of his direct mail campaign. This experiment was set in motion before the Democratic challenger unleashed a wave of attacks linking the incumbent to the scandal-plagued Republican governor. Like the Texas experiment, which also involved an incumbent fighting off accusations of scandal, this one was conducted in the context of an unexpectedly close race.

Advocacy Mail, 2004

An environmental organization conducted a large-scale direct mail campaign in a closely contested Midwestern state. The campaign consisted of two mailers reminding people to vote and to consider environmental issues when voting. The mailers, which used photographic images, portrayed environmental concerns such as clean water and leaving a natural legacy for future generations.

Nonpartisan Mail, 2006

Melissa Michelson, Lisa García Bedolla, and Donald Green collaborated with several organizations participating in the California Votes Initiative in order to test the effects of various forms of direct mail on low-propensity voters from Asian American, Latino, and African American communities.[23] In the days leading up to the June primary, some organizations conducted tests of postcards reminding people to vote in the upcoming election. In some cases, these postcards were accompanied by handwritten notes encouraging the recipient to vote. Other organizations used bilingual mailings with more professional graphics and layout. These experiments were replicated in November, but this time many of the groups included a simplified voter guide (sometimes in the recipients' putative native language, if the voter file indicated that they were born outside the United States) designed to introduce them to the candidates and ballot measures. In all, more than two dozen such experiments were conducted.

Jason Barabas, Charles Barrilleaux, and Daniel Scheller conducted an innovative study designed to test which, if any, ballot measures in Florida might pique the interest of potential voters.[24] They sent a single mailing to samples of registered voters both across Florida and specifically in Leon County. Each of the more than half-dozen mailings alerted voters to the importance of one ballot measure. The authors compared the mobilization effects of these mailings to those of a generic GOTV mailing.

One of the most unusual mail experiments conducted to date was inspired by Mark Grebner, a Michigan political consultant specializing in direct mail.[25] His idea was to shame people into voting by showing individuals their own and their neighbor's voting records in past elections. Mark Grebner not only developed the capacity to mass mail information about voters' participation; he also conducted some rather sophisticated experimental tests of his ideas. These tests were refined by a team of researchers including Alan Gerber, Donald Green, and Chris Larimer. In the days leading up to Michigan's August primary, Mark Grebner randomly distributed four kinds of direct mail: an appeal to civic duty, an appeal to civic duty combined with a message indicating that researchers would ascertain whether the recipient voted by looking at public records, an appeal to civic duty combined with a printout of whether each member of the household had voted in the past two elections, and an appeal to civic duty combined with a printout of whether each voter on the block had voted in the past two elections.

Partisan Mail, 2006

In a small-scale but nonetheless interesting study, Julia Gray and Philip Potter compared the effectiveness of high- and low-quality printing of mailings encouraging voter support for a Republican candidate for local office in Kentucky.[26]

Issue Advocacy, 2006

Inspired by pilot experiments conducted by Christopher Mann in 2005, several environmental organizations sought to increase turnout by encouraging voters to register to vote by mail.[27] These organizations sent mailings to their members or voters who were thought to be sympathetic to environmental conservation. Some of the mailings were about the environmental implications of the coming election and encouraged recipients to vote. Others encouraged recipients to vote by mail, arguing that it would make voting easier and more convenient given the many competing demands on their time. Similarly, large-scale experiments conducted by Christopher Mann in collaboration with groups seeking to encourage women to vote examined a wide array of different messages, including the distinction between strictly nonpartisan messages and advocacy messages.[28] This study represents the first experiment to provide a head-to-head comparison of nonpartisan and advocacy mail.

Lessons Learned

The four lessons emerging from these studies are rated according to the system detailed in chapter 2: three stars are for findings that have received solid confirmation from several experiments, two stars are for more equivocal findings based on one or two experiments, and one star is for findings that are suggestive but not conclusive.

★★★ *On average, direct mail has a weak effect on voter turnout.* To date, twenty-eight experimental studies have assessed the effects of direct mail. Pooling the results of these experiments without regard to whether the content of the mailing is partisan or not indicates that one vote is generated for every 500 people who receive a piece of mail. Since the average mailing address on a voter registration list contains 1.5 registered voters, this rate translates into one additional vote for every 333 pieces of mail sent.

★★ *Nonpartisan GOTV mail has proven more effective at mobilizing voters than partisan or advocacy mail.* Comparing the thirteen nonpartisan mail studies to the fifteen partisan and advocacy mail studies, we find nonpartisan mail to be somewhat more effective, on average, at boosting turnout. Nonpartisan mail increases turnout at a rate of one additional vote per 200 recipients. Partisan and advocacy mailings, on average, appear to have no effect.

Some of the initial partisan mail studies suggest that these mailings succeed as a way to "motivate the base." Both the Democratic mail sent by state assembly candidates and the Republican mail sent by a congressional candidate had the greatest impact on the "prime" partisan supporters. Although these early studies were large, the evidence that partisan mail motivates the base is not statistically overwhelming, and this hypothesis has since received limited support from other studies of partisan mail. Now it appears that, on average, partisan mail has no effect on turnout.

It should be emphasized that this broad-gauge comparison of nonpartisan mail with other types of mail does not establish that nonpartisan content per se generates higher turnout. The contrast we observe could have to do with who receives the mail and the electoral context in which they receive it. We must be cautious because no experiment to date has pitted campaign mail against strictly nonpartisan mail. That said, it could be argued that partisan mail fails to mobilize because the message is primarily about why one should vote for a given candidate or cause, not why one should vote. This hypothesis remains provisional, particularly in light of the null findings for advocacy group mail, which does emphasize the importance of voting.

★ *Partisan mail campaigns that have a sharp negative tone may diminish turnout slightly but probably have no effect.* The 1999 study of a Connecticut mayoral race found that nine pieces of negative mail had a weakly demobilizing effect. Those who received the mail were 1 percentage point less likely to vote, an effect that is not statistically distinguishable from zero. A much smaller study of a Florida mayor's race found negative mail to have a positive effect.

★ *The mobilizing effects of nonpartisan direct mail appear to taper off after six mailings per address.* The 1999 nonpartisan mailing campaign in New Haven found that turnout among those sent civic duty appeals was highest among those who received six mailings as opposed to none, two, four, or eight.

★★ *Subtle variations in message content have little effect.* In the New Haven 1998 experiment, Neema Trivedi's 2004 experiment, the two Florida 2006 experiments, and Christopher Mann's elaborate studies of mail from advocacy groups, variation in the content of direct mail failed to produce a statistically meaningful difference in outcomes. The one exception of note is the 1999 New Haven study suggesting that "close election" appeals have no effect when the election is obviously a blowout, but even here the statistical evidence that civic duty appeals worked better is not overwhelming. The lack of message effects is unquestionably the finding that readers of the first edition of *Get Out The Vote!* found hardest to swallow. It is also the finding that researchers have been gunning for, expecting to find that varying the type of GOTV message would lead to bigger or smaller effects. This has led to a surge in experiments that, ironically, have only served to bolster the conclusion that subtle variations don't matter. The same may be said for unusually expensive and high-quality mailings, such as those enclosing voter guides. It is sometimes suggested that voters respond if campaigns send a costly signal of how much their vote matters. Here, the mailings were expensive and, in some cases, reached out to ethnic voters in their first language, yet they had nothing more than the usual weak effect. Even handwritten notes were not noticeably more effective than conventional mail.[29]

★★ *Shaming voters by showing them their own voting record and/or that of their neighbors increases turnout.* The Michigan experiment in 2006, which involved 180,000 households, uncovered unexpectedly powerful effects. Showing voters their own voting record produced a jump of 5 percentage points in turnout or one additional vote for every twenty recipients. Showing recipients both their own voting record and that of their neighbors boosted the effect significantly to 8 percentage points, implying that one vote would be gained for every twelve recipients. This experiment marks an important exception to the idea that variations in message have no effect. That is why the previous "lesson learned" is qualified by the word "subtle." Messages that confront people with their voting record are anything but subtle. It should be noted that, when calculating the average effects of nonpartisan direct mail, we have excluded all shaming treatments, so as not to inflate the apparent effectiveness of nonpartisan mailings.

★★★ *There is no evidence of synergy between mail and other GOTV tactics.* Several experiments have examined whether mail enhances the effects of phone calls or visits. Only Emily Cardy's study of mail and phones in the 2002 gubernatorial primary found any hint of synergy, and this result is offset by an overwhelming array of studies. The 1998 New Haven experiment provided no support for the hypothesis that mail works better among those who are called or visited on their doorstep. The same may be said for other large studies: the 2002 NALEO and the 2006 California Votes Initiative studies showed no interaction between mail and other types of GOTV tactics. No evidence of synergy emerged from the 2004 or 2006 issue advocacy studies.

Cost-Effectiveness

Our assessment of the effects of nonpartisan mail suggests that it increases turnout by one vote for every 200 people who are sent a piece of mail. The typical address on a voter registration file contains 1.5 voters on average, so if mail is addressed to all voters at a household, voter turnout increases by one vote for every 133 pieces of mail. Since the effects of mail seem to level out after about six mailings, let us suppose that no more than six pieces of mail are sent to each household. At $0.75 per piece of mail, it takes $100 of mail to produce one additional vote. At $0.50 per piece of mail, this figure drops to $67 per vote. This estimate makes direct mail substantially more expensive than other nonpartisan GOTV tactics, such as door-to-door canvassing or, as we show in the next chapter, certain types of phone banks. This conclusion holds even more strongly for partisan and issue advocacy campaigns, which on average have a poor track record of generating increases in turnout.

What about mail that confronts people with their voting record in past elections? Although this type of mail is both inexpensive and highly effective, we would warn readers against using this tactic. This type of mail is like lightning in a bottle, an interesting but dangerous curio. It is interesting because it reminds us that mail is indeed capable of producing big effects and that, in some cases, the message does matter. But it is dangerous because many people who receive this mail become irritated at the prospect of a campaign snooping on them and scolding them in front of their neighbors. Your phone will ring off the hook with calls from people demanding an explanation. Whatever gains you make in turnout will be offset by public outcry against your campaign. The question is whether this type of mail could be repackaged in a more palatable manner. Perhaps one could avoid the *sturm und drang* of surprising unsuspecting voters by working within an organization, getting its members to pledge to vote at the start of the campaign. The leadership of the group could start a voting hall of fame, both to publicize the good work of voters and to communicate the fact that members' voter turnout will be monitored. In other words, it may be possible to transform the shaming effect into a get-the-recognition-you-deserve effect. Time will tell whether campaigns figure out how to convert this lightning into useful current.

Assessment and Conclusions

Direct mail is expensive, and its capacity to mobilize voters is typically rather limited. Nevertheless, direct mail makes sense for certain types of campaigns. If the campaign lacks the people power needed to distribute door hangers or the time to manage these on-the-ground efforts, direct mail is a sensible alternative. Direct mail has the further advantage of allowing centralized control of very large campaigns, which explains why national organizations turn to direct mail when targeting hundreds of thousands of voters. Our results indicate that direct mail does nudge voter turnout upward, but it is important to be realistic about what to expect from such a campaign. Appendix B provides a useful and rather sobering statistical overview of how various mail campaigns have fared.

Finally, it should be stressed that we have focused exclusively on voter mobilization. Mail that advocates on behalf of a candidate or issue may win votes through persuasion, not mobilization. Partisan campaigns may justify the use of direct mail on the grounds that it changes *how* people vote even if it does not change *whether* people vote. It turns out that experiments designed to detect these persuasive effects have had mixed results, a theme to which we return in chapter 10.

CHAPTER SIX

Phone Banks:
Politics Meets Telemarketing

You know them, you hate them: unsolicited telephone calls, typically occurring while you are eating dinner, bathing the kids, or settling down to relax for the evening. Phone calls from survey takers, telemarketers, or even campaign volunteers are rarely welcome. Nevertheless, every election year vast quantities of time and money are devoted to get-out-the-vote phone calls, some by paid professional callers, some by volunteers and paid campaign staff, and some by prerecorded messages. Opinions about the effectiveness of phone calls vary widely. Some campaign experts regard them as an indispensable ingredient of a successful campaign, while others contend that "telemarketers have killed off the usefulness of this technique."[1]

In this chapter, we discuss the various ways in which campaigns use the telephone in an attempt to mobilize voters. After laying out the steps required to orchestrate phone canvassing, we evaluate the experimental evidence about the effectiveness of volunteer phone banks, commercial phone banks, and prerecorded messages.

Our findings suggest that phone banks work to the extent that they establish an authentic personal connection with voters. Prerecorded messages seem ineffective. Commercial phone banks that plow through get-out-the-vote scripts at a rapid pace and with little conviction do little to increase turnout. Phone banks staffed by enthusiastic volunteers typically are effective in raising turnout, although the vagaries of organizing volunteers for a sustained period of time often limit the number of people who can be reached in this manner. When commercial phone banks are carefully coached—and paid a premium to slow their callers down—they can be as effective as the average volunteer phone bank. Managing a phone bank campaign therefore requires attention not only to the mechanics of making a lot of calls but also to the quality of each call.

Types of Phone Campaigns

There are five basic requirements for a telephone canvassing campaign: staff to make calls, several phone lines, a central location where callers can be supervised, a target list of potential voters (preferably with an up-to-date list of phone numbers), and a script that callers read or paraphrase. How these ingredients are put together depends on whether the phone bank in question is making prerecorded or live calls and, if the latter, whether the calls are made by campaign activists, paid staff, or professionals hired by a commercial phone bank. Before evaluating the performance of each type of phone bank, we first describe some of the practical aspects of each type of operation.

Professional Phone Banks

With the advent of commercial telemarketing firms, the technology used to conduct large-scale calling campaigns has become commonplace. Equipped with automatic dialers and computer-assisted interviewing technology, a large number of national and regional firms are capable of contacting hundreds of thousands of households each day. Commercial phone banks, moreover, require relatively little lead time; with the script and target list in hand, a telemarketing firm typically requires only a matter of hours before phone canvassing can get under way. The capacity to generate large numbers of calls with little lead time gives phone banks an edge over other GOTV tactics during the waning days of a campaign. That is why at the end of a campaign the remaining contents of the war chest are often dumped into a commercial phone bank.

Even if you plan to conduct your calls during the last weekend before Election Day, make time beforehand to shop around and develop a thoughtful and well-executed phone campaign. Phone banks offer a wide array of pricing options, reflecting at least in part the fact that their callers and training practices vary in quality. As we show in this chapter, the quality of the calls plays a crucial role in determining whether or not they actually generate votes.

The typical campaign has little use for the data collected by telemarketing firms, but you should request this information anyway for accounting purposes. Unless you are a regular customer, you will have to pay phone banks a deposit up-front, usually based on a setup fee and an estimated cost per completion. Be sure that you have a clear understanding of what counts as a completion before signing the contract and, after the calls have been completed, examine the records of whether and how target names were contacted in order to ensure that the charges are fair.

Put your own name (and the names of relatives and campaign workers who agree to be guinea pigs) onto the target list, so that you can track what the phone bank is doing. You also should take advantage of one of the high-tech perks of using a commercial phone bank, namely, the ability to listen in on GOTV calls. Monitoring the calls, especially early in the calling campaign, can be critical to your quality control efforts. It is not unusual to encounter a particular caller who is misreading the message, going too fast, or speaking with an accent that your target audience will find jarring. Monitoring calls also gives you an opportunity to discover whether the phone bank is charging you for "break-offs," that is, calls in which the recipient hangs up after a few seconds.

Robo Calls

A second approach to telephone canvassing is to contact voters with a prerecorded message known as a robo call. The recorded message may be provided directly by the candidate, by a member of the candidate's family, or by a prominent local or national figure endorsing the candidate. A nonpartisan campaign might enlist the help of a government official such as the secretary of state or might find a celebrity who is willing to deliver its nonpartisan message. Depending on the amount of demographic information that is available for individual voters, you can design different messages for different groups—one for young people, another for women, still another for Latinos.

The advantages of robo calling are that the calls are consistent in quality, relatively inexpensive, and easy to produce on short notice. They are designed as much for answering machines as for live respondents. Those who tout their virtues frequently recount anecdotes of voters who come home from work only to discover a memorable message on their answering machine from a movie star or a former U.S. president.

Robo calls, like live calls, require a list of phone numbers, but once these fixed costs have been paid, the unit costs of robo calling are much lower. Robo calls are usually priced in the neighborhood of $0.05 apiece or less, which is roughly one-tenth the cost of live calls. (Again, be sure that you are being charged per completion not per attempt.) Thus establishing some minimal level of name recognition among 100,000 households would cost just $5,000. Getting out votes, however, is a more difficult task than getting your candidate's name into circulation, so the key question is whether robo calls actually increase recipients' likelihood of going to the polls.

Volunteer Phone Banks

A third option is to organize a calling effort yourself. A homegrown phone bank may be staffed by activists supporting your campaign, by paid staff, or by a combination of the two. For the purposes of explaining how a phone bank operation is put together, we lump activists and paid volunteers together under the heading "volunteers," but bear in mind that these two types of workers are very different. It should be clear by the end of this chapter that callers who genuinely believe in the cause that they are calling for are much more effective than those who view this work as just another job.

Recruitment

Your first task is to recruit callers. Intuition suggests, and our research confirms, that callers who establish rapport have the greatest success in turning out voters via the telephone. Indeed, the principal advantage of organizing a volunteer phone bank is that the callers will convey an authentic sense of enthusiasm and commitment. The ease with which such callers can be found will depend on the nature of your campaign and those active within it. An articulate and motivated group of callers can move mountains; their evil twins (the ones who fail to show up, show up late, or accomplish little once they arrive) can be an expensive and demoralizing headache.

It is important to recruit more volunteers than you will actually need, because many who promise to appear will not show up on calling day. Twice the number needed is a reasonable rule of thumb. Providing some enticement for callers can be useful. Depending on the pool of volunteers and the time of day that the phone bank operates, donuts and coffee beforehand or a pizza party afterward are options. As mentioned in the chapter on door-to-door canvassing, it is usually cheaper—and perhaps wiser, from the standpoint of finances and morale—to pay workers with food and drink than with hourly wages.

Location

In principle, you can coordinate a phone bank in a decentralized manner, with callers working from home. Although less expensive, this type of arrangement creates potentially serious supervisory problems. Even if the callers are doing their work, you cannot monitor whether they are staying "on message" and conveying the proper tone. For this reason, most campaigns prefer to have phone bank volunteers make their calls from a central location. In assessing alternative sites, factors that must be taken into consideration include acoustics, physical layout (caller privacy has advantages, but so does a layout in which callers can be seen by one another and by the organizers), and facilities such as parking, restrooms, and perhaps even a refrigerator or soda machine.

Obviously, geographic location will loom large if your campaign plans to make long-distance calls using landlines, but clever campaigns nowadays rely on the free cell phone minutes that campaign volunteers often have for weekend calls. Indeed, a new industry has grown up around the coordination of cell phone calls made by political activists, who visit websites in order to pick up a list of target phone numbers. Unlike the typical campaign worker, these activists are sufficiently motivated to complete these calls without prodding from a supervisor. Groups such as MoveOn.org made vast numbers of cell phone calls using this model in 2004 and 2006, and one suspects that the next step will be to make these calls using web-based phone services so that campaigns can verify that target numbers have been called.

Work Shifts and Phone Capacity

After identifying your labor pool and workplace, try to determine how many calls you can expect to complete in the days remaining in the campaign. With an up-to-date list of phone numbers and a chatty script, a competent caller will complete sixteen calls per hour with the intended targets.[2] You can use this figure to calculate the number of person-hours that will be required in order to meet your objectives. For example, if you seek to complete 16,000 calls, your labor pool will need to furnish 1,000 person-hours. If the calls will be made on weekday evenings from 5:00 to 9:00 p.m. and on weekends from 9:00 a.m. to 6:00 p.m., a single phone line used to full capacity will generate thirty-eight hours of calls per week. If the calls will be made over two weeks, you will need fourteen phone lines.

Of course, the supply of labor may not cooperate with these simple calculations. Although the usual problem is having too few callers, phone bank organizers sometimes fail to plan for surges in the number of canvassers who report for duty. A GOTV phone drive that we studied in Houston, for example, foundered because the phone bank attracted more than 200 volunteers for only twelve phones. The inevitable outcome was disappointment for the organizers and frustration for the volunteers. If your campaign has the potential to snowball into something large, it is best to err on the side of having too many phones (or have ready access to cell phones). Sometimes a large supportive business will permit volunteers to make their calls from its offices after hours. Just remind your callers not to leave empty soda bottles on the mahogany furniture.

Beware of the Automatic Dialer

One way to drive a volunteer phone bank campaign into the ground is to use an automated or "predictive" dialing machine. This technology dials many numbers simultaneously and alerts callers when someone has picked up. While the caller is being summoned to the line, the person who has picked up hears the telltale silence of a telemarketing call about to commence. Unless the targets of your phone calls are especially lonely or curious, they will hang up moments before the conversation begins. Hand-dialed phone banks have completion rates in the 50 percent range, but an automated dialer can lower those rates to 15 percent or less. In more than one study, we have seen tens of thousands of target phone numbers devoured in a single evening, not because the calling crew was particularly large, but rather because large numbers of target voters hung up at the start of the call. If your phone bank has a computer dial the phone numbers, have your callers on the line as each number is dialed to prevent the deadly silence.

Training

Although volunteers should devote as much time as possible to the central task of contacting voters, it is important to begin your phone drive (and to welcome each new group of volunteers) with a brief training session on how to deal with a variety of contingencies. Should callers leave messages on answering machines or voice mail? How should they respond to voters who are hostile to the candidate or to the GOTV effort? How important is it for callers to stay on script? Should they speak only with the person or persons named on a calling sheet, or should they give their pitch to anyone who answers the phone? How should they respond to voters who request more information about the campaign or who ask to be called back at another time? And what information should callers record on the calling sheet as they place calls?

With regard to this last question, you may wish to have callers record not just the names they contact but also those who are not at home, those for whom recorded messages were left, and invalid telephone numbers or numbers that did not correspond to the voter named on the list. This information will enable you to track the progress of the GOTV effort and to direct volunteers to make a second or third attempt if time permits. The training session should provide volunteers with answers to all of these questions. A consistent written protocol to cover all likely situations—distributed and carefully explained to volunteers—will make things easier for them and will minimize unforeseen problems. Provide all callers with a printed instruction sheet and a copy of the script to keep near the phone. This is especially important for volunteers who arrive late and miss some of the training.

Preparing a Script

The final task of the planning process is to script the pitch that volunteers will deliver to the voters they contact. Whether your script should be formal or more casual will depend on the specific goals of the phone drive, the characteristics of targeted voters, and the enthusiasm of the volunteers. Callers should be instructed on whether to adopt a crisp professional tone or to engage in a more conversational and unstructured discussion. Using a standardized script has advantages. A reasonable degree of consistency among your callers is guaranteed, and less supervision is required. Volunteers, especially those without past experience with phone banks, will have the psychological comfort of clearly understanding what is expected of them. Nonetheless, research suggests that more conversational calls—perhaps because they are unhurried and responsive to the reactions of the recipient—have a greater impact on voters than tightly scripted calls.

Cleaning up Your Phone List

Nothing is more demoralizing to a group of volunteer callers than dialing nonworking numbers (see box 6-1). Nonworking numbers are less

Box 6-1. Building a Targeted Phone List

Public voter files and even commercially distributed voter lists are often loaded with outdated phone numbers. Regardless of how you develop your list, if you are conducting a phone bank and have the resources, you probably should hire a phone-matching firm to match names with updated phone numbers or conduct an initial round of robo calls in order to weed out nonworking numbers. When shopping for a firm, find out how recently the phone numbers were updated for your target jurisdiction. To keep the cost down, pare down your list to the persons you intend to call. Lastly, if your target list is very small, and you have the time, patience, and volunteers to do so, you could even look up phone numbers the old-fashioned way, using local directories.

of a problem when working with professional phone banks, because they charge you per completed call. But nonworking numbers represent a major nuisance for volunteer phone banks, especially those attempting to target mobile populations. Here is where robo calls come in handy. A GOTV robo call is inexpensive, and it can provide you with immediate information about which of your target numbers is out of service. Don't expect the GOTV robo call itself to have any effect on turnout, however.[3]

Confirming All Details

To protect against last-minute glitches, it is advisable to confirm all the details about a week before the phone drive is to begin. Items to check include the continued availability of the calling center, the required number of phones, adequate parking, and amenities for callers.

Even if your campaign is blessed with experienced and motivated volunteers, it is always advisable to call volunteers ahead of time to remind each of them of their commitment to participate. If the phone drive is being conducted on several successive evenings, you might assign one volunteer each evening to spend a few minutes contacting those who are signed up for the next day, or you could place these calls yourself. Despite your best efforts to remind and encourage volunteers, however, expect less than 100 percent attendance, even among the people who repeatedly promise to show up.

Supervision and Assistance during the Phone Drive

Campaign staff or a volunteer coordinator should be present on-site throughout the phone drive. If you are calling from several locations, each requires a supervisor. Volunteers may raise questions, need encouragement, drift off message, or waste time musing about the range of possible toppings that could embellish the next pizza. Supervision will ensure that volunteers stay on task and that the phone bank proceeds smoothly. Good training will minimize the amount of oversight required.[4]

Experimental Research on Telephone Calling

Several dozen experiments have assessed whether phone calls mobilize voters. As we review the experimental literature, we first consider the mobilizing effects of robo calls, both partisan and nonpartisan. Next, we summarize a series of experiments on the mobilizing effects of commercial phone banks. Finally, we discuss the rich array of volunteer phone banks that have been subjected to experimental evaluation.

Robo Calls: Inexpensive . . . And You Get What You Pay For

In a study conducted in Seattle in November 2001, a nonpartisan group hired a robo call vendor to place 10,000 calls with a recorded message from the local registrar of voters reminding citizens to vote in the next day's municipal elections.[5] The turnout rate among those who were called was no higher than that of the control group. This pattern held for those who voted in person as well as those who voted absentee. Of course, it could be argued that the registrar of voters lacked the pizzazz of a movie star or a famous politician. But the Seattle experiment nonetheless shows that reminders to vote do not in and of themselves raise turnout rates. The significance of this point should not be underestimated. "Forgetting" Election Day is not why registered voters fail to cast ballots. Low voter turnout reflects low motivation, not forgetfulness.

Celebrity callers seem no more effective at mobilizing voters. In 2002 the National Association of Latino Elected Officials made robo calls to mobilize Latino voters in five states.[6] Two calls were placed to each voter, one from a Spanish-language-television anchorwoman and another from a local radio or television celebrity. Both messages were conveyed in Spanish (except in one region, where one of the calls was in English).

Robo calls again appeared to have a miniscule effect on turnout. Despite the enormous size of this experiment, which involved more than 250,000 people in the treatment group and 100,000 in the control group, the mobilizing effects of robo calls were so weak that they could not be distinguished statistically from zero.

The same goes for an experiment using a pair of messages recorded by actress and recording star Vanessa Williams.[7] During the final weekend of the 2004 presidential election campaign, either a GOTV message or an "election protection" message targeted large samples of black and white voters in North Carolina and Missouri, both non-battleground but somewhat competitive states. Neither message had any effect on either racial group in either state.

Perhaps the problem is that people don't turn to celebrities for political advice. Looking for a more authoritative voice, faith-based mobilization groups in an area with a large Catholic and Latino population encouraged local priests to record bilingual robo calls encouraging voter participation. These experiments were much smaller in scale than the massive experiments mentioned above, but the result was the same: no effect.[8]

Perhaps the problem is that for political advice to be credible, it must come from a party's top political leader. The opportunity to test this hypothesis on a grand scale presented itself in a 2006 Texas Republican primary. One of the candidates for reappointment as state supreme court justice was endorsed by the popular Republican governor, Rick Perry, who had initially appointed him to the seat. Governor Perry recorded a robo call encouraging Republicans to vote in the primary in support of his nominee, whom he praised as a true conservative. Here was a Republican governor speaking to his fellow Texas Republicans about why they should reelect his conservative appointee. A robo call experiment was conducted involving hundreds of thousands of Republicans who had been "microtargeted" as Perry supporters. The results indicate that those in the treatment group, on average, voted at 0.4 percentage point higher than the control group, but despite the enormous sample, the effect is not statistically distinguishable from zero.

The results suggest that robo calls have minimal effects on turnout. Pooling all of the results from robo call experiments together suggests that one vote is generated for every 900 people who receive a robo call (either live or on their answering machine). This effect is so small that it falls well short of statistical significance, which is to say that the true average effect could well be zero. Granted, from the standpoint of cost-efficiency, even a tiny positive effect might make this inexpensive technology worthwhile. Experiments conducted to date, although encompassing more than a million observations, have yet to isolate this tiny positive effect. Robo calls might help you to stretch your resources in ways that allow you to contact the maximum number of people, but don't expect to move them very much, if at all.

Commercial Phone Banks

Although more influential than robo calls, calls from commercial phone banks often have weak effects on turnout. In 1998 we conducted two nonpartisan campaigns using a single commercial phone bank.[9] The smaller of the two campaigns was conducted in New Haven; a much larger study was conducted in neighboring West Haven. In both cities, the elections were rather quiet affairs, with relatively little campaign activity. In both experiments, the group receiving phone calls voted at rates that were no greater than the rates of the control group receiving no calls. None of the three scripts—one stressing civic duty, another, neighborhood solidarity, and a third, the possibility of deciding a close election—had any appreciable impact.

Curious as to whether this result was due to the failings of a single phone bank, we replicated the 1998 experiments on a grand scale in 2002.[10] Congressional districts in Iowa and Michigan were divided into two categories, depending on whether they featured competitive or uncompetitive races. Within each category, 15,000 randomly selected individuals at distinct addresses were assigned to be called by one of two commercial phone banks, each delivering the same nonpartisan message. Thus 60,000 people in all were called in the treatment group, and more than 1 million names were placed in the control group. In the 2002 study, the treatment effects were just barely on the positive side of zero. Taken at face value, the results suggest that these phone banks mobilized one additional voter for every 280 people they spoke with, but the effects were not statistically distinguishable from zero. Another massive study in Illinois, which called voters before the 2004 November election using a similar nonpartisan script, found somewhat larger effects.[11] This time one vote was generated per fifty-five completed calls. However, this study is counterbalanced by a pair of large nonpartisan experiments in North Carolina and Missouri, which found conventional calls to have meager effects, just one vote generated per 500 contacts.[12]

The findings from experimental tests of commercial phone banks have not sat well with those in the phone bank industry. In a blistering attack on these results published in *Campaigns & Elections* magazine, Janet Grenzke and Mark Watts denounce these results on the grounds that the use of nonpartisan scripts "betray[s] basic misunderstandings about why and how GOTV efforts are conducted and to whom they are directed." "Effective GOTV campaign messages," Grenzke and Watts argue, "are [written for] and aimed at partisan audiences."[13] Their claim is that *real* campaign calls—the ones that seek to persuade people to support a candidate or issue—mobilize voters. That's a testable proposition. Let's see what the evidence says.

John McNulty conducted an experiment examining the effects of advocacy calls made by a campaign seeking to defeat a municipal ballot measure in San Francisco.[14] Close to 30,000 calls (about half resulting in successful contact) were made by a commercial phone center located in the Midwest. The script was very brief:

Hello [name]. I'm calling on behalf of the Coalition for San Francisco Neighborhoods, reminding you to oppose Proposition D. Proposition D is a risky scheme that allows the PUC [Public Utility Commission] to issue revenue bonds without voter approval. These bonds would be paid back through higher utility rates. Can we count on you to join us in opposing Proposition D next Tuesday?

Consistent with other findings concerning the delivery of brief scripts by commercial phone banks, one vote was produced for every 200 successful contacts. A much larger experiment conducted by Christopher Mann tells the same story. GOTV phone calls before the 2006 general elections had no effect, regardless of whether these calls were made using nonpartisan messages or messages advocating support for a minimum wage measure.[15]

Turning from ballot measures to candidates, the pattern of results remains unchanged. Emily Cardy examined the results of an experiment in which a commercial phone bank called to persuade voters identified as pro-choice to support the pro-choice candidate in a 2002 Democratic gubernatorial primary.[16] Again, the turnout effects were minimal, amounting to roughly one vote for every 250 contacts. Weaker findings emerge from a hotly contested 2004 congressional primary in which a pro-choice interest group sought to encourage voters to vote in support of a pro-choice challenger to an incumbent in a solidly Democratic district. This large experiment found no difference in turnout rates between the treatment and control groups.

The notion that advocacy phone calls are better at mobilizing voters receives no support from an array of large and well-executed experiments. However, it could be argued that these experiments stop short of making explicit partisan appeals. What happens when one tries to mobilize Republicans and Democrats using either nonpartisan scripts or scripts that urge them as partisans to back a party's candidate? Costas Panagopoulos conducted this experiment in an Albany, New York, mayoral contest.[17] Targeting registered Democrats or Republicans, callers from a commercial phone bank read either partisan or nonpartisan scripts. The partisan scripts were drafted by seasoned political consultants from each party. Consistent with the pattern of findings described above, neither the partisan calls nor the nonpartisan calls had an appreciable effect on turnout; if anything, the nonpartisan script worked slightly better.

Before giving up on commercial phone banks, we must consider the possibility that the effectiveness of these calls hinges on the manner in which they are delivered. Having eavesdropped on many hours of commercial phone canvassing, we know that many callers rush through the scripts. Their mechanical style conveys little enthusiasm about voting. These callers, who can forge through fifty or so completed calls per hour, behave much as one would expect given the incentives of piecework and the eagerness of supervisors to move on to the next calling campaign.

In 2002 David Nickerson evaluated a youth-oriented voter mobilization campaign in which a commercial phone bank was paid top dollar to deliver its GOTV appeal in a chatty and unhurried manner.[18] The script required the reader to pause for questions and to invite respondents to visit a website in order to learn more about their polling location. A good deal of coaching ensured that this appeal was read at the proper speed. Between one and four calls were made to randomly selected subgroups of young people over the four-week period leading up to Election Day. The phone bank kept records of each person they contacted, so that when respondents were contacted a second time, the script took notice of the fact that the previous conversation was being resumed. Because the experiment was very large and spread over more than a dozen regions, the results provide an unusually nuanced assessment of whether and when calls are most effective.

The bottom line is that these calls produced a substantial and statistically significant increase in voter turnout in the target group, but only among those called during the final week of the campaign. In other words, calls made during the first three weeks of a month-long GOTV campaign had no apparent effect on voter turnout. Calls made during the last week produced one vote for every twenty contacts. These results suggest that a phone call's impact is greatest close to Election Day. But here's where things get murky. A follow-up experiment conducted by Costas Panagopoulos randomly assigned the timing of nonpartisan calls before a mayoral election in Rochester, New York, in 2005. [19] The calls were made by a commercial phone bank using conventional nonpartisan scripts that were somewhat shorter and less interactive than the scripts used by the phone bank that Nickerson studied. The Rochester results show no increase in the impact of phone calls closer to the election; the calls had weakly positive effects regardless of whether they were made a few days or a few weeks before Election Day. One interpretation is that timing is crucial to high-quality efforts and that more conventional commercial phone bank efforts have weak effects even when the calls are made close to Election Day.

As further proof that a carefully supervised phone bank campaign can work, another commercial phone bank was trained by Youth Vote staff in Denver (see box 6-2). An even lengthier script was prepared for the callers, who were selected on the basis of age, told about Youth Vote's mission, and given Youth Vote buttons to wear while making calls. Youth Vote staff sat with the callers on-site as they made their calls, to ensure the quality of the operation. When the election was over, turnout figures showed this phone bank to be quite successful, increasing turnout by one voter for every eighteen people contacted.

These findings suggest that the quality of the phone call makes all the difference. If this hypothesis is correct, a given phone bank can produce large or small effects, depending on the manner in which it conducts its calls. To test this hypothesis, an experiment was conducted in 2004, calling voters in North Carolina and Missouri. [20] A large phone bank deployed three kinds of nonpartisan scripts: a standard script akin to the ones used above; a longer, chattier script in which people were asked whether they knew their polling location, which was provided on request; and a still longer script in which people were encouraged both to vote and to mobilize their friends and neighbors to vote. The results are suggestive, if a bit puzzling. As expected, the standard script had weak effects, raising turnout by just 1.2 percentage points among those contacted. Also as expected, the medium script had a fairly large effect, raising turnout by 3.4 percentage points. This statistically significant

Box 6-2. A "Conversational" Youth Vote 2002 Script

Hi [first name]. My name is [your full name], and I'm calling on behalf of the Youth Vote Coalition [pronounce slowly and clearly as it is hard for many people to understand "Youth Vote" the first time they hear it]. This is not a sales call, and we are not affiliated with any particular political party or candidate. Youth Vote is a national nonprofit, nonpartisan organization composed of diverse groups all working together to increase voter turnout among eighteen- to thirty-year-olds.

The reason we are contacting you is to thank you for registering to vote. You have taken the first crucial step in giving yourself the power to make your voice heard in our democracy. However, even more important than that is the fact that you actually DO vote on Election Day. This year's Senate race in Colorado is especially important and could have national implications in determining the balance of power in Congress. It is expected that less than 500 votes may determine the outcome of this race. Your vote can make a difference. Thus we encourage you to take the time to vote in the upcoming election on TUESDAY, NOVEMBER 5th, between the hours of 7 a.m. and 7 p.m.

Have you received your voter registration card in the mail?

[If yes:] OK, that tells you where your polling location is. But just so you know, your polling location is at [name of place and address]. Again, you can vote between the hours of 7 a.m. and 7 p.m. and will need to show your voter registration card and/or a government-issued picture ID. Lastly, we would like to provide you with a toll-free phone number and websites for obtaining nonpartisan information on the candidates and issues in your area. The number is 1-888-Vote-Smart (1-888-868-3762), and the websites are www.vote-smart.org [make sure you say vote-dash-smart.org] and www.youthvote.org.

Well [person's first name], I'd like to thank you for your time. Again, remember to mark your calendar to vote on Tuesday, November 5th, and encourage your friends and family to vote, too. Have a good evening.

increase implies that one vote was generated for every thirty completed calls. The puzzling result is the fact that the chatty recruit-your-friends script had an unexpectedly weak effect, one vote per sixty-nine completed calls. Apparently, coming up with the right chatty script is still more art than science.

Volunteer Phone Banks

The relaxed, authentic style of most volunteer phone banks provides the right ingredients for success. A wealth of experimental evidence, however, cautions that volunteer phone banks are often, but not always, effective. For example, in the weeks leading up to the November 2000 elections, the Youth Vote coalition of nonpartisan organizations targeting young voters had mixed success in generating votes.[21] Of the four sites in the experiment, two showed large effects (Albany and Stony Brook), and two showed weak effects (Boulder and Eugene). Overall, one vote was generated for every twenty-two contacts. When Youth Vote repeated this experiment in 2001—this time targeting voters of all ages—the effects were weaker but still positive.

In 2002 the volunteer phone banks were pitted against the commercial phone bank described above in an effort to determine which approach produced more youth votes.[22] This time, the volunteer phone banks were given a very ambitious goal—to contact thousands or even tens of thousands of voters. Many sites got a late start in organizing their campaign and were forced to turn to paid staff, in some cases from temporary employment agencies. Turnover among callers was high, and supervisory staff was stretched thin by responsibilities other than the phone bank. This meant that local sites frequently relied on callers with minimal training. The net result was a flop: the local phone banks increased turnout at a rate of one voter for every fifty-nine calls.

The importance of enthusiasm and training is illustrated further by three successful efforts in 2002. A volunteer calling campaign funded by the Michigan Democratic Party attempted to contact 10,550 registered voters between the ages of eighteen and thirty-five and completed calls with 5,319 of them.[23] The net effect was to raise turnout significantly among those contacted: one additional vote was produced for every twenty-nine people contacted. NALEO's local phone bank campaign, which was directed toward Latino registered voters in Los Angeles and Orange counties, raised turnout significantly among those contacted,

---

Box 6-3. An Ethnic Mobilization Script

The National Association of Latino Elected Officials used the following
script, in English or Spanish, depending on the language spoken by the
respondent:

> Good evening. My name is [your name]. I'm calling on behalf of
> NALEO. I am calling to remind you that the upcoming election will be
> held on Tuesday, November 5th. Your vote will help build a stronger
> community. Do you plan to vote on Tuesday, November 5th?
>
> [If the response is yes:] Your participation in the upcoming election
> means better schools, better jobs, and safer neighborhoods. To keep
> our community growing, we have to vote. Don't forget to vote in the
> upcoming election on Tuesday, November 5th. The polls will be open
> from 7 a.m. to 8 p.m. Thank you and have a good evening.
>
> [If the response is no:] Your vote is very important in the upcoming
> election. Your vote can ensure better schools, better jobs, and safer
> neighborhoods. To keep our community growing, we must vote.
> NALEO encourages you to vote in the upcoming election on Tuesday,
> November 5th. The polls will be open from 7 a.m. to 8 p.m. Thank you
> and have a good evening.

---

producing one vote for every twenty-two contacts.[24] A nonpartisan
phone bank in Los Angeles County, organized by University of Southern
California professor Janelle Wong, targeted ethnic Chinese voters and
raised turnout significantly.[25]

Again, this is not to say that volunteer phone banks staffed by enthusiastic callers are a surefire success. Several of the other Asian groups
that Wong targeted in Los Angeles County were unmoved by the GOTV
appeal. It may be that the brevity of her voting reminders and the lack of
ethnic appeal robbed the scripts of some of their impact (see boxes 6-3
and 6-4 for sample scripts).

Another good example of what committed volunteers are capable of
achieving is illustrated by an experiment conducted by Joel Middleton in
coordination with MoveOn.org. In a 2006 special congressional election
in California, MoveOn directed its decentralized web-based phone bank

Box 6-4. A Reminder Script

Janelle Wong of the University of Southern California organized a multilingual phone bank in Los Angeles that made nonpartisan turnout appeals to 1,598 registered voters with Chinese, Japanese, Korean, Indian, and Filipino surnames. The script was very brief, consisting of little more than a reminder to vote:

Hi. May I please speak to Mr./Mrs./Ms. [last name or full name]? My name is [your name], and I'm a student at USC. I'm calling from CAUSE-Vision21. I'm not trying to sell you anything. I just wanted to call and remind you to vote on Tuesday, November 5. If you have any questions about voting, you can call this hotline: 888-809-3888.

effort at voters who were identified as potential supporters of the Democratic candidate. The net result was one additional vote for every twenty-six contacts, which is a strong and statistically reliable effect.

The MoveOn experiment illustrates one further point, which is that a follow-up call just before Election Day can boost the effect of an initial call. This finding corroborates an earlier experiment conducted by the Public Interest Research Group (PIRG) in New Jersey. Before the 2003 state legislative elections, PIRG conducted a phone bank campaign targeting young voters. The experiment involved randomly assigning those who received the first call to a second round of Election Day phone calls. Interestingly, the effects of the second round of calls were large, but only among those who in the first round of calls said that they intended to vote. Clearly, this experiment needs to be replicated before the recontact-the-intended-voters adage becomes authoritative. But there is mounting evidence to suggest that this adage should be taken seriously in the meantime. Recontacting intended voters is precisely what the Southwest Voter Registration and Education Project did in its large-scale November 2006 campaign in Los Angeles, and its results mark the strongest phone-calling effect of any volunteer phone bank: one additional vote for every eleven contacts.

Overall, volunteer phone banks have a fairly good track record of mobilizing those whom they contact. The rule of thumb that emerges from our review of this literature is that one additional voter is produced for every thirty-eight contacts. The real question for volunteer phone banks is not whether they work under optimal conditions but rather whether they can achieve a sufficient volume of calls to make a difference. It is the rare volunteer phone bank that can complete the 38,000 calls needed to generate 1,000 votes. The experience of Youth Vote in 2002 suggests that striving to expand the quantity of calls can jeopardize their quality.

Lessons Learned

The lessons emerging from these studies are rated according to the system detailed in chapter 2: three stars are for findings that have received solid confirmation from several experiments, two stars are for more equivocal findings based on one or two experiments, and one star is for findings that are suggestive but not conclusive.

★★★ *Robo calls have a very weak effect on voter turnout.* Thus far, none of the experiments using robo calls has been able to distinguish their effects from zero. Our best guess, based on experiments involving more than 1 million voters, places the vote production rate somewhere in the neighborhood of one vote per 1,000 contacts, but given the shaky state of the evidence, robo calls may have no effect at all. If you are attempting to mobilize voters in a constituency with millions of people and willing to gamble that robo calls do work, this tactic may be a cost-effective option, given the very low cost per call. But do not expect to notice the effects of a robo call campaign, since optimistically it takes roughly 1 million completed calls to produce 1,000 votes.

★★★ *Volunteer phone banks are often effective, but their quality varies, and their capacity to contact large numbers of people is often limited or unpredictable.* The average volunteer phone bank generates one vote for every thirty-eight completed calls, but there is significant variation among volunteer phone bank efforts. Of the nineteen distinct experimental studies of volunteer phone banks, seven found effects of less than one vote per fifty contacts, and five found effects of better than one vote per twenty-five contacts.

★ *Volunteer phone bank scripts that consist only of a brief reminder seem to produce votes at the lower end of the volunteer phone bank spectrum.*

Wong's study of brief volunteer phone calls produced a weaker-than-average effect, and so did the volunteer phone bank organized by Jason Barabas and his colleagues, which called to remind Florida voters that certain ballot measures would be presented in the 2006 election.

★★ *Live calls conducted by professional phone banks typically produce weak effects.* A standard commercial phone script of approximately thirty seconds in length (with little interaction between caller and voter) on average increases turnout by 0.55 percentage point among those contacted. Due to the very large size of the ten experimental studies that have measured it, this estimate is statistically distinguishable from zero and implies that one vote is generated for every 180 completed calls. Telemarketing firms charge a substantial premium for more conversational and interactive scripts, as longer scripts increase the costs of training and supervision, while cutting the number of completed calls per hour. These augmented phone bank efforts appear to be significantly more influential. The experiments gauging the effects of high-quality calls suggest that they generate one vote per thirty-five contacts.

★★ *The effectiveness of professional phone banks has little to do with the specific reasons for voting stressed in the scripts.* Any reasonable script will work or not work, depending on whether it is delivered in an unhurried manner. The three nonpartisan scripts used in the 1998 New Haven and West Haven experiments were equally ineffective, as were the three scripts used in the 2002 Youth Vote campaign. Experiments that directly compare partisan and nonpartisan scripts—the 2005 Albany experiment conducted by Costas Panagopoulos and the 2006 Missouri experiment conducted by Christopher Mann—found no difference in effectiveness.

★★ *Recontacting people who earlier expressed an intention to vote boosts the effectiveness of a calling campaign.* Volunteer phone banks have had good success conducting a second round of calls close to Election Day targeting those who earlier said that they intended to vote. Either people who express an intention to vote are especially receptive to reminders or they feel obligated to honor their previous commitment when reminded of it.

★ *Calls are most effective during the last week prior to the election.* Calls made earlier than this do not appear to influence voter turnout. This intuitively appealing hypothesis is supported by an experiment involving a well-trained and carefully supervised professional phone bank in 2002 but is not supported by a subsequent experiment involving a conventional call from a commercial phone bank. An ineffective phone bank tactic does not become effective simply because it is deployed on the eve of the election.

Cost-Effectiveness

Gauging the cost-effectiveness of alternative phone bank strategies is no simple matter, because the effectiveness of phone banks varies markedly depending on how the callers are trained and supervised. When commercial phone banks deliver brief scripts that involve little conversation between caller and voter, they generate votes at the rate of one per 180 completed calls. At a rate of $0.50 per completed call, that amounts to $90 per additional vote.[26]

In contrast, top-of-the-line commercial phone banks cost $1.50 per completed call. It is easy to burn a lot of money paying this type of phone bank to make early calls and to call each respondent repeatedly, but a properly targeted campaign seems to pay off. Suppose this phone bank had contacted voters just once during the last week of the campaign. Assuming that votes were produced at a rate of one per thirty-five contacts, the cost per vote would be $53 per vote. Obviously, this rate would fall if you were to bargain down the price to, say, $1 per contact. Bear in mind, however, that these figures presuppose a great deal of supervision and training, without which the quality and effectiveness of the calls may well deteriorate.

Volunteer phone banks staffed by activists produce votes at an average rate of approximately one per thirty-eight contacts (contacts here exclude messages left with housemates). If volunteers are paid at a rate of $16 per hour and make sixteen such contacts per hour, then one additional vote costs $38. If you have the good fortune of working with talented volunteers, who generate votes at a rate of one vote per twenty completed calls, this rate falls to $20 per vote. Obviously, lower wage rates mean better cost-efficiency, but higher supervision and training costs work in the opposite direction. Most important, the cost of recruiting and maintaining a sufficient number of volunteers to staff a sizable phone bank campaign drives up the costs of a volunteer operation.

So, as you reflect on your own circumstances, ask yourself the following questions: How much dependable and committed labor can I muster and at what hourly rate? Do I have easy access to the resources that make a volunteer phone bank run smoothly (for example, phones, supervisory staff)? Finally, what are the opportunity costs of choosing either a commercial or a volunteer phone bank?

The last question deserves special consideration in the light of your campaign's goals. Using a commercial phone bank to propel you to victory may make the celebration a somewhat lonely affair. Those who lament the professionalization of politics point out that the advent of commercial phone banks means that fewer local people participate in campaigns and that the pool of political activists gradually diminishes. If you rely on local activists, you may be able to ask them for labor and political support in the future.

Assessment and Conclusions

Although telephone communication is more than a century old, it continues to evolve rapidly. Cell phones, once the province of science fiction, are now as common as the microwave oven. Yet more than 90 percent of registered voters still live in households with "landline" telephones as well. A large and growing number of residences have caller identification or privacy manager technology, yet fewer than 5 percent of all calls from commercial phone banks are blocked as a result. New rules concerning "do not call lists" designed to prevent telemarketers from making unsolicited calls do not apply to live political phone banks, but they may discourage vendors who distribute phone databases for both political and other purposes from gathering these numbers. Several states have passed legislation restricting the use of robo calls, even robo calls by political campaigns. No one knows how these legal and technological trends will play out in the future. Phone campaigns could become considerably more difficult.

As it stands, phone-based GOTV campaigns are a hit-or-miss affair. Robo phone calls may produce wonderful anecdotes about people coming home from work to find a phone message from their favorite celebrity, but the miniscule effect of these calls on turnout continues to defy scientific detection. Our best guess is that robo calls generate one vote per 1,000 calls, but to detect an effect this small requires an enormous experiment in which 4 million voters are divided equally between treatment and control groups. Live calls made by the typical telemarketing firm are somewhat more effective but also more costly. Commercial phone banks, when well coached and carefully supervised, can do an excellent job of producing votes, but their cost-effectiveness depends on the premium charged to deliver a longer, more conversational appeal. In terms of cost per vote, high-quality volunteer efforts have an edge over other types of phone banks—when they take shape as planned. Too often, they fall flat and fail to attract sizable numbers of motivated callers. Falling back on temporary workers means incurring all the hassles of maintaining a phone bank operation with very little payoff in terms of votes.

The ability to tailor a phone bank to serve your purposes has much to do with the resources at your disposal. Can you recruit capable volunteers? Do you have the time and energy to devote to overseeing a volunteer phone bank? If you hire a commercial phone bank, will you be able to work out a deal whereby you help to coach and monitor the callers?

The scientific understanding of phone banking has grown dramatically in recent years, as experiments increase in number and sophistication. Yet many questions about phone banks remain unanswered. Can volunteer efforts be made more effective, perhaps by assigning people to be in charge of mobilizing their friends and neighbors? Do phone calls directed to specific individuals have indirect mobilizing effects on other voters living at the same address? Are robo calls incapable of having a big influence on the recipient, or are there ways to give them greater impact, perhaps by "personalizing" them in some fashion? Can the MoveOn.org model of coordinating cell phone calls by enthusiastic activists provide an ample supply of callers, or do their numbers and effectiveness dwindle over time or across elections? Campaigns may yet discover the optimal mixture of technology and political enthusiasm.

CHAPTER SEVEN

Electronic Mail:
Faster, Cheaper, but Does It Work?

Every new form of communication technology opens new opportunities for mobilizing voters. The explosive growth of the Internet has drawn an increasing number of Americans into the world of electronic mail. According to national surveys, 70 percent of the population used e-mail in 2006, up from 57 percent in 2003 and 46 percent in 2000.[1] Because both voting and computer use are correlated with income, e-mail usage is especially common among registered voters.

From the vantage point of campaigns, electronic mail has three attractive properties, at least in principle. First, if a group or campaign has access to e-mail addresses, it may reach large numbers of people instantly at very low unit cost. Second, e-mail enables recipients to forward messages easily to their friends, which creates the possibility of extending the influence of a given mailing. Finally, the content of e-mail is very flexible. It is easy to design mailings that direct recipients to websites, which in turn instruct them how to register, where and when to vote, how to find out more about the candidates, and whom to contact in order to become more involved in a campaign.

The downside of e-mail is that recipients are overrun with unsolicited communication, known as spam. Many e-mail servers are equipped with filters that automatically reject or reroute spam. And even when spam wends its way past these filters, there is no guarantee that the recipient will read the message after examining the subject line (the title of the e-mail). Even if the recipient reads a GOTV message, there remains the further question of whether this medium actually generates votes. It is one thing to present recipients with options that they can choose immediately from the comfort of their chair, such as visiting a website that tells them where to vote, and another to motivate them to get out of that chair on some future date in order to cast a ballot.

In this chapter, we evaluate the effectiveness of get-out-the-vote appeals conveyed by electronic mail. After describing the nuts and bolts of assembling an e-mail campaign, we examine five large-scale experiments that assessed the effects of nonpartisan and partisan e-mail on voter turnout. Three of these studies involved e-mail from nonpartisan groups, one was from a political party to its regular e-mail distribution list, and one was from an environmental advocacy group to its members. Although these five studies do not exhaust the range of ways in which mass e-mail can be used to mobilize voters, they do show a clear and consistent pattern. None of the studies found higher rates of voting among those who were randomly targeted with e-mail. We conclude the chapter by discussing some promising ways that e-mail's effectiveness might be enhanced and, finally, by reviewing some intriguing experimental evidence suggesting that text messaging—sending brief written messages to cell phones—raises voter turnout.

The Nuts and Bolts of an E-Mail Campaign

Depending on your familiarity with computers, the prospect of sending a mass mailing of e-mail is either daunting or a source of techie excitement. Regardless of whether you distribute the e-mail yourself or rely on a commercial firm, the basic requirements are the same. You need a mailing list and a message. The challenge is to find the right list and the right message.

Lists

Like phone and direct mail campaigns, e-mail campaigns require a target list. These lists come in three forms. The first is an "opt-in" list of e-mails—addresses supplied by individuals who wish to be contacted by your campaign. Lists of this kind are hard to come by because they require advance work on somebody's part. For example, when registering new voters, you can encourage them to provide their e-mail address so that you can remind them when and where to vote. Some commercial vendors sell opt-in lists, obtained by asking vast numbers of e-mail addressees whether they are willing to receive political communications via e-mail. What counts as opting in varies from vendor to vendor. High-quality opt-in lists include only those people who actively consent to receive political e-mail. Low-quality lists contain names of people who did not object when offered the opportunity to receive political spam. This type of opt-in list might be called a "neglected to opt out" list, since many of the people on it simply failed to read or answer their e-mail. The quality of an opt-in list determines its price. Low-quality opt-in lists go for $0.10 per name. High-quality commercial opt-in lists are often quite expensive, somewhere on the order of $0.50 per name. Bear in mind that $0.50 buys one brief live phone call or ten robo calls.

The second type of list is an administrative database maintained by a particular group or organization. For example, colleges typically maintain a directory of their students' e-mail addresses. Political organizations periodically e-mail loyalists, resulting in a fairly reliable collection of e-mail addresses and high (by Internet standards) percentages of people who open the e-mail. Depending on your connections and the purposes of your campaign, you may be able to use or purchase these lists. For example, the nonpartisan organization Votes For Students (VFS) was able to purchase the e-mail databases of nineteen colleges, comprising hundreds of thousands of e-mail addresses. The advantage of administrative lists is that they often are linked to mailing addresses, information that allows you to target people in your jurisdiction.

Finally, many commercial vendors supply generic lists of e-mail addresses. How they obtain these addresses is often a mystery. One common technique is to create a program that searches through millions of web pages, harvesting all of the e-mail addresses listed therein. These lists tend to be dirt cheap ($50 will buy millions of addresses). But it is anybody's guess as to whether they contain any registered voters in your jurisdiction. Unless you are especially interested in getting the word out to people in faraway places, you should avoid generic lists.

Messages

An e-mail message should be thought of as three distinct components. The first is the subject line. This line frequently determines whether your message makes it past spam filters designed to prevent mass mailings (such as yours). The more personal the message, the less likely it is to be stopped by filters or shunted to a bulk mail box. There are, of course, all sorts of sleazy tricks to get past these filters, such as using the subject line "MESSAGE RETURNED, NAMESERVER ERROR." Do not resort to these tactics. It is hard to imagine that voters who open an e-mail with this misleading subject line will be receptive to the GOTV message that awaits them. Take the high road and formulate a short phrase that might plausibly encourage recipients to vote in the upcoming election. For example, "Need help finding your polling place in today's election?" or "Lincoln County elections today: Polls open from 6 a.m. to 8 p.m." This has the added effect of getting the message across even to those who do not open your e-mail.

The second component of an e-mail is the text. How the text looks to readers will depend on the mail browser they are using. Some may read the text as though it were printed by an old-fashioned typewriter; others may be able to appreciate your choice of font and type size. Before sending a message, do a trial run with a few types of mail browsers to see how it will come across. One style of e-mail is to present people with a few simple messages, with web links to follow if they seek additional information. Another is to hit people with a wall of words, as though they were delving into a newspaper story. The former has the advantage of being accessible to most voters, although the latter seems popular among universities, where students sometimes forward authoritative-sounding e-mails to their friends.

The final aspect of e-mail is graphics. Primitive e-mail readers will not display them, and neither will newer ones that are designed to filter unsolicited and perhaps distasteful images. But most e-mail users see graphics when they open up an e-mail. One advantage of sending graphics is that they make the message more vivid and memorable.

Another advantage of sending e-mail to html-compatible e-mail browsers is that your e-mail server is alerted when the message is loaded, enabling you to count the number of messages that have been opened. In the experiments described below, this information was crucial: without it, researchers would not have been able to distinguish an e-mail campaign that failed because no one read the messages from an e-mail campaign that failed because the messages, when read, failed to motivate people to vote.

Experimental Evidence Concerning E-Mail

Evaluating the effectiveness of an e-mail campaign is no mean feat. It is easy to send e-mail, but hard to link e-mail addresses to individual voters.

This problem bedeviled the first experimental study of e-mail, conducted during the 2000 campaign by John Phillips of Yale University.[2] His approach was to conduct a postelection survey, by e-mail, of 6,000 young registered voters whose names had been placed into treatment and control groups. The problem with this strategy is that people who received the e-mail encouragement to vote, and did so, might be especially inclined to respond to the survey. In addition, this approach relies on self-reports about voter turnout. The fact that this study found a series of three e-mails to have negligible mobilization effects is suggestive but not reliable.

Fortunately, a golden opportunity for an evaluation of GOTV e-mail presented itself in the form of the Votes For Students campaign in 2002. Votes For Students, as the name suggests, is a nonpartisan organization designed to encourage voter participation by college students. Led by an imaginative and energetic group of University of Minnesota undergraduates, VFS collaborated with colleges to assemble an enormous database of student e-mail addresses.

VFS programmers created a computer platform capable of sending large quantities of e-mail and of monitoring the rate at which these messages were opened. In order to allow for the possibility that students might forward the VFS e-mail to friends, these experimental e-mails were sent out in varying "density" to each campus. Some campuses received a high density of e-mail—90 percent of the students received VFS messages. On other campuses only one-third of the students received VFS messages. If students in the treatment group were infecting students in the control group, the low-density schools should show bigger treatment effects than the high-density schools.

The content and frequency of the e-mail varied considerably from school to school, as illustrated in box 7-1. Students attending the University of Minnesota were treated to a dose of school spirit, inasmuch as the six e-mails encouraging voter participation typically ended with the cheer "Go Gophers!" In most other cases, students received four e-mails because Votes For Students obtained the school's e-mail database later than expected. An early October e-mail conveyed information about how to register to vote. A late October message provided information about how to obtain an absentee ballot. A few days before the election, students were reminded of the importance of voting. A final reminder was sent on Election Day.

As expected, many of the VFS e-mails went unopened. Combining all of the sites, 20 percent of the recipients appeared to open at least one of

Box 7-1. Text of the Six E-Mail Messages Sent to University of Minnesota Students

1. Subject line: Deadline Oct. 15, Register to Vote Online Today
As college students we have made excuses for too long about why we don't vote. We need to stop ignoring our duty and just do it. Votes For Students is a nonpartisan organization that gives you all the voting tools needed to stop making excuses. By clicking on the link below, you can get a voter registration form, access an absentee ballot online, and more. As college students, let's stop neglecting democracy. VOTE. Oh, and enjoy homecoming. GO GOPHERS!

2. Subject line: Online Voter Registration: Deadline Tuesday
Fellow U of M students
For the past two years we have seen huge tuition increases because not enough students vote. We as students need to change that. It is now possible by clicking on the link below to download a voter registration form and get access to an absentee ballot online. Take advantage of how easy it is to vote these days and do your part to stop the tuition increases. VOTE. Oh, and enjoy homecoming. GO GOPHERS!

3a. Subject line: Request an Absentee Ballot Online Today
College students are some of the busiest people around. We know because we are students like you. To make your life easier we have taken away all the hassles of voting this fall. By clicking on the link below, you can get voter registration forms, access an absentee ballot online, and more. Take advantage of how quick and easy voting is this fall. Oh, and enjoy homecoming. GO GOPHERS.

3b. Subject Line: Reminder: Get your Absentee Ballot Today
As we saw in Florida, one vote can make a difference, your vote. Votes For

the VFS e-mails. At a minimum, students were exposed to a series of e-mail subject lines that called attention to voter registration deadlines and the impending election.

The massive size of the experiment enabled David Nickerson to pinpoint the effect of e-mail with a high degree of precision.[3] After the election was over, certain colleges furnished both home addresses and campus addresses for the students in the treatment and control groups. He

Students is a student-run, nonpartisan organization working to give you everything you need to make your vote count. By clicking on the link below, you can get a voter registration form, access absentee ballots online, and more. Register, VOTE, make a difference. Oh, and enjoy homecoming. GO GOPHERS!

4. Subject line: Express you opinion on politics
Votes For Students would like to hear your opinion. Tell us what you think of politics and you will be eligible to win cash prizes of up to $500. By answering the question below as well as a short series of questions that will follow, you can help us learn about the student voice. Tell us your opinion and, more importantly, VOTE.

5. Subject line: Vote Tuesday, Nov. 5
Voting in Minnesota is as simple as voting gets. With same-day voter registration, Minnesota citizens can vote even if they missed earlier registration deadlines. All you need to do is take a picture ID (student ID is acceptable) and proof of your address. Do your part. VOTE Tuesday, November 5.

6. Subject line: Vote Today: Vote Tuesday, Nov. 5
A single vote can make a difference. Your vote. As we have seen in recent elections, one vote has the power to decide the future direction of our country. Your vote will impact the way our government addresses terrorism, education, the economy, and every other aspect of your life. And in Minnesota every citizen over eighteen can go to the polls and make a difference. All you need to do is take a picture ID (student ID is acceptable) and proof of your address. Do your part. VOTE today.

then matched these names and addresses to the voter rolls in order to see which students registered or voted. Undoubtedly, some of these addresses were out of date, but the capacity to match names accurately was identical for the treatment and control groups, and the results remained unchanged when he increased the stringency of the matching criteria.

In his analysis of the results, David Nickerson looked for evidence that students in the treatment group registered to vote and voted at higher rates than students in the control group. Neither proved to be the case. Although "click-through" data showed that Votes For Students directed thousands of people to a website that enabled them to register to vote online, the treatment group was no more likely to be registered to vote than the control group. Either the people directed to online registration failed to register, or they would have registered anyway, without the e-mail stimulus. By the same token, the turnout rates were no higher for the treatment group than for the control group. For example, the registration rate among the 3,312 Eastern Michigan University students in the treatment group was 48.4 percent. The registration rate among the 6,652 students in the control group was 49.7 percent. The voter turnout rate in the treatment group was 25.3 percent, compared with 26.4 percent in the control group. Weak registration and turnout effects were observed at every college site. Based on more than 50,000 experimental subjects in five sites, David Nickerson concluded that overall e-mail has a weakly negative effect on registration and turnout.

The next step in this line of research is to investigate whether e-mail is more effective when sent to people who allow their e-mail address to be part of an opt-in list.[4] Before a Houston municipal election in 2003, Youth Vote targeted an opt-in list containing the e-mail addresses of more than 12,000 registered young voters. The treatment group was sent a series of three e-mails encouraging them to become informed about the coming election and to visit the Youth Vote website, which between 5 and 8 percent did following each e-mail. Turnout, however, was not affected by this intervention. When David Nickerson tabulated the voter turnout rates for the treatment and control groups, he found that among the 6,386 people in the control group turnout was 9.2 percent. Among the 6,386 people in the treatment group turnout was 9.0 percent. In sum, it appears that young voters were unresponsive to both the Votes For Students e-mail and the Youth Vote e-mail.

What about sending e-mail to a more diverse age range? Or sending e-mail to people who specifically request to be on a mailing list reminding individuals to register and vote? Before the 2004 presidential election, a progressive organization called Working Assets sent GOTV e-mails to individuals who had visited its website and requested information about registration and voting. In all, 161,633 people who supplied their name and address received subsequent e-mail GOTV reminders. These reminders took several forms, two of which were studied. One reminded people that their state's voter registration deadline was approaching and encouraged them to vote. Another message, sent to those in same-day registration states, informed potential voters that they could vote even if they had not yet registered. Both of the messages encouraged their readers, saying, "Can one vote make a difference? One vote can make a difference! Just ask the folks in Florida."

Participants in the study came from seven states. David Nickerson found that in all seven states those assigned to the treatment group were slightly less likely to register than their control group counterparts. Turnout rates were not affected by the intervention.

The Nickerson studies, taken together, suggest that e-mail is a poor vehicle for boosting registration and turnout. But Nickerson's reports have one limitation: all of his experiments involved nonpartisan messages. The next question is whether messages from a political party to its e-mail list of core supporters would produce larger effects. To test this hypothesis, Alissa Stollwerk collaborated with the Democratic National Committee to assess the effects of three e-mails encouraging voter turnout in support of the Democratic mayoral candidate in the 2005 New York City general election.[5] The e-mails were sent in the late afternoon on election eve, on the morning of Election Day, and during the mid-afternoon of Election Day. The subject lines referred to voting, and the text of the e-mail itself implored Democrats to "vote to ensure that our representatives protect the values and beliefs that we all treasure." Of the 41,900 people in the treatment group, 13 percent opened at least one of the e-mails.

The partisan reminders, however, had no effect on voter turnout. Among the 41,900 people in the treatment group, the turnout rate was 58.7 percent. Among the 10,513 in the control group, turnout was 59.7 percent. Like the Nickerson studies, the Stollwerk study has a very small margin of error. Although it seems unlikely that partisan e-mail reduces turnout, the Stollwerk study demonstrated that its positive effects are probably very small. The fact that the Nickerson and Stollwerk experiments generated the same result—no effect—provides yet another indication that what matters is not so much the message, as the mode by which it is communicated.

Perhaps New York City Democrats were less than passionate about their party's mayoral candidate. Perhaps more passion would be generated if an environmental 501(c)(4) were to e-mail members of environmental groups.[6] Such a campaign was undertaken before the 2006 November election when this organization urged support for a county bond measure designed to "preserve our last remaining open space for our children and our grandchildren before it is lost to development." The three e-mail messages, sent before the election, contained graphics and text designed to emphasize the urgency of protecting rivers and streams as sources of clean drinking water. A brief postelection phone survey of 2,024 respondents evenly divided between treatment and control groups was conducted in order to assess the e-mail campaign's effectiveness. Among those assigned to receive the e-mails, 14.1 percent recalled receiving them.[7] Self-reported turnout was 80.9 percent in the control group and 79.9 percent in the treatment group. Validated turnout for the entire sample ($N = 18,818$), including those without phone numbers, was 52.0 percent in the treatment group and 52.4 percent in the control group.

Lessons Learned

The lessons emerging from these studies are rated according to the system detailed in chapter 2: three stars are for findings that have received solid confirmation from several experiments, two stars are for more equivocal findings based on one or two experiments, and one star is for findings that are suggestive but not conclusive.

★★★ *Nonpartisan e-mail designed to encourage voter participation has negligible effects on voter registration.* Although thousands of recipients of these e-mails followed links to sites where they could register online, registration rates for the treatment and control groups were almost identical. Absent these e-mail campaigns, the people who registered online would have registered anyway.

★★★ *E-mail appears to have negligible effects on voter turnout.* Studies of both nonpartisan and partisan e-mail found e-mail communication to have no positive effect on voter turnout. This finding holds across a range of age groups, target lists, and message styles.

Assessment and Conclusion

Given the current state of the evidence, the cost assessment of mass e-mail is rather dismal. Setting up a target database and hiring technical staff to design and distribute e-mail involve substantial start-up costs. The marginal cost of sending each e-mail is minimal, but unfortunately, the effects on registration and turnout are minimal as well.

Although a series of high-quality experiments have failed to find evidence of e-mail's effectiveness, it is too soon to give up on this medium. Given the tiny marginal costs of sending e-mail, it does not require much of an effect for e-mail to be a cost-effective means of mobilizing voters. The challenge for e-mail campaigns, then, is to experiment with a variety of approaches, in search of an appeal that works reliably. Disappointing as the results of the five experiments are, they are hardly proof that e-mail campaigns are doomed to fail.

Could the way forward be to send more personalized e-mail, perhaps propagated by friends encouraging each other to vote? A pilot experiment designed to test this proposition showed some promising initial results. Tiffany Davenport conducted a friends-to-friends e-mail experiment, in which each sender's network of friends was randomly assigned to receive either a mass GOTV e-mail (presumed to have no effect) or a personal e-mail note encouraging voter turnout.[8] Her preliminary results suggested that personalized friend-to-friend contact substantially increases turnout vis-à-vis the mass e-mail control group. This line of research may pave the way for a new generation of mobilization campaigns. Using the vast number of social connections provided by Facebook and other online communities may be the secret to making e-mail effective.

Or could the key be whether one's electronic messages rise above the fray of incoming communications? Allison Dale and Aaron Strauss conducted an experiment involving more than 8,500 telephone numbers of people who had registered to vote with one of three nonpartisan groups, sending half of them text messages from various nonpartisan groups urging them to vote the following day.[9] Their results showed a powerful effect of 3.1 percentage points and, when read in conjunction with two prior experiments on text messaging, suggest that this type of communication raises turnout by approximately 2.6 percentage points.[10] (As usual, there was no evidence of significant variations in the effect depending on whether the GOTV communication conveyed a "civic duty" or a "close election" message, and providing the number of a polling location hotline did not increase the effect.) Interpreted in light of the e-mail studies showing no effect, this intriguing result suggests that the mode of text communication is crucial. But what is it about receiving a message on one's phone that makes it so powerful? This finding seems to defy the basic thesis that impersonal communication is ineffective. Or does it instead show that the reason personal communication works is that it, like text messages on one's phone, commands the voter's attention?

CHAPTER EIGHT

Using Events to Draw
Voters to the Polls

It is the rare campaigner who looks forward to the prospect of calling and canvassing for weeks on end. Even people who genuinely love to talk with voters blanch at the prospect of contacting several hundred households. At the same time, most people who enjoy politics and political organizing relish the prospect of coordinating and attending campaign events.

Campaign events may take many forms. Events such as Election Day festivals attract potential voters by turning the polls into social gathering places. Forums and debates attract potential voters by bringing them into close contact with candidates, perhaps providing an opportunity for citizens to question candidates directly. Voter education seminars stimulate interest in the electoral process and provide information about how, when, and where to register and vote.

Over the years, we have found that many organizations that lack the capacity to conduct large-scale GOTV efforts are nonetheless quite good at organizing and publicizing events. This chapter aims to assess the effectiveness of these efforts. The results, though preliminary and tentative, suggest that events may represent a valuable supplement to conventional voter mobilization campaigns.

Campaign Events in Historical Perspective

Since the late 1880s, state laws have gradually distanced the individual voter from the hoopla surrounding Election Day. Before the introduction of the secret ballot, voters cast their votes in front of their peers. The political parties supplied printed ballots of varying colors. Voters could scratch out the party's suggested names and write other names instead, but these marks and the partisan complexion of the ballot were apparent to party onlookers. In Connecticut, for example, voters were required to place their filled-out ballot on the ballot box; if no one challenged their right to cast a ballot at that point, their ballot was placed in the box. The reforms of the late nineteenth century replaced party-printed ballots with ballots distributed by the state, required party workers to remain seventy-five feet or farther from the polling place, and provided booths for voters to cast their ballots in secret. A century later, in an effort to make voting more convenient, several states instituted early voting periods and no-fault absentee voting, further isolating the voter.

The net effect of these reforms has been to change the character of Election Day. Before the reforms of the 1880s, voters often lingered for hours at the polls, consuming the free booze and entertainment that the parties provided. As historian Richard Bensel points out, polling places were sometimes located in saloons or other gathering places where a raucous, freewheeling atmosphere prevailed. Voting in federal elections was a men-only affair in those days, and brawls and catcalls frequently accompanied the act of voting. Bensel reports that the jurisprudence of that era set the bar rather high for charges of voter intimidation, requiring only that "a man of ordinary courage" must be able to cast his ballot.[1] Nonetheless, voting rates were much higher than anything seen in the twentieth century.

Once voting was moved out of sight of onlookers and party officials, Election Day whiskey ceased to flow, and crowds no longer congregated at the polls. A century later, reforms allowing people to vote by mail or in advance of Election Day further diminished interaction between voters and the social significance of Election Day itself.

The events leading up to Election Day have also changed. Consider, for example, the presidential election of 1884, in which 71 percent of eligible voters cast ballots. What did campaigning look like in the heyday of voting? Connecticut was a "battleground state" in this election, giving Grover Cleveland a narrow 51.3 percent victory statewide. The city of Hartford had a steady stream of campaign events—parades, speeches, and rallies—that drew large numbers of people in the evenings and on weekends. The Hartford *Courant* paints a picture of one procession:

A grand parade of uniformed republican clubs took place in the Eighth ward last evening. . . . All along the line of the march there were fine illuminations of private residences, displays of flags, burning of colored fires, and large numbers of people in the streets to witness the procession. On Grand and Lawrence streets there were some particularly fine displays, and the whistle of the Billings & Spencer company's factory on the latter street blew a continuous salute while the procession was passing. . . . At one place on Park there was a pyramid of six or eight children in front of a house with fancy dresses, and waving flags, making a beautiful tableau, as illuminated with colored lights. . . . There were nearly 600 men in line, including the drum bands.[2]

These kinds of events are difficult to imagine today. Unless a presidential candidate makes a personal appearance, rallies are rare. Processions are even rarer.

The one enduring feature of old-fashioned elections is the candidate forum. At the state and national level these debates are nowadays highly scripted events directed at a television audience, but they nonetheless offer an opportunity for interested viewers to get a sense of the candidates' issue positions and personal style. At the local level, they attract smaller audiences, but often serve the purpose of encouraging candidates to address the concerns of specific segments of the electorate and allow voters to size up the styles and issue stances of the candidates.

Although it is not possible to measure the impact of nineteenth-century campaign events, it is possible to test the effectiveness of contemporary events, some of which are designed to create the same feelings of interest and engagement. In this chapter, we discuss three such interventions. The first is a set of experiments measuring the impact of Election Day festivals, patterned after those of the late nineteenth century (minus the liquor and fistfights). The second set of experiments looks at candidate events. Some studies randomly encouraged voters to watch debates on television, but one study looked at a campaign event called "Candidates Gone Wild," which was a cross between a candidate debate and an offbeat talent show. Lastly, we examine an intervention targeting high school seniors in which an energetic researcher came to high schools, talked about the importance of voting, and then walked students through the voting process using their precinct's voting machine. Although very different, all three brought people together to share a common election-related experience.

Election Day Festivals

In 2005 and 2006 Elizabeth Addonizio, Donald Green, and James Glaser set out to explore the feasibility of creating a more festive and community-focused atmosphere at the polls.[3] This line of inquiry turns the usual approach to GOTV on its head. Researchers and policymakers tend to focus on the *costs* of voting and ways to reduce those costs. But rarely do they address the potential *benefits* of casting a ballot. This line of research attempted to quantify the impact of imbuing polling places with the attractiveness of a local fair.

These poll parties, while inspired by those of the nineteenth century, departed from their historical models in significant ways. Elections and Election Day activity are highly regulated today, and most state and federal laws prohibit not only vote buying but any kind of quid pro quo inducement to vote. Researchers were therefore informed by local and state officials that the parties had to be advertised and carried out in such a way as not to link the casting of a ballot with the receipt of food and entertainment. Provided that these restrictions were respected, the festivals were well within the bounds of election law. And unlike the social activities surrounding elections in the nineteenth century, which catered to the tastes of male voters, these parties were meant for general audiences, including children. The empirical question the researchers thus addressed was whether these family-friendly, alcohol-free variants of the old-time poll party raise turnout.

Over the course of two years, the authors coordinated a series of sixteen experimental festivals. These festivals were held in a wide array of locations, ranging from middle-class, all-white suburbs to poor, largely minority inner cities. All of the festivals followed a common model, which was developed in New Hampshire, where the authors conducted a pilot study before municipal elections held in the spring of 2005. The authors began with two towns—Hooksett and Hanover—that had similar populations and voting rates. A coin was flipped, and the researchers organized a party in Hooksett, leaving Hanover as the control group.

The festival was preceded by a week of publicity and local organizing. Flyers were handed out at town meetings, and posters were displayed in local stores and meeting spots. On the Saturday before Election Day, the regional newspaper included a flyer advertising an "Election Day Poll Party," giving the location and time. The local paper also advertised the event. On the Sunday before Election Day, a story describing the party appeared in one of the papers. At the same time, three dozen lawn signs advertising the event were planted on busy streets in town. Finally, two prerecorded thirty-second phone calls were directed to 3,000 Hooksett households. Both extended an invitation to the party and gave details about its hours (3:00 to 7:00 p.m.) and location.

Election Day turned out to be a beautiful spring day, perfect for an outdoor event. The festival took place immediately outside the polling place, on the front lawn of the local middle school. A large tent was set up, surrounded by signs encouraging people to enjoy free snacks, drinks, and raffles. A cotton candy machine, expertly staffed by political science professors, attracted a steady stream of children. People of all ages milled about the party tent, eating, drinking, and listening to music supplied by a local disk jockey. People at the party seemed aware of the event before coming to the polls to vote. They had read the flyer, received the calls, or heard about the various advertised activities from other residents.

Judging from the size of the crowd it attracted and party-goers' positive evaluation of event, the party was deemed a success. Hooksett, despite having no contested candidates on the ballot, garnered a higher voter turnout rate than Hanover. After replicating the experiment in a local election in New Haven in 2005, the authors attracted the involvement of Working Assets in 2006, which coordinated local festivals in every region of the country during the primary and general election season. In each site, target precincts were identified, some of which were randomly assigned to a treatment group in which a festival was held. Turnout rates of the treatment and control precincts were compared; because these additional sites were not matched in terms of past voter turnout rates, a multivariate analysis was conducted to control for past turnout differences across precincts.

Across all thirty-eight precincts, the results indicated that festivals— or to be more precise, the festivals and the preelection publicity surrounding them—increased turnout by approximately 2 percentage points. Because many of these precincts were small, the festivals together generated approximately 960 additional votes at a cost of $26,630 in 2006 dollars. These figures imply a cost per vote of $28, which puts festivals on the same general plane as other face-to-face tactics.

These figures also convey some important accounting lessons. If you want to make your festival dollar go further, hold your event in a large precinct or in a place where people from multiple precincts come to vote. Or better yet, in places that have consolidated voting locations to accommodate early voting, hold your festival on a weekend and advertise to the entire city.

The main challenge in holding a festival is drawing a crowd. In effect, the turnout problem shifts from getting people to vote to getting people to attend (and then vote). Building festival attendance is as yet more art than science, but the authors offer some ideas worth exploring. A lineup of all-school musical performances serves the dual purpose of providing performers and an appreciative audience of family members. Jurisdictions that allow for voting by mail allow festival planners to hold their parties after church or as part of a prelude to a weekend concert or sporting event. Partisan house parties could bring friends together to congregate for drinks and snacks before walking en masse to a nearby polling place. Variations on the festival theme are almost limitless. The challenge of putting together a successful festival stems from the fact that contemporary Americans do not associate festivals with elections, and some election officials worry that even a nonpartisan festival might appear to serve some partisan purpose. It might take a festival or two for locals to see social gatherings as an expected and attractive aspect of coming to vote.

Candidate Debates

To what extent does watching a debate increase a person's probability of voting? Social scientists have often speculated that exposure to the candidates and the issues they discuss causes voters to become more interested in the campaign and therefore more likely to vote. However, experimental evidence is thin. Just two studies have randomly encouraged people to watch candidate debates. Bethany Albertson and Adria Lawrence report the results of an experiment conducted in 2000, which showed that people who are randomly encouraged to watch the presidential debates are significantly more likely subsequently to report an intention to vote.[4] The problem with this study is that it relied on self-reports in the context of a follow-up interview; it did not document whether people actually voted. A study by Sendhil Mullainathan, Ebonya Washington, and Julia Azari in the context of the 2005 mayoral election in New York City overcame this problem by randomly encouraging people to watch the mayoral debates a few days before the election and measuring their behavior using public records.[5] Again a positive effect was found, although it falls short of statistical significance. Taken together, these studies hint that viewing debates may increase voter turnout.

What about attending a debate in person? Live debates are the kind of event that can be staged relatively easily among down-ballot candidates, and the question is whether these events have any effect on those who attend. David Nickerson studied a creative attempt to bring out the lighter side of a meet-the-candidates event.[6] The event, called "Candidates Gone Wild" (CGW), was hosted by the Oregon Bus Project and a local counterculture newspaper in the hopes of boosting young people's interest in local politics. David Nickerson describes the event as "a high-energy amalgam of a political debate, the Gong Show, and David Letterman's Stupid Human Tricks." The show took place in Portland two weeks before its 2006 primary election, and candidates for county and city offices were invited to participate. Candidates had an opportunity to make themselves known and to show their lighter side. CGW was held in a local theater, and several hundred potential voters attended the event. Tickets were sold in advance for $3.

The CGW study was small but cleverly designed. For the purposes of the experiment, fifty tickets to CGW were set aside. After the remaining 950 tickets were sold, Oregon Bus Project volunteers signed interested individuals up for a lottery to distribute the fifty remaining tickets. Those signing up became the subjects of the study. To register for the lottery, individuals had to fill out a card with their full name, address, phone number, and e-mail address. In the end, 100 people signed up for the lottery, and fifty names were randomly selected to receive tickets. A post-election survey confirmed that, for the most part, the lottery winners attended the show, and the control group did not.

Before describing the effects of the program on turnout, let's first consider how the event affected voters' opinions, based on a postelection interview that David Nickerson conducted with thirty-nine of the participants. Given the content of a program like Candidates Gone Wild, one might expect the audience to become more informed about the election and to feel more connected to the politicians and their political system in general, resulting in higher turnout rates. In fact, the findings are mixed. A significantly higher proportion of the treatment group could correctly identify whether the seven candidates who participated were challengers or incumbents, but the treatment group was no better than the control group at answering four factual questions about the candidates. (The particular questions were selected because the content was mentioned during CGW.) All in all, voters who attended CGW seemed to be more familiar with the candidates but retained little substantive information two weeks after the event.

The picture is similarly mixed with regard to attitudes about politics. When asked to agree or disagree with a series of statements, members of the treatment group were no more likely to express interest in politics or to think that voting is particularly important. This finding echoes Ebonya Washington's study of the New York mayoral election, which also found debates to have little effect on interest in the election. Nevertheless, participants in the CGW treatment group were far more likely than their control group counterparts to think that local elections are important.

The most striking finding in this study is the turnout effect. Although the treatment and control groups expressed similar attitudes about voting, the average rate of turnout was substantially higher in the treatment group. Among the ninety-one people whose vote could be validated using public records, turnout in the control group was 17 percent, compared to 31 percent in the treatment group. The small size of this experiment means that its results must be interpreted with caution, but the results remain intriguing. The "random invitation" design is an underutilized experimental approach, and more experiments are needed to verify the results of these three promising studies.

First-Time Voter Program

By the spring of their senior year, a large proportion of high school students have reached voting age, but only a small proportion vote. The First-Time Voter Program is a school-based outreach effort aimed at encouraging high school seniors to vote. The program consists of three elements. A young researcher, rather than a high school teacher, leads the seminar. Unlike a course taught in a classroom, the seminar's format is informal and interactive. The seminar focuses on providing students with the experience of registering to vote and casting a ballot using the type of voting machine that is used in their jurisdiction.

This intervention, developed by Elizabeth Addonizio, is designed to make young voters feel more comfortable with the voting process.[7] Focus group studies of young people suggest that they sometimes feel apprehensive about voting for the first time. Rather than feel self-conscious or confused in front of others, young voters abstain. The seminar therefore begins informally, with the instructor establishing rapport with the students. She asks them about their perceptions of voting and Election Day and explains why she first decided to vote. She invites them to participate: "No need to raise your hand, just jump right in." The presenter talks about why people vote and describes the offices that are up for election at the local, state, and federal levels and the policy areas that are controlled by public officials at each level. She asks the students questions about what they know about voting and whether they have ever gone to vote with a parent, friend, or guardian. The lack of exposure to the voting process is echoed in almost every school that participates in the program. Most students say that they have never seen an official voting machine, they do not know how to vote, and although they will soon turn eighteen, nobody has offered to teach them about voting or called on them to participate in the voting process.

In an effort to connect the voting process to the students' lives, the presenter also discusses the relevance of voting to issues students often care about. For example, the presenter discusses the significance of elections by pointing out that elected officials have control over policies affecting drivers' licenses, town curfews, the use of cell phones in public places or while driving, and the amount of money available to fund scholarships and other educational programs. Accounts from several schools suggest that students enjoy the realization that just about every area of their lives is affected by elected officials. The presenter explains the importance of becoming informed about the candidates, asks the students how they might learn about the candidates and the issues relevant to the election, and describes the sources available to them to learn more.

The presenter also talks to the students about young voters as a group. She explains how eighteen-year-olds received the right to vote in the wake of the Vietnam War. She talks to them about how young people at that time believed that if they could be drafted and called upon to serve their country they should be able to select the leaders who would make these decisions. She asks the students what issues they care most about. They frequently notice that they have similar concerns to one another, and they frequently talk about themselves as a group.

In the next part of the program, for about fifteen minutes, the presenter explains the voter registration requirements and procedures. She then distributes voter registration cards, explains where to get the cards and how to fill them out, and (in some of the schools) collects the completed voter registration cards of eligible students. The presenter also explains the rules for absentee balloting and what to do if the student is away (for instance, at college) on Election Day.

Finally, in the third part of the program, the presenter opens the voting machine and shows the students how it works. She invites the students up to the machine. One by one, the students are given the opportunity to practice voting on the machine. They seem to enjoy the actual voting part of the program, and many ask if they can cast a second or third vote. It often becomes a game for the students to vote for certain candidates or cast write-in ballots with the names of their friends and teachers.

Although students are not forced to register or to cast a practice vote, they are encouraged to do so. Generally, about 90 percent of the students cast a ballot, and about 20 percent cast more than one ballot. After the students have voted, the presenter congratulates the students for casting their first vote. The First-Time Voter sessions tend to run about forty minutes, involving about twenty to thirty students per session. An effort is made to keep the sessions as small and as intimate as possible. The number of sessions per school varies with the total number of students to be accommodated.

In order to evaluate the effectiveness of this program, Elizabeth Addonizio conducted a series of experiments. Before fall and spring elections in 2003 and 2004, seniors in participating high schools in Connecticut, Indiana, Kentucky, Nebraska, New Hampshire, and New Jersey were randomly divided into two groups, one of which was assigned to participate in a voter mobilization effort. The total population for the study consisted of the 840 students who were old enough to vote at election time. Experiments were conducted in different states at different times to allow for variation in the salience of the election and the socioeconomic level of the population under study. The experiment was replicated in areas with competitive and noncompetitive local, statewide, and presidential elections and in high- and low-socioeconomic communities in order to determine whether the competitiveness of the election and the affluence of the community influence the effects of the mobilization effort.[8]

Addonizio's results indicated that students attending the First-Time Voter Program had turnout rates that were approximately 9 percentage points higher than their control group counterparts. These effects were quite consistent across different electoral and socioeconomic settings.

Because the program encourages young people to vote in several ways, it is not clear which aspects of the First-Time Voter Program are responsible for this large effect. It may be that students vote because their participation in the program helps them to overcome their apprehension about using a voting machine. Or it may be that the convivial atmosphere of the program succeeds in creating a feeling of connection with the community and interest in participating in local affairs. Teasing apart the different aspects of the program is an avenue for future research. For practitioners, the program shows that relatively brief events can induce significantly higher rates of participation among low-propensity voters. The question is whether the treatment effects are enduring (and create voters out of nonvoters) or whether the treatment merely speeds up the acquisition of voting habits, causing eighteen-year-olds to vote as though they were in their middle to late twenties.

Conclusions and Thoughts for Further Research

The findings of this chapter may be summarized using our usual rating system: three stars are for findings that have received solid confirmation from several experiments, two stars are for more equivocal findings based on a few experiments, and one star is for findings that are suggestive but not conclusive.

★★ *Election Day festivals increase voter turnout.* The array of small-scale experiments conducted to date suggests that, at least in low-salience elections, festivals draw voters to the polls. The effects observed in these elections tend not to be large, but festivals appear to provide a cost-effective means of increasing turnout.

★ *Viewing candidate debates on television or in person increases turnout.* Experimental findings remain ambiguous, but they suggest that viewers vote at higher rates even if they do not show higher overall levels of interest in politics.

★★ *Seminars that convey information about how to vote and why voting is important increase turnout among young voters.* Although the mechanisms underlying this effect remain unclear, group discussions about and experience with the voting process appear to produce substantial increases in voter turnout. These effects are similar in magnitude to the effects of door-to-door canvassing.

The varied and sometimes offbeat interventions described in this chapter serve as reminders that scientific discoveries draw their inspiration from many sources. One important and underutilized source is our own history. We tend to view our politics as fundamentally different from the electoral battles that predated television sets and Progressive reforms. We tend to view ourselves as markedly different from our poorer and more insular predecessors. And yet, experiments continually turn up evidence that old-fashioned campaign tactics work. The simple fact that experiments show the efficacy of low-tech, personal mobilization techniques suggests that the distant past ought to be mined more frequently for ideas about how to mobilize voters.

The experiments reported in this chapter underscore, among other things, the importance of making civic engagement engaging. Festivals, madcap candidate events, and even casting mock votes are sources of fun. Although the Progressive reformers were bent on making elections sober affairs (literally) that turn on issues rather than petty bribes, their insistence on imbuing polling places with what Bensel calls a "morgue-like atmosphere" meant that elections ceased to attract interest as social events. How much of the precipitous drop in voter turnout rates between the 1880s and 1920s is due to this transformation remains unclear. What does seem clear is that the process is, at least to a limited extent, reversible.

CHAPTER NINE

Using Mass Media
to Mobilize Voters

The three traditional forms of mass media—television, radio, newspapers—have long been staples of both campaign craft and social science inquiry. Presidential, senatorial, and gubernatorial campaigns spend enormous resources trying to reach voters through paid advertisements and so-called "earned media," such as public appearances and announcements that attract news coverage. For decades social scientists have studied the ways in which these campaigns are shaped by efforts to attract media attention and by the ways, in turn, that voters are influenced by what they see, hear, and read. During the 1930s, at the dawn of modern social science, teams of researchers set out to measure the effects of political propaganda on voters' opinions and behavior. Unfortunately, despite several decades of research by thousands of scholars, little progress has been made.[1]

The basic problem is that social scientists have seldom gauged the media's influence using field experiments. Most research on the media's influence relies on surveys. Survey researchers ask respondents what they have been watching and perform a statistical analysis to assess the correlation between media consumption and political attitudes or behaviors. This research design suffers from two drawbacks. The first is that respondents are often asked to characterize their viewing patterns in vague terms (for example, How many days per week do you watch television?), which means that the "treatment" is measured with error. The second problem is that media consumption reflects personal tastes. It may be that those who watch Fox television news are, on average, more sympathetic to Republican policies than nonviewers, but does exposure to Fox news *cause* viewers to become more sympathetic to Republican policies? Or does Fox news simply attract viewers who tend to have Republican sympathies? Survey data cannot distinguish between these two hypotheses. At most, survey data can narrow the comparison to those people who have similar background characteristics (they grew up in similar places, had similar experiences, and so forth). But narrowing the comparison is not the same thing as forming truly comparable groups of viewers and nonviewers. We are left to speculate about whether the Fox news effect is real or illusory.

In response to this conundrum, social scientists have turned to laboratory experiments in order to assess whether the mass media influence political attitudes and behaviors. Laboratory studies expose subjects randomly to different media, and random assignment means that we can trust the treatment and control groups to be comparable. However, laboratory studies have at least three limitations. First, they typically expose subjects to the media in a contrived way. Subjects might be invited into the lab and asked to watch a news program. Or subjects may be asked to read newspaper articles as part of a copyediting exercise. The manner in which these subjects are exposed to the media is potentially quite different from how they would receive these messages under ordinary conditions. Second, laboratory researchers tend to measure outcomes in ways that make it difficult to interpret an experiment's practical consequences. Rarely do laboratory experiments measure actual voter turnout; instead, as part of a post-treatment interview, they measure whether subjects say that they are likely to vote. Third, college students make up an overwhelming preponderance of subjects in media experiments. One is left to wonder whether the experimental results that college students generate apply to the broader population of voting-age adults.

The bottom line is that, although university library shelves sag with books and articles purporting to measure the effects of the mass media, rarely have these effects been measured using field experiments. And when we further restrict our attention to the effects of the mass media on voter turnout, we are left with only a handful of studies, most of which were conducted within the past few years. Ordinarily, we would exclude from our review any nonexperimental study, but in this chapter we discuss a small number of quasi-experiments as well. In future editions of this book, these studies are likely to be superseded by randomized experiments.

This chapter provides a summary of research findings for readers who are thinking about conducting a media campaign to encourage voter turnout. Because media campaigns tend not to be do-it-yourself affairs (campaigns with sufficient resources to conduct this type of campaign generally rely on consultants to produce and distribute advertisements or public service announcements), we focus our attention primarily on the research findings rather than on the how-to aspects of conducting a media campaign.

Do Persuasive Campaign Ads Mobilize?

One of the most intriguing theories about the media's influence holds that television hoopla signals to voters the importance of an upcoming election. The idea is that the content of political ads is secondary; what matters is the fact that the airwaves and newspapers are filled with ads and political banter. When voters see or hear a lot of political ads, they infer that an important election is coming up. Elections that are perceived to be important attract higher rates of turnout. What makes this theory interesting is the notion that campaign ads—even those that make no mention of voting or Election Day—produce higher turnout.

Although this theory has intuitive appeal, it has been challenged by scholars studying what might be termed "natural experiments." Natural experiments involve comparisons of groups that approximate treatment or control groups. Consider, for example, the way in which accidents of geography cause some people to be inundated with television ads, while others receive none at all. These accidents are especially common where presidential ads are concerned. People living within the same state are sometimes subjected to widely varying numbers of presidential ads, depending on their proximity to media markets that serve battleground states. For example, voters in western Maryland receive Pittsburgh television broadcasts. In the last presidential election, Pennsylvania was a pivotal battleground state, and both presidential contestants aired thousands of ads on Pittsburgh television stations during the final weeks of the campaign. These ads were directed at those in Pennsylvania, but they were just as pertinent to Maryland voters, who voted in the same presidential election but whose Electoral College votes were sure to go to the Democrats. Unlike their counterparts in western Maryland, voters in central Maryland saw almost no ads because their television stations did not emanate from Pennsylvania. The same intrastate contrasts may be found in several others states, such as Indiana and Georgia, which border battleground states. Within states, the idiosyncrasies of geography cause some counties to be blanketed with ads while others remain untouched.

Because this study is not a randomized experiment, its findings must be read with caution, as the treatment and control groups may differ in ways that affect turnout rates. Nonexperimental studies that seem to be sound might nevertheless contain hidden biases, and their conclusions must be interpreted as provisional, pending experimental confirmation.

With this warning in mind, we note the weak correlation between advertising volume and turnout. Examining 128 geographic zones in which people living in the same state were subject to different amounts of televised presidential campaign advertising, Jonathan Krasno and Donald Green found no evidence that exposure to ads during the final weeks of the campaign increased turnout in the 2000 election.[2] The largest volume of advertising exposure—enough advertising to expose each member of the television audience approximately 132 times— raised turnout by less than 1 percentage point. Scott Ashworth and Joshua Clinton came to a similar conclusion when comparing different regions of New Jersey, some of which received a torrent of presidential ads from Philadelphia, while others received no ads, as they were in the New York City broadcast area.[3] Again, there was no evidence that those exposed to an avalanche of presidential ads voted at higher rates.

Sometimes presidential ads are blamed for decreasing turnout. Attack ads are said to polarize the electorate and alienate moderates. But Krasno and Green found no support for this theory. Perhaps more important, neither did Joshua Clinton and John Lapinski, researchers who tested this hypothesis by exposing large numbers of viewers randomly to positive and negative ads aired on WebTV.[4] Their analysis of voting records found no effect on turnout. Apparently, attack ads do not demobilize voters, and more upbeat ads do not mobilize voters. Regardless of their tone, campaign ads have little effect on turnout.

For campaigns, the finding that thousands of gross ratings points fail to increase turnout in presidential elections can be read in two ways. First, the finding implies that one should not count on persuasive ads to mobilize. Perhaps the lack of effect reflects the fact that televised campaign advertising, like partisan direct mail, tends to focus almost exclusively on candidates and issues. Rarely do they mention voting or Election Day. Perhaps campaign ads could mobilize if voting were a more prominent theme, but the ads we see have little effect.

A second interpretation holds out the hope that campaign ads mobilize voters in nonpresidential elections. The hypothesis is that voters do not need any reminders about the significance of an upcoming presidential election. Presidential campaigns dominate the news every day for weeks leading up to the election. The situation may be quite different in state or local elections. Below, we revisit both issues, as we consider whether advertisements that encourage voting in presidential and other elections, in fact, increase turnout.

Conveying Social Norms

Another theory about why the media might influence voter turnout is that media messages express "social norms," ideas about what kinds of behaviors are appropriate. Just as radio, newspapers, and television tell us what fashions are in style, they also tell us how right-thinking people regard Election Day.

With this theory in mind, Lynn Vavreck and Donald Green sought to link voting to the strong feelings of patriotism that flourished after the September 11, 2001, terrorist attacks on the United States.[5] The idea was to employ evocative imagery to suggest that voting is a patriotic responsibility. Two ads were created by a team of UCLA film students. The first used a sequence of still images of inspiring American scenes (firemen hoisting a flag, the AIDS quilt, and children playing) as the percussive cadence in the background escalated in complexity and volume. The female narrator observed, "Even as the world changes, your role as a citizen remains the same." At the end, the images coalesced into the shape of the United States, under which the tagline read, "Shape your country, vote this Tuesday."

The tone of the second ad was much darker, this time addressing the fear of violent extremism. The ad flashed still images of swastikas, notorious dictators, and frightening moments from famous wars defending freedom. The voiceover challenged viewers with an ironic observation about the pictured dictators: "Not interested in politics? That's OK. Really, that's OK. Plenty of others are." The anti-democratic images increased in speed as the same percussive cadence increased in volume. At the end, the tagline read, "Stand up for democracy, vote this Tuesday." Unlike the first ad, which identified voting with national pride and solidarity, the second ad warned viewers to consider the negative consequences of neglecting their civic responsibilities.

In order to test the effects of these ads on voter turnout, an experiment was conducted in the context of four statewide elections during 2003. In Kentucky and Louisiana, statewide offices were contested, and Kentucky's gubernatorial election was relatively competitive. In New Jersey and Virginia, legislative elections were by and large low-salience affairs. Across all four states, a total of 156 cable television systems were randomly assigned to four groups: a control group receiving no ads, a group receiving the "shape your country" ad, a group receiving the "stand up for democracy" ad, and a group receiving a mixture of both ads.

The ads ran from October 30 through November 3, immediately before the general elections of 2003, on TNT, USA, and Lifetime networks in New Jersey, Virginia, and Kentucky. In Louisiana, the ads ran on the same networks from October 30 to November 14, the date of the Louisiana election. These cable networks were selected because of their broad appeal and high ratings during prime-time viewing hours at this time of year. Each ad ran twice on each channel every night before the election, for a total of thirty spots in each cable system in New Jersey, Virginia, and Kentucky and ninety-six spots in Louisiana. After the election, voter turnout data were obtained for zip codes that were encompassed by a single cable system.

The pattern of turnout suggests that the ads may have led to a very small boost in turnout. A simple comparison of the control group to all of the treatment groups suggested an increase of approximately half a percentage point, an effect that is not statistically distinguishable from zero. When one controls for past voter turnout, the "shape your country" ad appears to be the most effective, although again the results fall short of statistical significance. In an attempt to bring more statistical precision to this estimate, Vavreck and Green also conducted an automated telephone survey of more than 25,000 registered voters living in the experimental cable television systems. Respondents in both the treatment and control groups were asked about whether they received cable television and whether they recently watched several specific shows, the idea being to identify comparable viewers in the treatment and control groups, some of whom randomly encountered the voter turnout ads. By refining the comparison in this way, the authors expected to observe larger treatment effects. Instead, this analysis again showed weak and statistically insignificant positive effects.

One pair of ads hardly exhausts the range of possible treatments that must be tested, but the lack of effectiveness of these ads tentatively suggests that television ads merely affirming the norm of participating in an election do not generate higher turnout rates in low- and medium-salience elections. The null result cannot be blamed on low rates of exposure to the ads because even when one compares likely ad viewers, the treatment effect remains small.

Emphasizing What's at Stake

Perhaps imploring people to vote is not enough. Perhaps media appeals must also include a persuasive reason why the issues at stake in an upcoming election merit viewers' participation. This hypothesis inspired an experimental test of television ads produced by the Rock the Vote organization, which was at the forefront of efforts to increase voter turnout among young people.[6] Rock the Vote has a long history of producing memorable and sometimes controversial public service announcements. Rock the Vote's 2004 ad campaign dealt with two themes, the prospect of a military draft and the high cost of secondary education.

In the "military draft" advertisement, a young couple dancing at a party discussed the man's new job. He was very excited to be working in promotions and hoped to start his own firm in six months. The woman interrupted him and said, "That's if you don't get drafted." The man was puzzled. She clarified, "Drafted, for the war?" He responded, "Would they do that?" The ad closed with everyone at the party looking into the camera and the words "It's up to you" on the screen. The voiceover said, "The draft. One of the issues that will be decided this November. Remember to vote on November 2nd." The closing image was of the Rock the Vote logo on a black screen.[7]

In the "secondary education" ad, a young man arrived at work with news that he had been accepted to college. His colleagues congratulated him, but one of them asked, "Books, room, board, tuition . . . how can you pay for all of that?" The ad closed with everyone looking into the camera, as the words "It's up to you" filled the screen. The voiceover was similar to the one above, but with education substituted for the draft.

The experimental evaluation conducted by Lynn Vavreck and Donald Green focused on twelve non-battleground states, in order to gauge the effects of the treatment with less interference from presidential campaign ads. Random assignment placed forty-two cable systems into the treatment group and forty-three into the control group. In this experiment, both ads were shown with equal frequency as many times as budget constraints would allow. During the last eight days of the election campaign, the ads aired four times per night in prime time on each of the following channels: USA, Lifetime, TNT, and TBS. Approximately two-thirds of American households subscribe to cable television, and according to the National Cable Commission, these are among the most popular cable channels.

Given the ads' content, the focus of the experimental evaluation was the 23,869 eighteen- and nineteen-year-olds living in these cable systems. For them, 2004 marked their first opportunity to vote in a federal election. The authors reported an increase of 3 percentage points in turnout in this age bracket, which is both large in absolute terms and statistically significant. Interestingly, the effect was strong among those up to twenty-two years old (the end of the college years) and small and insignificant for older people. This experiment provides the first clear evidence that televised ads can increase turnout within a targeted audience. Equally interesting is the fact that turnout among other age groups was only mildly affected. Although the ads were placed on programs watched by a wide age spectrum, only young viewers seem to have responded with higher levels of turnout. This finding again suggests that ads are effective only when they engage viewers with messages about the importance of the upcoming election.

What's at Stake and Who's on the Ballot

Persuading people of the importance of an upcoming presidential election is one thing; persuading them of the importance of an upcoming municipal election is quite another. Few local elections are closely contested; incumbent mayors tend to win more than 90 percent of their bids for reelection. Moreover, the issues at stake in local elections tend to be less lofty and engaging than the topics that usually take center stage in federal elections. As a result, it is not uncommon to see municipal elections attract less than one-third of all registered voters to the polls.

The question is whether turnout in municipal elections responds to a mass media campaign that calls attention to the significance of local elections, provides some basic information about the contestants, and tells voters when the election will take place. Costas Panagopoulos and Donald Green tested this proposition by conducting an experiment in seventy-eight mayoral elections occurring in November of 2005 and 2006.[8]

In the thirty-nine randomly selected treatment municipalities, radio ads were placed by a professional ad buyer on local radio stations that were thought to reach a broad cross section of the electorate. For each city assigned to the treatment group, between fifty and ninety gross ratings points (GRPs) were purchased. A gross ratings point is a metric used to gauge the size of the projected audience. Each GRP represents enough advertising to expose 1 percent of the media market to the ad once; fifty GRPs is enough to expose 50 percent of the media market once or 1 percent of the media market fifty times. The quantity of advertising is relatively small compared to what a political campaign might purchase in a hotly contested race, which leaves open the question of whether more intensive (and expensive) advertising campaigns might be more effective.

The script was customized for each location. For example, the following sample script was used for Syracuse, New York:

> Many people don't realize how important local government is. But think about it. Your local government is in charge of things that affect your life every day: police protection, transportation, garbage collection, tax assessment. From fire departments to libraries to safe drinking water—it's all part of local government.
>
> Here's where you come in: Voting. If you're a registered voter in SYRACUSE, you have an opportunity to shape the direction of your city by electing the mayor and other local officials. On Tuesday, November 8th, residents of SYRACUSE will vote to decide whether to RE-elect Democratic MAYOR MATTHEW DRISCOLL or to support his opponent, Republican JOANNIE MAHONEY.
>
> Take part in shaping your city's future. Be sure to vote on November 8th.
>
> Paid for by the Institution for Social and Policy Studies, a nonpartisan organization that encourages citizens to take an active role in their communities.

Note that this script was strictly nonpartisan. It neither endorsed a candidate nor hinted which one might be better at addressing local issues. And unlike the Rock the Vote ad, it neither tailored its message to specific subgroups nor used vignettes to dramatize the importance of the upcoming election.

The results of this experiment were positive but inconclusive. In twenty-three of the thirty-nine pairs of local elections, voter turnout was higher in the treatment group. The average rate of turnout in the treatment group was approximately 1 percentage point higher than in the control group. Although these results are encouraging, they fall short of statistical significance in the sense that there is roughly a one-in-four chance of coming up with a 1 percentage point estimate simply by chance even if the true effect were zero.

Murky results are not at all unusual in science, and the best way to clear the fog is to conduct larger and more telling experiments. In 2006 Panagopoulos and Green conducted a follow-up experiment in which Spanish-language radio stations encouraged listeners to consider the significance of the imminent congressional elections.[9] As in the mayoral experiment, the script (in Spanish) described some of the important issue domains that are affected by federal elections, presented the names of U.S. House of Representatives candidates, and mentioned when the election would occur. Because Spanish-language radio is rarely heard by non-Latinos, the focus of the evaluation was voter turnout among those with putatively Latino surnames.

Preliminary results from 204 congressional districts indicate that the radio ads generated a significant boost in turnout among voters with Hispanic surnames and, as predicted, no increase in non-Hispanic turnout. As additional results from this study become available, the statistical precision of this estimate will become clearer. For the moment, it appears that radio ads stressing the stakes of the upcoming election nudge turnout upward and may represent a cost-effective way to increase turnout.

Newspapers

Notwithstanding the fact that newspapers have played a central role in democratic politics for centuries, they have rarely been the subject of experimental inquiry. Those who study nonexperimental data have often speculated that newspapers supply political information and increase voter turnout. This argument has been bolstered recently by a clever analysis of a natural experiment associated with the rise of television during the 1950s. Matthew Gentzkow demonstrated that, as television stations acquired licenses across the country, newspaper readership fell, and so did voter turnout.[10] This thesis implies that a profound transformation in voter turnout could lie on the horizon. Newspaper readership has plummeted among young people, and the average daily reader grows older each year.

The question is what would happen to voter turnout if people were randomly induced to read a daily newspaper. A path-breaking experiment conducted by Alan Gerber, Dean Karlan, and Daniel Bergan provided several hundred Virginia households living in the Washington area with free newspaper subscriptions in 2005.[11] One group of households was randomly assigned to receive the conservative *Washington Times,* while another group was randomly assigned to receive the more liberal *Washington Post.* A control group of households received no subscription. Subscriptions were distributed during the final weeks of the statewide election campaign in Virginia, enabling these researchers to test whether receiving a daily newspaper boosts turnout.

Among the 2,571 people whose names could be matched to voter turnout records, turnout was 56.3 percent in the control group, 57.4 percent among those assigned to the *Washington Post,* and 56.1 percent among those assigned to the *Washington Times.* Overall, the subscriptions generated a half percentage point gain in turnout, concentrated primarily among those who had voted in the two most recent general elections. This finding falls short of conventional standards of statistical significance, which is to say that one could obtain an estimate this large due simply to chance. Nevertheless, this is an interesting result that is made even more intriguing by the fact that the difference in turnout between treatment and control groups grew even larger in the 2006 midterm elections that occurred a year later. Could it be that receiving a daily paper sets in motion growing involvement in elections?

A related question is whether turnout rises when newspaper readers are presented with half-page advertisements encouraging them to vote in local elections. This experiment is a twist on the mayoral experiment involving radio, except that it targets newspaper readers, who tend to be high-propensity voters. Costas Panagopoulos conducted a pilot study involving four pairs of towns, all of which held municipal elections during 2005.[12] The towns were each paired according to past voter turnout, and one member of each pair was randomly assigned to receive a half-page ad in its local newspaper on the Sunday before the election. The ad stressed the importance of local issues and urged voters to cast ballots on Tuesday.

Due to the small size of the pilot study, the results are by no means conclusive. Turnout was higher in the treatment town in three of four pairs. Of course, this kind of outcome would be expected merely by chance one-third of the time. Nevertheless, this finding merits further investigation, because if newspaper ads really do boost turnout by 1.5 percentage points, as this pilot study suggests, the implied cost per vote would be very attractive. Fortunately, newspaper experiments are relatively easy to conduct across a broad array of settings. One could, for example, place ads in randomly assigned college newspapers and look at turnout in different campus precincts. Or one could pick locations such as Los Angeles or Queens and randomly assign some of the ethnic newspapers to treatment and control groups, looking for interethnic variation in turnout. Given how straightforward it is to experiment with local newspapers, it is shocking that the academic study of newspapers has so rarely employed experimental designs.

Conclusion

Only recently have field experiments been used to study the mobilizing effects of the mass media. The first edition of *Get Out The Vote!* could only foreshadow forthcoming experiments; this edition can now place some bounds on what is reasonable to expect from a media campaign. Future editions will surely bring greater refinement to these conclusions, which are rated according to the system detailed in chapter 2. Each of the conclusions is rated with one star, indicating that the findings are suggestive but not conclusive.

★ *The sheer volume of political ads is a poor predictor of voter turnout.* Mere exposure to a large number of campaign ads does not, in itself, raise voter turnout in presidential elections. The conclusion derived from natural experiments involving television ads fits well with the experimental finding, noted in chapter 5, that partisan direct mail tends to have little effect on turnout.

★ *Television ads that specifically urge voter turnout have the capacity to mobilize targeted viewers.* The Rock the Vote ads, which used vignettes to dramatize the significance of the upcoming election, produced statistically significant increases in turnout among eighteen- and nineteen-year-olds. The ads had minimal effects on voters older than twenty-two.

★ *Broad-based television ads that encourage voter turnout appear to have weak positive effects on voter turnout.* The two experiments testing the effects of ads that urged voters to "shape your country" or "stand up for democracy" increased turnout by less than a quarter percentage point.

★ *Radio campaigns that stress the importance of upcoming local elections appear to have some positive effect on voter turnout.* These effects are in the neighborhood of 1 percentage point, although this estimate remains statistically imprecise.

★ *Daily exposure to newspapers raises turnout, at least among those who do not ordinarily receive a daily paper.* Virginians given free subscriptions to Washington daily newspapers became more likely to vote in subsequent state and federal elections.

★ *Newspaper ads urging voters to participate in upcoming local elections appear to increase turnout.* These results are statistically imprecise but suggest a possible effect of between 1 and 2 percentage points.

How do the media results fit with our general pattern of results in this book? On the one hand, mass media appeals resemble direct mail or robotic phone calls in the sense that they are delivered in an impersonal and mechanical fashion. On the other hand, the Rock the Vote experiment suggests that vignettes that dramatize the meaning of an upcoming election can be influential, perhaps because they succeed in simulating a personal appeal. If our interpretation of the pattern of results presented in this book is correct, the success or failure of any mobilization campaign hinges on whether it increases the audience's motivation to participate. Evidently, some, but not all, ads succeed on this score, and the challenge for those who launch media campaigns in the hopes of raising voter turnout is to craft a message that truly motivates the audience.

What do our findings suggest about the cost-efficiency of using the mass media to raise voter turnout? Any calculation of dollars per vote must be regarded as tentative, but the following numbers provide a good starting point for discussion. The 2003 televised public service announcements had disappointing effects, apparently raising turnout by just 0.22 percentage point. However, the cable systems that were targeted contained more than 2.3 million registered voters, so the ads generated just over 5,000 additional votes. The total cost of producing, distributing, and running the ads was $76,700 (in 2007 dollars), which puts the cost per vote at approximately $15. The Rock the Vote ads were shown on cable television systems comprising more than 350,000 voters and had an average treatment effect across the whole age spectrum of 0.56 percentage point (mostly concentrated among young voters). The total number of votes generated was approximately 2,000. We do not know the cost of producing the ads, but distributing and airing them in the experimental study cost $30,700 (in 2007 dollars), which again implies $15 per vote. This rosy cost-per-vote estimate must be interpreted with extreme caution, given that the estimated effects are subject to a great deal of statistical uncertainty, but they remind us that television reaches vast audiences, and even a small effect goes a long way.

As for radio, the results are again subject to some interesting, if tentative, back-of-the-envelope calculations. The mayoral election experiments cost a total of $112,000 in order to increase turnout by an average of 0.79 percentage point in the treatment towns. These thirty-nine towns contained an average of 50,000 registered voters, so the radio ads generated roughly 15,400 votes, which comes to $7 per vote. The cost calculations for the 2006 Spanish-language radio experiment are likely to be similar, given the low cost of advertising in this market.

Finally, the cost per vote for newspaper advertising also seems attractive. The average city in Panagopoulos's sample contained 31,500 registered voters. Raising turnout among registered voters by 1.5 percentage points in an average city implies an increase of 473 votes. On the cost side of the equation, purchasing a half-page of newspaper advertising cost approximately $2,500 per city. Paying $2,500 to produce 473 votes—at just about $5 per vote—is a bargain. The question is whether the apparent effect holds up when the experiment is replicated. But even an effect of 0.5 percentage point implies a cost per vote of $15.

The bottom line seems to be that the mass media represent a potentially cost-effective means of raising turnout. The effects of mass media campaigns—at least the ones that have been studied experimentally—are not large in percentage point terms. Indeed, it is hard to detect the effects of a media campaign without access to an experiment involving scores of observations, so an organization running an advertising campaign of this type should not expect to see a big boost in turnout. Nevertheless, television, radio, and newspapers are inexpensive in many parts of the country. Advertisers of commercial products tend to target places with lots of consumer dollars. As a result, regions that are less affluent offer a bargain to groups who are interested in generating votes rather than sales.[13] Thus whether media campaigns are cost-effective may hinge on where they are conducted. A thrifty campaign interested in mobilizing large numbers of people efficiently could, it seems, run an efficient campaign outside the major media hubs.

Next Steps in Media Research

The first and most obvious next step in this line of research is to replicate and extend the existing experiments so that issues of cost-efficiency can be assessed more precisely. Thus far, media experiments have generated promising findings, but the results showing small but cost-effective voter mobilization effects are nowhere near as robust as the findings in well-established areas of GOTV research. Until more experimental results come in, we cannot rule out the possibility that the effects are zero, in which case cost-effectiveness goes out the window. Those in the advertising business like to joke that half of all money spent on television is wasted; the problem is that you don't know which half it is. Our view is more skeptical: How do they know that only half is wasted?

A further question is whether media campaigns amplify the effects of ground campaigns. Organizations that conduct both types of campaigns sometimes offer anecdotes suggesting that the media campaign makes it easier for canvassers to strike up a conversation with voters who have heard about the organization and perhaps endorse its electoral aims. This hypothesis does have an air of plausibility, but like many claims about synergy, it must be viewed with skepticism until supported with experimental evidence.

Finally, there remains the question of what kinds of people are most strongly influenced by the mass media. The Rock the Vote ads seem to have had their strongest effect on new voters (eighteen- and nineteen-year-olds), suggesting that media campaigns do not merely accentuate the voting propensities of established voters. The newspaper subscription experiment suggests the opposite: established voters are most strongly influenced by daily exposure to newsprint. The radio experiments do not address the question of how subgroups are affected. The issue of which forms of media communication most strongly influence which segments of the electorate is in need of more experimental research. Without it, campaigns are at a loss to know whether and how to target their messages for maximum cost-effectiveness.

The array of unanswered questions about long-standing forms of mass communication is the great irony of media research. Given the amount of money at stake, one would think that the experimental literature would be extensive and nuanced. Instead, a half-century after the development of television and nearly a century after the development of radio, we know relatively little about their effects on voting behavior. As field experimental inquiry gains momentum, that is likely to change.

CHAPTER TEN

What Works, What Doesn't, and What's Next

The dozens of experiments summarized in this book provide a useful benchmark for anyone seeking to launch or evaluate a voter mobilization campaign. When we began our experimental research in 1998, we were struck by the fact that even people running very expensive campaigns were operating on little more than their own intuition about what worked. The academic literature in existence at that time was little help. Experimental studies were rare, and the ones that found their way into print reported what we now know to be outlandish findings. One study, based on interviews with fewer than 100 college students, purported to show that calling people up on election eve and asking them whether they intended to vote increased their probability of doing so by more than 20 percentage points.[1] Bear in mind that the callers did not implore people to vote; they merely inquired about their plan to vote, yet generated a massive "self-prophesy effect." Another study, also based on a few dozen voters, purported to show that partisan mail increased turnout 19 percentage points.[2]

With a mix of optimism and skepticism, a growing number of researchers have spent the last decade replicating the studies that claimed to have discovered giant effects. After all, if these effects were truly as the scholarly literature reported, low voter turnout could be cured with a nationwide survey or a massive direct mail campaign. Alas, we and other researchers have found that an ordinary mailing has a modest effect on turnout, raising it by a fraction of a percentage point. Asking people whether they intended to vote proved to be a nonstarter as well. An experiment by Jennifer Smith, Alan Gerber, and Anton Orlich debunked the notion of a "self-prophesy effect."[3] More than 1,000 Connecticut voters were queried about their intentions to vote, but turnout remained unchanged. Similarly, another researcher, Christopher Mann, found that preelection phone interviews by *Washington Post* pollsters had no effect on turnout.[4] The list of registered voters who were slated for calls had the same voting rate as a randomly selected control group that was left alone. Merely asking people about their views of the candidates or their intentions to vote did not increase their chances of voting.

With the benefit of hindsight, these findings make perfect sense. Live calls from commercial phone banks have weak effects, even when the callers ask voters whether they can be counted on to vote. If urging people to vote and extracting a verbal commitment from them has little impact, it would be amazing if one could raise turnout rates just by asking people whether they *intend* to vote. As for direct mail, we now know that one cannot reliably detect its small effects unless one studies thousands of voters. A study of a few dozen people—or even a few hundred people—may discover huge effects simply due to chance. Looking back, it seems clear that these sensational findings can be attributed to something called "publication bias." Academic journals are averse to publishing statistically insignificant findings, which means that smaller studies must report larger results if they are to find their way into print. As a result, the experimental studies that find their way into print tend to give a misleading picture of what works.[5]

And those are just the experimental studies. If we expand the discussion of unreliable evidence to include nonexperimental research—focus groups, surveys, and case histories that do not involve control groups—the litany of unsupported claims becomes nearly boundless. These claims are not necessarily false, just untrustworthy. Take voter guides, for example. Focus group researchers found that people shown a simplified voter guide reported that it increased their enthusiasm about voting.[6] Survey researchers found that people living in areas that provided voting guides and sample ballots were more likely to vote, even after taking their age, education, and other background attributes into account.[7] The effect seemed especially strong among young people and those who never went to college, leading the authors to recommend that states routinely mail voters sample ballots. However, when this proposition was tested experimentally using sample ballots distributed through the mail, a series of large studies found no effect on turnout.[8]

Once the red herrings have been cleared from the path, the experimental results form an intelligible pattern. We begin by summarizing what *does not* work:

✔ Mobilizing voters is not merely a matter of reminding them that Election Day is near. Prerecorded messages reminding people to vote do little, if anything, to raise turnout, even when the prerecorded voices are those of well-known and credible people. Even live calls from commercial phone banks that briefly remind people to vote have weak effects.

✔ Mobilizing voters is not just a matter of putting election-related information in front of them. Canvassing and direct mail campaigns that have distributed voter guides have produced disappointing results.

✔ Telling people why they should vote for a particular candidate or cause does not, in itself, lead people to vote at higher rates. Putting a partisan edge on a mailing or a phone call does not seem to enhance its effectiveness.

Having ruled out several widely held notions about how to mobilize voters, we now offer some hypotheses suggested by the experimental results:

✔ To mobilize voters, make them feel wanted at the polls. Mobilizing voters is rather like inviting them to a social occasion. Personal invitations convey the most warmth and work best. Next best are phone calls in which the caller converses with the respondent, as opposed to reading a canned script. Mailed invitations typically don't work very well.

✔ Building on voters' preexisting level of motivation to vote is also important. Calling back a voter who has previously expressed an intention to vote appears to be a powerful mobilization tactic.

✔ Many nonvoters will vote if they think that others are watching. Some of the strongest experimental effects occur when voters are reminded that voting is a matter of public record.

All three of these hypotheses share a common theme: the decision to vote is strongly shaped by one's social environment. One may be able to nudge turnout upward slightly by making voting more convenient, supplying voters with information, and reminding them about an imminent election, but these effects are small in comparison to what happens when voters are placed in a social milieu that urges their participation. That said, providing social inducements to vote is neither easy nor cheap. So a natural question is whether, when cost is taken into account, effective GOTV tactics are also cost-effective.

Summarizing the Cost-Effectiveness of GOTV Tactics

Table 10-1 summarizes our assessment of the bottom line. What does it cost to make a voter out of someone who would otherwise abstain? Each of the GOTV tactics is characterized in terms of costs and benefits. In constructing our dollars-per-vote estimates, we err on the side of caution and provide figures only for those tactics that have been shown to work. In other words, table 10-1 reports the cost-effectiveness of tactics whose average impact has been demonstrated to be greater than zero. Tactics such as robo calls or television, whose mobilizing effect has yet to be distinguished statistically from zero, are excluded from this segment of the table. Interested readers may look back at previous chapters for our speculations about the cost-effectiveness of these unproven tactics.

As you examine this table, remember that the attractiveness of any GOTV tactic depends on the resources available to your campaign and the constraints within which it must operate. If your campaign is long on enthusiastic volunteers but short on money, you might consider leafleting, canvassing, or conducting a volunteer phone bank. If your campaign has money but lacks volunteers, you might invest your money in carefully supervised commercial phone banks or perhaps direct mail.

One of the most important lessons to draw from table 10-1 is that conventional GOTV campaigns seldom work miracles. Canvassing 100 registered voters at their doorstep will not generate 100 votes. A more realistic estimate is seven additional votes. Similarly, sending a nonpartisan piece of direct mail to 10,000 registered voters will not bring 10,000 people to the polls. The average number of additional voters you should expect from this type of direct mail campaign is fifty.

We are not saying that GOTV work is fruitless. Our point is rather that an ambitious GOTV campaign requires a serious investment in both quality and quantity. In order to generate 1,000 votes, your door-to-door canvassing effort may need to contact 14,000 registered voters. Or you could send nonpartisan mailings to 130,000 households, place door hangers on 125,000 doors, or hire a commercial phone bank to speak briefly with 180,000 registered voters. Each of these approaches relies on the *scale* of a well-crafted GOTV operation to generate appreciable numbers of additional votes.

Table 10-1. Cost-Effectiveness of Get-Out-the-Vote Tactics[a]
Updated for *Get Out the Vote,* second edition

GOTV effort	Start-up and overhead costs	Ongoing management	Effectiveness per contact[b]	Is effect statistically reliable?	Dollar cost per vote (excluding start-up and management costs)
Door-to-door	Labor intensive: recruit, prepare walk lists	Substantial ongoing training and supervision	One vote per 14 contacts (plus effects of spillover)	Yes	At $16 per hour and 6 contacts per hour, one vote costs $29
Leafleting	Labor intensive: recruit, prepare walk lists and leaflets, determine polling locations	Minimal: monitor walkers, check work	One vote per 189 voters reached by leaflets	Not significantly greater than zero	*
Direct mail, partisan	Resource intensive: design, print, mail	Intensive during start-up, then postal service takes over	No detectable effect	Large number of studies show average effect cannot be large	*
Direct mail, nonpartisan	Resource intensive: design, print, mail	Intensive work with consultants, then postal service takes over	One vote per 200 recipients	Yes, but borderline significant	At $0.50 per piece, one vote costs $67
Phone, volunteer	Labor intensive: amass enthusiastic callers and secure phone bank	Ongoing training and supervision	One vote per 38 contacts	Yes	At $16 an hour and 16 contacts per hour, one vote costs $38
Commercial live calls, without special coaching	Resource intensive: obtain phone list	Ongoing or sporadic monitoring	One vote per 180 contacts	Yes	At $0.50 per contact, one vote costs $90
Commercial live calls, with special coaching, long scripts	Resource intensive: obtain phone list, carefully select calling firm	Extensive monitoring	One vote per 35 contacts	Yes, but based on few studies	At $1.50 per contact, one vote costs $53
Robo calls	Obtain phone list, recording talent	None	One vote per 900 individuals called	Not significantly greater than zero	*
E-mail	Moderately labor intensive: amass e-mail lists, compose message(s)	Most of the work is in the start-up	No detectable effect	Large numbers of studies show average effect cannot be large	*
Election Day festivals	Labor intensive: arrange advertising and organization	Requires staff on hand to host and supervise events	Raises precinct-wide turnout by 1–2 percentage points	Yes, but based on few studies	Roughly $28 per vote
Television	Resource intensive: hire consultants	None	Raises zip-code-wide turnout by 0.5 percentage point	Not significantly greater than zero	*
Radio	Resource intensive	None	Raises city-wide turnout by 0.8 percentage point	Not significantly greater than zero	*

a. Costs may vary due to local circumstances and market conditions.

b. "Contact" is defined as follows: for door-to-door canvassing, talking to target voter; for phone calls, talking to target voter; for mail, mail sent; for leaflets, leaflet dropped at door. For leafleting and door-to-door canvassing, calculations assume that the average household has 1.5 voters.

* Cost-effectiveness is not calculated for tactics that are not proven to raise turnout.

Another approach is to place even greater emphasis on the quality of GOTV work. A call or visit by a charismatic candidate, as opposed to a volunteer canvasser, might well produce larger effects. If you are contemplating a campaign that emphasizes quality, keep things in perspective. Even if your supertreatments are twice as effective as the most effective door-to-door canvassing campaign, you will still need to contact 7,000 registered voters to produce 1,000 votes. To sway election outcomes involving large numbers of voters, high-quality campaigns must also be high-quantity campaigns.

Further Thoughts on Cost-Effectiveness: Mobilizing Voters over the Long Haul

Voter turnout campaigns tend to focus on the here and now. They work to generate votes during the waning days of the campaign, and when the polls close, the campaign closes shop as well. Apart from influencing the outcome of an election, what lasting effects do GOTV campaigns have?

One of the most interesting findings to emerge from GOTV research is that voter mobilization campaigns have enduring effects. The New Haven residents who were randomly assigned to receive direct mail or face-to-face canvassing in 1998 were more likely to vote in both the election held in November 1998 and the mayoral election held in November 1999.[9] This study has since been replicated with nine other canvassing populations.[10] The treatment groups in the Michigan social pressure experiment not only voted at higher rates in the August primary; even though they received no further mailings, they were also significantly more likely to vote the following November. Taken together, these studies show that for every 100 voters mobilized in a given election, an additional thirty-three will participate in the following election. If we assume a geometrically declining rate over time, 100 additional votes in this year's election will produce a total of forty-eight additional votes in all subsequent elections.

The long-term impact of voter mobilization has profound implications. First, it suggests that voting is a habit-forming activity. Someone who votes in this election is more likely to vote in the next election. Someone who skips an election is less likely to vote in the future. America's low turnout rates may reflect the fact that we have the most frequent elections on earth. One might liken sleepy municipal elections to gateway drugs; by enticing so many people to abstain from voting, they weaken voting habits.

Second, this finding casts a different light on the usual way of evaluating the costs and benefits of a GOTV campaign. The typical approach is to think only in terms of votes produced in the current election. A more realistic calculation would take into account the future effects of this year's voter mobilization drive. If your campaign generates 1,000 additional votes at a cost of $40,000, this price amounts to $40 per vote for the current election. But if we also include the 330 votes in the next election, the price falls to $40,000/1,330 = $30 per vote. This added efficiency is an important consideration for political parties and other organizations that have a long-term interest in producing votes, especially if the alternative is to spend money on persuasive messages that may have no long-term impact once the current slate of candidates has moved on.

Synergy?

One common refrain among those who design campaigns is the importance of "touching" voters with a steady stream of campaign communication. Touch them first with a mailer, then with a phone call, then with another mailer, a robo call, and so forth. When thinking about the cost-effectiveness of this approach, it is important to be clear about exactly what is being claimed. A GOTV campaign consisting of a mailer and a phone call probably will produce more votes than a campaign consisting of just a phone call or just a mailer. The notion that "more is better" is not really at issue here. When consultants speak of an "integrated" campaign in which the whole is greater than the sum of the parts, they are suggesting that those who receive mail are *especially* responsive to the ensuing phone call (or vice versa). Suppose that mail increases turnout 1 percent and phone contact increases it 2 percent. The claim is that mail and phone together increase turnout more than 3 percent because the mailing warms voters up to the message that they receive via phone.

This claim has been tested in no fewer than ten experiments, and the results decisively reject the synergy hypothesis. In the 1998 New Haven study, mail did not increase the effectiveness of phone calls, and phone calls did not enhance the effects of door-to-door canvassing. In the 2000 NAACP National Voter Fund study, those who received mail were as (weakly) influenced by phone calls as those who received no mail. The

2002 NALEO experiment failed to support the hypothesis that robo calls enhance the effectiveness of direct mail or vice versa. Neither direct mail nor robo calls amplified the effects of live calls. The same may be said of nonpartisan live calls and direct mail sent by groups mobilizing Asian Americans in 2006 and of live calls, robo calls, mail, and canvassing directed at predominantly Latino neighborhoods in California. Three studies of mail, robotic calls, and live calls by environmental organizations in the 2004 and 2006 elections showed no synergy. Emily Cardy's study of direct mail and phone calls on behalf of a gubernatorial candidate did show some (albeit statistically insignificant) signs of synergy, raising the possibility that the hypothesis applies to partisan messages, but a recent study of partisan mail, phone calls, and canvassing in another gubernatorial contest found no evidence that combinations of different treatments had especially strong effects. In sum, experimental researchers have searched long and hard for the El Dorado of synergy only to conclude that combinations of GOTV appeals do not appear to deliver a bonus of votes.

Perhaps the reason for the lack of synergy has to do with the mechanisms by which GOTV campaigns work. Getting a piece of direct mail rarely creates a personal sense of belonging, so the subsequent phone call does not build on a growing predisposition to vote. Conversely, for those who have received a phone call, the ensuing mailer does not have special resonance. Although it is possible to imagine a situation in which one GOTV tactic amplifies the effect of another, experiments have not detected these interaction effects, which explains why this book is organized into chapters that look at GOTV tactics one at a time rather than in special combinations.

Frontiers of GOTV Research

Although the rigorous investigation of voter mobilization has come a long way in the past decade, unanswered questions abound. These open questions fall into two broad categories. The first category is practical: What is the best way to allocate resources over the course of a campaign? The other category is theoretical: Why do certain mobilization tactics work better than others?

One of the basic practical questions that confronts any campaign seeking to increase turnout is how much energy to devote to voter registration. Unfortunately, beyond the unsuccessful attempts to use e-mail to encourage registration, no publicly available experiments have assessed the efficiency with which resources devoted to registration translate into additional votes. This gap in the literature means that we cannot say what kinds of registration campaigns work best or, perhaps more important, whether various types of registration drives produce more votes per dollar than voter mobilization campaigns.

We know far more about whether encouraging one's supporters to vote by mail will increase voter participation. Campaigns prefer to have their supporters cast mail-in ballots. First, when supporters vote by mail well in advance of Election Day, the campaign no longer needs to expend resources communicating with them. Second, campaigns like to be seen as offering a service to people who receive their mailings; this builds rapport and may be useful in subsequent fund-raising and recruitment efforts. Third, and most relevant for us, it is thought that encouraging voters to vote by mail raises their probability of voting. As a result, campaigns often expend considerable resources early in the campaign encouraging targeted individuals to become absentee voters. Here, the experimental evidence is much clearer than the evidence on voter registration.[11] Mail and phone calls can induce recipients to vote by mail, but they do not, on average, produce an increase in voter turnout rates. Evidently, inducements to vote by mail cause people who would otherwise vote in person to vote by mail. They do not cause people who would otherwise not vote to cast a ballot.

This news is unfortunate for campaigns, because it means that there is no easy way around the challenge of efficiently raising turnout well in advance of Election Day. The question then becomes whether it is worthwhile to begin GOTV efforts early, say, two months before the election. This is a question that GOTV researchers have sought to answer, but the experimental results have been murky. The reason is that it takes a very large experiment to differentiate the effects of early and late GOTV work. The requirements of the experiment become even greater if the research seeks also to estimate the effects of different numbers of contacts. The existing evidence hints that canvassing and calling late in the campaign works best, but it remains unclear how effective early calls and visits are. As academics are fond of saying, further research is needed.

Turning to the unanswered theoretical questions, the main challenge is to isolate the active ingredient that causes some GOTV tactics to work and others to fail. This research agenda remains in its infancy. Earlier in this chapter, we speculated about mechanisms that might account for the sizable effects of canvassing, certain forms of repeat phone contact, and "shaming" mail. But those were just speculations. The task for researchers is to define these mechanisms more precisely and to spell out testable propositions that will help to prove whether that mechanism is operative. Consider, for example, the hypothesis advanced by Julia Gray and Philip Potter that canvassing works because it conveys a "costly signal" to voters.[12] Canvassing is difficult and time-consuming, and when voters see a campaign doing it, they infer that the campaign and election are worth special attention. According to the costly signal hypothesis, even direct mail can be as effective as canvassing if it causes voters to infer that the campaign has committed serious resources to it. The line of experimentation that these researchers have initiated is designed to test whether the active ingredient in voter mobilization is impressing voters with a costly signal, as opposed to other mechanisms, such as conveying the message that others value the voter's participation. Regardless of whether this particular hypothesis pans out, the Gray and Potter research agenda points to where the increasingly refined GOTV literature is heading. Having sketched the contours of what works in a rigorous scientific fashion, experimental researchers are now asking why.

In Search of Supertreatments

One of the most exciting challenges in GOTV research is to use intuitions about why certain GOTV tactics work to aid the search for unusually powerful methods of increasing turnout. The literature on synergy suggests that supertreatments are not likely to be found in special elixirs that combine conventional treatments. Instead, recent experiments imply that supertreatments are likely to turn up when powerful social-psychological forces are harnessed. For example, the strong tendency for people to guard their reputation and self-image is illustrated in the striking finding from chapter 5 that a single mailing can produce an increase of 8 percentage points in turnout by revealing a person's past voting record to the neighbors.

On the frontier of GOTV research lies the investigation of similar social influences, such as the effects of friends and family members communicating the importance of voting, expressing interest in the electoral process, and intimating their disdain for those who fail to fulfill this civic obligation. A related topic is the study of how social networks can be used as mobilizing agents. Can workplaces, religious groups, online communities, and other social ties be used to bind people together into blocs of voters? In the heyday of machine politics, it was common for "block captains" to mobilize a specific list of voters. The idea of recruiting people to be responsible for turning out a small group of friends, neighbors, parishioners, or co-workers is essentially an attempt to harness the formidable social influence that peers exert on each other. Perhaps peer influence could be enhanced by linking other forces, such as the feeling of obligation to honor a commitment to vote expressed to a friend, particularly if that friend intimates that voting is a matter of public record. The question for researchers is whether these social influences, separately or in combination, in fact produce large increases in voter turnout and, if so, whether the effects can be reproduced inexpensively on a large scale, perhaps using new communication technologies.

Conducting Your Own Experiment

The experiments described in this book have only begun to scratch the surface of all that can be learned about making GOTV campaigns more efficient. While reading this book, you may have thought of some experiments of your own. You may be running for office, wondering how you can use the lessons learned from your upcoming campaign to improve the efficiency of subsequent campaigns. Or perhaps you remain unpersuaded by the experimental results presented in this book and want to see for yourself whether they hold up.

With a bit of thought and planning, you should be able to put a meaningful experiment into place. You do not need an advanced degree in social science, but it is important to proceed carefully and methodically so as to guard against the problems that sometimes confront this type of research. Here is a brief overview of how experiments are designed, conducted, and analyzed.

Spell out Your Hypothesis

Although it sounds like a class assignment, a useful first step in any experimental project is to write, in a single sentence, the claim that you will be testing. This will force you to clarify what the treatment is and who the subjects are. For example, "Among voters with Latino surnames, Spanish-language mailers increase turnout more than English-language mailers," or "Candidates are better able to mobilize voters through door-to-door canvassing than are the activists who work for candidates," or

"Election Day rides increase voter turnout among those who live more than a mile from their polling place."

Define Your Target List

Create a list of voters who will be targeted for the GOTV intervention you are evaluating. Depending on how your campaign is organized, the lists of targets may be individual people or places (such as voting precincts or media markets). For example, your list may consist of Latino voters in Fresno County. If there are some areas or people that your campaign absolutely must treat, exclude them from the list to be randomized. These must-treat observations are outside your experiment.

Determine How Many People (or Places) You Wish to Assign to the Treatment and Control Categories

The larger the numbers in each category, the more precise your results will be. However, do not assign more people to the treatment group than you have the resources to treat. Apportion your experimental groups so that your contact rate in the treatment group will be as high as possible. Box 10-1 offers some sense of how precise your estimates will be under different allocation schemes.

Divide the List into Treatment and Control Groups

Creating random treatment and control groups is easy to do with a spreadsheet program such as Microsoft Excel. Box 10-2 walks you through the steps of randomly sorting and subdividing your target list.

Random sorting is useful even if you are apprehensive about excluding a control group. Suppose you are conducting a phone canvass. Sort your phone list so that it is in random order. Call names on the randomly sorted list, starting from the top and working your way down. When your campaign is over, any names that you did not attempt to call represent your control group. The names that you did attempt to call represent the treatment group.[13] Nothing about the campaign's execution has changed, but now it becomes amenable to rigorous evaluation in the event that you failed to attempt to call all of the names on your target list. This approach is ideal for evaluating campaigns whose goals outstrip their resources.

Box 10-1. Calculating the Precision of an Experiment

With calculator in hand, you can easily anticipate the precision of an experiment. Let C represent the contact rate (the proportion of people in the treatment group that you actually contacted). A typical contact rate for a phone experiment is 0.5, for example. Let N represent the number of people on your list. Let N_T stand for the number of people in your treatment group and N_C, the number of people in your control group. The margin of error in your study is plus or minus the square root of N divided by the square root of $(C^2 N_T N_C)$. So, if your contact rate is 0.5, 9,000 people are in the treatment group, and 1,000 people are in the control group, then your margin of error is 0.067, or 6.7 percentage points. In other words, if you add and subtract 6.7 percentage points from whatever result you obtain, you will have a 95 percent chance of bracketing the true effect of your intervention. If that margin of error seems uncomfortably large, increase the sample size, make the control group and treatment group closer in size, or improve the contact rate.

Box 10-2. Random Assignment

Random assignment to treatment and control groups is easily accomplished with a spreadsheet program such as Microsoft Excel. First, open the spreadsheet containing the list of voters. Second, place your cursor on an empty cell in the spreadsheet and click the equal sign in order to call up the equation editor. Enter the formula RAND() and hit enter. A random number between 0 and 1 should appear in the cell. Third, copy and paste this random number into a column beside the columns in your data set. Now every row in your data set should contain a random number. Fourth, highlight all of the columns in your data set and click DATA > SORT. A box should appear asking you to indicate which column(s) to sort by. Choose the column that corresponds to the column of random numbers just generated. Click OK. Fifth, having sorted the data in random order, add a new column to your data set. This new column will indicate whether each person is assigned to the treatment group. If you want 500 people in your treatment group, put the number 1 into the first 500 rows and the number 0 into the remaining rows.

Resist the temptation to evaluate your campaign without randomization. Making all the calls you can, in the order that they arrive from the list vendor, and then dubbing the remainder a control group may produce misleading results.

Check the Randomization

Random assignment should, in principle, create treatment and control groups that have similar background characteristics. To ensure that you have conducted the randomization properly, check to see that the treatment and control groups have approximately the same rate of voter turnout in some recent election (before your intervention). If this information is not available, check to see that the average age in the treatment group is approximately the same as the average age in the control group. If the treatment and control groups differ appreciably, you may have made a computer error or gotten an unlucky draw. Redo your randomization.

Administer the Treatment to the Treatment Group Only

Be vigilant about adhering to the treatment and control assignments. Do not contact anyone on the control list! The easiest way to keep the experiment from going awry is to release only the treatment names to the phone bank or direct mail vendor. Send leafleteers and door-to-door canvassers out with the names of people in the treatment group only and remind them not to knock blindly on every door.

Maintain Records of Who Was Contacted

Maintain records of who was contacted, even if that person is someone in the control group who was contacted by mistake. You will need this information in order to calculate the effect of actually receiving your intervention.

Archive Your Campaign Materials

Once you have successfully carried out this protocol, archive your campaign materials and write a brief description of the experimental procedures. While you wait for registrars to furnish voter turnout information, and before you forget the details, write up the description of the experiment and how it was conducted. Create a physical or electronic archive of your campaign materials—your scripts, recorded messages, mailings, and so forth. Be sure to collect whatever data you need from canvassers (for example, walk sheets with contact information) and callers before these materials disappear.

Calculate Turnout Rates

When voter turnout data become available, calculate the turnout rates of the people in the treatment and control groups. You can do this by hand or by computer using the subjects' names and voter identification numbers. Remember, your treatment group consists of those individuals assigned at the outset to the treatment group, regardless of whether you were able to contact them or not.

Analyze the Results

Analyze the experimental results. The difference in turnout between the original treatment and control groups—ignoring for the moment whether persons in the treatment group were actually treated—tells you quite a lot. (Note: Do not discard people in the treatment group who weren't home or were found to have moved.) If the turnout rate in the assigned treatment group is higher, your intervention succeeded in raising turnout. This difference is known as the intent-to-treat effect, because it does not take notice of the possibility that only some of the assigned treatment group were actually treated.

Next calculate the contact rate. Divide the number contacted in the treatment group by the number assigned to the treatment group. If your contact rate is less than 100 percent, divide the intent-to-treat effect by the contact rate. This number indicates the effect of the treatment on those who were actually treated. Consider the following example. Your control group votes at a rate of 42 percent. Your treatment group votes at a rate of 47 percent. Your contact rate is 50 percent. So the effect of the treatment on the treated is $(47 - 42)/0.5 = 10$ percentage points.

Perform a Statistical Analysis

A bit of statistical analysis can indicate how likely it is that the difference you are seeing was produced by chance. Why worry about chance? Sometimes just by luck of the draw you may underestimate or overestimate the effectiveness of the treatment. We have developed some (free) web tools

Box 10-3. Simplified Web Software for Analyzing Experimental Data

For the convenience of first-time experimenters, we have created a website (research.yale.edu/vote) that reads in experimental results and generates a statistical analysis. You supply six numbers: the number of people that you (1) assigned to the treatment group, (2) assigned to the control group, (3) successfully treated in the treatment group, (4) inadvertently treated in the control group, (5) found to have voted in the treatment group, and (6) found to have voted in the control group.

To see how the program works, suppose you wish to analyze results from Melissa Michelson's door-to-door canvassing experiment in Dos Palos, California. Prior to the 2001 election, she assigned 466 people with Latino surnames to the treatment group and 298 Latinos to the control group. Of the people in the treatment group, 342 were successfully contacted. No one in the control group was contacted. In the treatment group, eighty-six people voted, whereas forty-one people voted in the control group. The six inputs are, therefore, 466, 298, 342, 0, 86, 41.

After entering these numbers in the appropriate boxes, click the SUBMIT button. You will see output that summarizes the research findings and estimates the size and precision of the treatment effects. Check the statistical summary that appears in the middle of the page to ensure that you have entered the data correctly. The computer will summarize the voting rates and contact rates based on the numbers you provided. Next, examine the "intent-to-treat" estimate. This number is calculated by subtracting the voting rate in the control group from the voting rate in the treatment group. In this example, the intent-to-treat estimate is 4.7, suggesting that assignment

to walk you through this process as painlessly as possible and to give you some pointers about how to interpret the numbers (see box 10-3).

Crafting an experiment requires planning and supervision, yet experience has shown that any energetic and well-organized researcher can learn to do it. For years we have taught a seminar that requires students to conduct a full-fledged randomized study. We also teach a summer workshop on experiments, attended by faculty, students, and nonacademics. Many of the participants have gone on to conduct clever and well-executed voter mobilization studies. One got a team of friends together to the treatment group raised turnout 4.7 percentage points. Beneath this figure is the standard error of the estimated intent-to-treat effect. The larger this number, the more uncertainty surrounds the intent-to-treat estimate. The "treatment effect" is estimated by dividing the intent-to-treat estimate (4.7) by the contact rate (0.73), which produces the number 6.4. Those who were actually treated became 6.4 percentage points more likely to vote. The uncertainty of this estimate is measured by its standard error, 3.7.

Finally, the statistical software makes three useful calculations. The first is the 95 percent confidence interval, which spans from −0.8 to 13.6. The true treatment effect has a 95 percent probability of lying within this range. The second calculation is the one-tailed significance of the estimated treatment effect. When conducting GOTV experiments, it is conventional to expect turnout to rise as a result of the treatment. The so-called "null hypothesis" is that the treatment failed to increase turnout. The one-tailed significance level states the probability of obtaining an estimate as large as the estimated treatment effect (in this case 6.4) by chance. When this probability is below 0.05, as is the case here, the estimate is said to be "statistically significant." Naturally, if the experiment were repeated, the results might come out differently. The "power" of an experiment describes the probability that it will produce a statistically significant estimate given the observed treatment effect. In this case, Michelson's experiment has a 54 percent probability of rejecting the null hypothesis given that the treatment effect is 6.4. The power of an experiment can be improved by raising the contact rate or increasing the number of observations.

to make GOTV calls on behalf of a candidate for governor; another designed and distributed nonpartisan direct mail; another organized a large-scale precinct walking campaign. More than a dozen such studies have been published or presented at academic conferences. One of the most gratifying aspects of writing a book like this is hearing about the imaginative experiments that readers have conducted, some of which are truly remarkable pieces of research.

Experimental research requires a fair amount of effort, but the biggest hurdle in conducting a successful experiment is conceptual. To design and execute a randomized experiment, you must first understand why a randomly assigned control group is essential. At every stage in the process of executing an experiment, people will whine about your insistence on a control group. They will propose instead that you simply consider the people the campaign happened to treat as the treatment group and that you consider the people the campaign failed to contact as the control group. In other words, they will propose that you forget about random assignment and just let them treat whomever they please. You will have to convince them that a randomly assigned control group is indispensable.

Why is it indispensable? Well, suppose you are interested in the effects of a GOTV phone call campaign, but you do not randomly assign subjects to treatment and control groups. Suppose that you naively compare the voting rates of the people you reached to the voting rates of the people you did not reach by phone (either because they didn't answer when you called or because you never called them). This comparison could be very misleading because there is no guarantee that the people who answered the phone have the same propensity to vote as the people who were never reached. This comparison requires a risky leap of faith. Experimenters hate it when scientific claims depend on leaps of faith.

When you balk at this dubious research design, its advocates may try to reassure you by suggesting that you can make the research design serviceable by comparing a select group of people who did or did not receive the call. The select group they have in mind are people who are similar in age, party attachment, and voter turnout rate in previous elections. Do not give in. What they are suggesting is a demonstrably flawed research design. Here's why. Even if the people who were treated have the same observed attributes as the people who were not treated, there is no guarantee that their *unobserved* attributes are the same. Learning that a person is home when you call reveals something about their likelihood of voting (that is, they have not moved, they are not dead, they are willing to pick up the phone when a stranger calls). Even if your phone calls had no effect on turnout, the people you reached will vote at higher rates than the folks you could not or did not reach.

In order to drive this point home to our academic colleagues, we conducted the following experiment: a couple of days before the November 2004 election, we called 15,000 registered voters in Illinois and urged them to buckle their seat belt when driving during the holiday season.[14] Not a word was said about voting or politics. Just seat belts. Obviously, the true effect of this call on voter turnout was zero. But sure enough, the people who actually received the buckle up message voted at a rate that was 5 percentage points higher than that of the people who were not called, even though the two groups shared exactly the same pattern of voter turnout during the previous decade. Why? Because this comparison excluded the dead, the moved, and the unfriendly from the treatment group but did not exclude them from the control group. If the comparison were properly constructed, the experiment would yield the correct answer. As expected, there was no difference in turnout between *assigned* treatment and control groups. The point here is that if your research design is flawed, you risk generating deeply misleading conclusions. Don't get fooled into thinking that you can patch up a flawed design by focusing on people who share the same observed characteristics.

What is the right way to test the mobilizing effects of a phone call? Randomly assign voters to receive a call or not. Keep track of the fraction of the treatment group that actually received the calls. Compare the voting rates among those originally assigned to the treatment and control groups and divide by the fraction of the treatment group that received the calls. (Or just use the web-based software described in box 10-3.) Because you are comparing the randomly assigned treatment and control groups, the groups have the same expected voting rate, and there is no bias in favor of finding that phone calls work (or don't work).

Another common concern among those who resist experimental research is that a campaign cannot afford to take a control group out of its list of targeted voters. This concern is often based on a somewhat unrealistic sense of how effective their mobilization campaign is likely to be (or how close the election is likely to be). If, for example, a state legislative campaign has resources to target 15,000 voters and you remove a control group of 1,500, two things happen. First, the campaign can reallocate its resources to the 13,500 and treat some of them more intensively. Second, your control group will cost the campaign votes in proportion to its effectiveness. Suppose the campaign is outstanding and both mobilizes and persuades a base of supporters. If left untreated, suppose the control group votes at rate of 45 percent and votes four to one in favor of your candidate. Had the control group been treated, this group would have voted at a rate of 50 percent and supported your candidate by a five-to-one margin. In the worst-case scenario, the campaign reaps no additional votes from the extra resources it reallocates to the treatment group and loses ninety-five votes. That is probably a much smaller number than the campaign envisioned when it worried about the loss of a control group. These kinds of calculations help campaign managers to see that the small short-term risks associated with an experiment are outweighed by the long-term benefits of acquiring knowledge.

Present Your Results

Once you have conducted your experiment, try to present it in a manner that enables it to contribute to the accumulation of scientific knowledge about campaigns. Here is a brief checklist of things to report to your audience.

✔ Describe the experimental setting. When and where was the campaign conducted? What other kinds of campaign activity or public debate might voters have been exposed to?

✔ Describe the experimental treatments. What were the interventions? When were they deployed and by whom? Present the phone or canvassing scripts. Show pictures of the mailings or e-mail.

✔ What were the experimental groups, and from what population were they drawn? Describe the randomization procedure used to assign the groups. Describe the number of observations assigned to each experimental group.[15] Show whether, as expected, the treatment and control groups have similar background attributes, such as average age or past voting rates.

✔ Were the treatments successfully administered to all of the people who were supposed to receive them? If not, what proportion of the treatment group actually received the treatment? Did the control group inadvertently receive your treatment? If so, what proportion of the control group was inadvertently treated?

✔ Briefly explain the source of your voter turnout information and how you dealt with cases in which people in the original treatment groups were not found on the rolls of voters. (Sometimes those not found are classified as nonvoters, and sometimes they are excluded from the analysis altogether.) Check whether the treatment and control groups have similar rates of being found on the voter rolls. Present the voting rates for each experimental group, including the number of observations used to calculate each voting rate.

These are the essential ingredients of any experimental write-up. Obviously, if you have the statistical skills, you can go into much more detail, but do not skip directly to a complex statistical analysis without first walking the reader through the simple facts of the experiment mentioned above. One of the most attractive features of experimentation is that it lends itself to a straightforward and transparent style of presentation.

Strategies for Increasing Electoral Participation

Although much of this book is directed to those who seek to sway elections, it also speaks to those whose larger purpose is to remedy low rates of voter participation. In contrast to the end of the nineteenth century, when turnout in presidential elections was over 70 percent, nowadays about three-fifths of the eligible electorate votes in U.S. presidential elections, and roughly one-third does so in federal midterm elections. Municipal and special elections sometimes spark voter interest, but more often than not they hover in the range of 30 percent turnout. It's not uncommon to see single-digit turnout in uncompetitive municipal elections (see box 10-4).

The question is what to do. Proposals abound. For simplicity, we group them into three categories. The first is a massive constitutional overhaul. Institute a new electoral system that encourages minor parties so that voters will be able to choose from a wide spectrum of candidates. Introduce a system of direct electoral control over policy. Consolidate elections at all levels of government so that voters have to vote only once every two years.

Although these ideas make wonderful discussion topics for magazines and college seminars, they cannot be considered serious proposals for policy reform. Even if one were convinced that proportional representation does a better job of attracting voter participation than other electoral systems (turnout patterns in countries like New Zealand, which have switched to a proportional representation system, call this assumption into question[16]), the chances that the United States will adopt such constitutional reforms are, as it were, statistically indistinguishable from zero. As for direct democracy, it is doubtful whether states that regularly present ballot initiatives and referenda to their citizens enjoy higher voter turnout as a result. And introducing direct democracy at the federal level would require a constitutional revision that fundamentally alters the dual system of representation that currently accords power on a per capita basis in the House of Representatives and on a per state basis in the Senate. Not likely any time soon.

Somewhat more realistic, if only because it is more concrete, is the idea of consolidating the election calendar. Compared with constitutional

---

Box 10-4. Further Reading on
Voter Turnout in the United States

The following books span a range of perspectives on why American voter turnout is low or declining. Diagnoses range from the media-centered campaigns to restrictive registration laws to the lack of vigorous party competition. Prescriptions range from civic education to new journalistic norms to changes in electoral rules.

Adam J. Berinsky, "The Perverse Consequences of Electoral Reform in the United States," *American Politics Research,* vol. 33, no. 4 (2005): 471–91.

David E. Campbell, *Why We Vote: How Schools and Communities Shape Our Civic Life* (Princeton University Press, 2006).

Benjamin Highton, "Voter Registration and Turnout in the United States," *Perspectives on Politics,* vol. 2, no. 3 (2004): 507–15.

Frances Fox Piven and Richard A. Cloward, *Why Americans Still Don't Vote and Why Politicians Want It That Way* (Boston: Beacon Press, 2000).

Stephen J. Rosenstone and John Mark Hansen, *Mobilization, Participation, and Democracy in America* (New York: Macmillan, 1993).

Ruy Teixeira, *The Disappearing American Voter* (Brookings, 1992).

Martin P. Wattenberg, *Where Have All the Voters Gone?* (Harvard University Press, 2002).

Raymond Wolfinger and Stephen J. Rosenstone, *Who Votes?* (Yale University Press, 1980).

---

revisions, this one poses fewer risks of unintended consequences. Consolidating the election calendar might increase voter turnout rates. Parties and candidates would channel their GOTV efforts toward a single campaign, the gravity of which would attract greater interest. The problem is generating the political will to impose uniformity on municipal, county, state, and federal election calendars. It is no accident that some jurisdictions choose to hold their elections at odd times; this is a calculated move by parties and interest groups seeking to diminish the influence of national election tides on their local or state elections.

A second group of proposals involves more modest policy changes related to voting procedures. Allow voters to cast ballots online. Allow ballots to be cast over a three-week period. Permit everyone who so desires to vote by mail. Create a national database that automatically reregisters people when they change addresses. Or institute same-day registration nationwide. One might reasonably anticipate that each of these ideas will be adopted one day, but the track record of this kind of tinkering is not impressive. Those who have examined the effects of changing balloting and registration rules on patterns of state turnout over time find that the introduction of same-day registration rules in Idaho, Maine, Minnesota, New Hampshire, Wisconsin, and Wyoming was associated with only modest gains in turnout.[17] Permitting early and absentee balloting also boosted turnout, but again only to a small extent. The Motor Voter Law, which made the registration process easier and more widely accessible, also had small positive effects. These innovations are arguably a step in the right direction, although the specter of voting fraud looms over proposals such as same-day registration and Internet voting. But even if they could be implemented without problems, they cannot be expected to produce substantially higher turnout rates.

The last category of proposals involves some form of voter education. Create hotlines and websites that provide free information about where to vote and what choices will appear on the ballot. Convene public debates among candidates so that voters can learn about where they stand on the issues. Encourage journalists to devote more attention to issues and less to the horse race competition between candidates. These well-intentioned proposals may be worthwhile for a host of reasons, but they seem unlikely to increase voter turnout appreciably. Candidate debates, like Sunday morning talk shows with politicians, typically attract appreciative but tiny audiences. Public interest websites attract little traffic. Journalists who write about policy debates rather than the vicissitudes of electoral fortunes find their work ignored by all but a small constituency of readers. Politics does not interest most people. It is noble but unrealistic to expect nonvoters to seek out edifying news stories, websites, or public events.

Our perspective on how to raise voter turnout is rather different. Examine a range of GOTV tactics and figure out which ones are effective and cost-efficient. By demonstrating what works (and what does not), this investigative approach provides an important signal to those engaged in electoral competition. If the market for campaign services learns from a reliable source that a particular GOTV tactic is a more cost-effective way of garnering votes, we eventually will see campaigns allocate more resources to this tactic.

We should emphasize the word "eventually" in the previous sentence. Findings from scientific studies are not likely to win converts overnight. People who run political campaigns are justifiably skeptical of what passes for research. And even if some of this skepticism could be put to rest by blue-ribbon panels executing studies of the highest quality, the problem of conflicting economic interests remains. Big money is at stake in the market for campaign services, and those who earn their livelihood in this line of work are unlikely to sit still as their product or domain of expertise is threatened. On the one hand, campaign managers sometimes profit from the services they sell, either because they hold a financial stake in firms with which the campaign subcontracts or because they expect to have an ongoing business relationship with the subcontractors. On the other hand, managers also have a financial incentive to win elections, so as to burnish their reputation en route to future consulting work. The tension between these two economic incentives comes into play when campaign managers are able to protect their reputation by employing well-accepted, profitable, but inefficient campaign tactics. In this case, they can have their cake and eat it, too, running "credible" campaigns whose activities make for handsome profits.

If we are correct in our suspicions concerning the cost-inefficiency of campaigns that rely heavily on mass media, direct mail, and conventional commercial phone banks, scientific evidence will hasten a gradual evolutionary process. Managers who run inefficient campaigns eventually will be pushed aside by those who prove more successful in electoral competition. Admittedly, the process of natural selection could take a long time to unfold. After all, there are many reasons why elections are won and lost, and the market may have difficulty identifying which tactics are truly associated with success. Perhaps that is how capital-intensive campaigning came to prominence in the first place. Nevertheless, the recent shift in campaign tactics toward more personal interaction with voters increases our confidence that political campaigns are attentive to and influenced by scientific findings.[18]

Frontiers of Campaign Strategy: The Relative Cost-Effectiveness of Turnout Versus Persuasion

A great many research questions must be answered before those seeking to sway elections will have reason to embrace GOTV activity as an especially attractive way to invest campaign dollars. The experimental research reported in this book examines only *whether* people vote, not *how* they vote. In order to show that cost-effective voter mobilization tactics are also cost-effective vote generation tactics, we need to see how they compare to persuasive communication. To what extent do phone calls, direct mail, and other campaign tactics affect voter preference? This line of experimental research is just coming into existence. Due to the constraints of the secret ballot, it is harder to study vote choice than voter turnout. Experimental researchers must either randomly assign their treatments at the level of the voting precinct, where vote choice can be counted in the aggregate, or gather individual-level data using a post-election survey.[19]

Experimental studies of persuasion, which were rare when the first edition of this book was written, have grown steadily in number and sophistication. The early studies, pioneered by Alan Gerber, focused on the persuasive effects of partisan direct mail by Democratic candidates for Congress, mayor, and state legislature in 1999 and 2000. He then followed up with a pair of studies gauging the effectiveness of partisan direct mail on behalf of a Republican congressional candidate running in the 2002 primary and then general election. Party mobilizing in Michigan in 2002 was the subject of an experimental evaluation by David Nickerson, and a Republican state senatorial incumbent was the focus of a pair of experiments in 2002 and 2004 by Jennifer Steen and Donald Green. In 2003 Kevin Arceneaux studied a Kansas City municipal election in which ACORN canvassed randomly selected precincts in support of a ballot measure designed to raise money to maintain bus service. In 2004 Kevin Arceneaux again worked with an interest group canvassing in inner-city neighborhoods in support of a ballot proposition in California but also broke new ground in studying the effects of a door-to-door campaign by a local candidate in New Mexico. The first experiment to look at the persuasive effects of radio was conducted by Costas Panagopoulos and Donald Green in the context of mayoral elections in 2005 and replicated in 2006. The 2006 election cycle was a watershed for persuasion research. Kevin Arceneaux and Robin Kolodny examined the effects of a liberal activist group that canvassed and called pro-choice women in two contested state legislative districts. David Nickerson studied the effects of an intensive door-to-door canvassing campaign in five Oregon State house districts. Donald Green studied the effects of an e-mail campaign that an environmental group directed toward its members urging opposition to a ballot proposition. Finally, in 2006, Alan Gerber, James Gimpel, Donald Green, and Daron Shaw collaborated on a pair of studies in collaboration with Republican campaigns in Texas. One study examined the effects of a multi-million-dollar television and radio campaign on vote preferences during the early months of a gubernatorial race; the other examined the effects of a robo call campaign on behalf of a state supreme court justice running for reelection.

This assortment of studies is much smaller than the corresponding literature on voter turnout, but some tentative conclusions have begun to emerge. By this point, the reader has become familiar with our ranking system characterizing the firmness of these conclusions and will not be surprised to see that no proposition receives more than two stars.

★★ *Persuasive efforts on behalf of challengers and open seat candidates seem to be more effective than persuasive efforts on behalf of incumbents.* Alan Gerber's study of a mayoral challenger's campaign found direct mail to be both effective and cost-effective. Panagopoulos and Green found that radio campaigns designed to increase the name recognition of both mayoral candidates have the effect of improving the challenger's showing at the polls, presumably because the challenger is less well known than the incumbent. Arceneaux's calling and canvassing results revealed strong effects in the context of an open seat contest in a primary election, and the same may be said of Cardy's study of phone and mail appeals in a gubernatorial open seat primary. Gerber's early studies of incumbent direct mail campaigns, in contrast, found weak effects on those targeted in general elections, a finding corroborated by other studies of direct mail and phone calls on behalf of incumbents in 2002 and 2004.

★ *Incumbents benefit from persuasive appeals made during primary elections.* Gerber's study of a 2002 congressional primary found that persuasive mail affected the incumbent's vote share.

★★ *Persuasive campaigns by interest groups are somewhat risky.* The Arceneaux and Kolodny study of calls and canvassing of pro-choice targets found that urging support for Democratic candidates on the basis of this issue had some positive effect among Democrats but caused Republicans to become significantly less likely to vote for these candidates. Nickerson's study of Oregon in 2006 found that, while registered Democrats responded in the expected direction to an intensive canvassing campaign on behalf of Democratic statehouse candidates, voters registered as Independents became markedly less likely to vote for these

Democratic candidates. Another risk of a campaign that seeks both to persuade and mobilize is that voters who are identified as supporters may ultimately prove to be lukewarm in their support. In Kansas City, ACORN did a splendid job of mobilizing its targeted voters, but apparently the people they mobilized did not vote lopsidedly for the sales tax increase that ACORN supported. In the randomly targeted precincts, the experiment revealed a strong turnout effect but little net gain in votes for the ballot measure. There are to date no experiments documenting an interest group's success in persuading targeted voters, but there are a couple of experiments showing that a group's endorsement of a ballot measure had no effect on vote choice.

★ *Robotic calls endorsing a candidate seem to have little effect on vote choice.* As noted in chapter 7, Governor Rick Perry recorded a robo call in support of the reelection of a state supreme court candidate whom he had appointed to the bench. The context for the election was a Republican primary. The election drew low turnout, but this race was closely contested and decided by roughly 1,000 votes. Although Perry was popular among Republicans, his recorded message had no detectable effect on precinct-level vote margins.

★ *Television advertising has strong but transitory effects on vote choice.* The Perry campaign launched its media campaign at a time when one other candidate was on the air in select markets. The Perry campaign's ads were randomly rolled out at different points in time in each media market. Tracking polls showed strong gains in Perry vote support as a function of when and where the ads appeared, with 1,000 gross ratings points translating into approximately 5 percentage points of Perry support. However, this support dissipated quickly after the ads were aired. Within one week, the effects were gone.

In sum, the experimental evidence on persuasion suggests that it is much more difficult than one might think. Intuition suggests that a credible source—a Republican governor speaking to Republicans or an environmental group speaking to its members—would have an easy time cuing voters about low-salience issues on the ballot. One would guess that down-ballot races and relatively obscure ballot measures would be susceptible to the influence of what political scientists sometimes term "opinion leaders." Evidently, voters are much less deferential than generations of scholars have supposed. Indeed, the boomerang effect that Nickerson or Arceneaux and Kolodny found in their studies of interest group campaigns suggests that the group and candidate's political party are the main cues to which voters attend. Independents voted Republican when canvassed by union members. Pro-choice Republican women voted Republican when they learned that a pro-choice interest group endorsed the Democrat. Perhaps Governor Perry's endorsement fell flat because it was not a partisan cue in the context of a general election.

Persuasion appears to work best in situations where candidates are struggling to gain name recognition and credibility. Converting Alan Gerber's findings into 2007 dollars, challenger spending generates additional votes at the rate of one vote for every $31. Radio-based campaigns designed to promote name recognition may be even more cost-effective, although these estimates remain too statistically imprecise to warrant fine-grain comparisons. The point is that persuasive appeals seem to work best for challengers, but they are far from cheap. The cost per vote seems to rise sharply as we move from challengers to incumbents, perhaps because whatever one does to burnish the incumbent's image seems to dissipate quickly, and voters return to their long-standing appraisal of the incumbent's personal traits and record in office.

Although much research remains to be done, the emerging literature on persuasion is encouraging to those hoping to find GOTV efforts to be cost-effective ways of producing votes. It turns out that minds are difficult and expensive to change, particularly in the closing days of an election campaign. Although by no means cheap or easy, mobilizing supporters may turn out to be the most cost-effective way to influence elections.

Scientific Frontiers

Many of the major advances in the history of science have occurred in the wake of the discovery of new measurement technologies. The telescope and the microscope are but two examples of instruments that produced a host of new measurements that, in turn, heralded rapid advances in theory-building and technological development.

The experimental approach to the study of voter mobilization is not only changing the way in which campaign tactics are evaluated, but also changing the way in which social science is practiced. For the first time, social scientists have at their disposal a method for measuring the causal effect of a treatment in a real-world setting. And as field experimentation has spread, social scientists have accumulated a diverse set of increasingly reliable measurements about what interventions work and under what conditions. These measurements, in turn, help to guide and refine the theoretical understanding of human behavior. In an earlier era, social scientists were able to speculate in a manner that was largely unconstrained by hard facts, because causal measurements were unreliable. As field experiments cause hard facts to pour in, theorizing necessarily becomes more challenging. Theories must account not only for today's well-established facts but also for the facts that experiments will soon unearth.

The field experimental movement has brought social scientists into the world and forced them to grapple with the practical problems that decisionmakers routinely confront. Social science is replete with theories of action, but how do they measure up when put to the challenge of urging people to vote? Theories of persuasion and opinion change abound, but what happens when these theories are forced to shoulder the burden of persuading voters to support a candidate or cause? Politics is a humbling laboratory from which few theories emerge unscathed. But politics also presents the behavioral scientist with extraordinary and untapped opportunities to learn about the factors that shape opinions and behavior.

Technical Results of Door-to-Door Canvassing Experiments

This technical appendix provides brief information on and results from each of the randomized experiments on door-to-door canvassing. With one exception, we report experimental results estimated without covariates (except for those covariates that reflect the strata within which randomization was performed).[1] This approach provides the most straightforward reading of the results, without danger of post hoc adjustment.

Before 1998, two randomized field experiments dealt with door-to-door canvassing: the classic work by Samuel Eldersveld and the relatively obscure study by Roy Miller, David Bositis, and Denise Baer.[2] Both may be credited with paving the way for later research. Indeed, these remain among the few experimental studies to examine partisan mobilization efforts. The Eldersveld study included both partisan and nonpartisan efforts; the Miller, Bositis, and Baer study mobilized voters on behalf of a Democratic primary candidate.

Like many seminal research articles, they suffered from some serious limitations. The samples were far too small to detect even large mobilization effects with appreciable statistical power. In addition, Eldersveld's method of analyzing the data was biased: he lumped together the uncontacted members of the treatment group and the control group. Miller, Bositis, and Baer were silent on the question of how their analysis dealt with people they were unable to contact. The enormous magnitude of the effects they reported suggests that they may have made the same error as Eldersveld. Despite their defects, these studies warrant the praise due research that is far ahead of its time.

In 2000 we published an essay reporting the first large-scale randomized field experiment conducted in political science.[3] Originally conceived as a pilot study to enable us to learn the ropes of both experimental research and voter mobilization tactics, the project grew into a far-ranging study of door-to-door activity, commercial phone banks, and direct mail, each conveying alternative messages. The door-to-door effort remains one of the largest conducted in a single site (New Haven, Connecticut). Turnout in the control group—those not assigned to any of the three forms of voter mobilization—was 42.2 percent ($N = 11,596$). Among those assigned to be contacted solely by door-to-door canvassing, the turnout rate was 46.3 percent ($N = 2,877$). Among those assigned to be contacted by door-to-door canvassing as well as mail or GOTV phone calls, the turnout rate was 44.8 percent ($N = 3,254$).[4] For purposes of maintaining comparability with other studies, our meta analysis defines contact as speaking with a targeted individual (as opposed to anyone in a targeted household); using this criterion, the contact rate among those assigned to the canvassing-only treatment group was 28 percent. There were no statistically significant differences among the scripts (civic duty, neighborhood solidarity, your vote counts in a close election) in terms of their effectiveness in mobilizing voters.

Before the 2000 elections, we conducted two types of door-to-door canvassing experiments.[5] A study in Eugene was randomized at the individual level, while studies in Boulder and Ann Arbor were randomized at the level of city blocks. The Eugene study saw turnout increase from 62.6 percent ($N = 771$) to 64.6 percent ($N = 1,145$) among people who were registered by Youth Vote; comparable numbers for a list of voters eighteen- to twenty-nine-years-old drawn from the city's voter file were 55.0 percent ($N = 1,007$) and 59.3 percent ($N = 1,003$). Unfortunately, treatment-on-the-treated effects were impossible to determine because canvassers did not keep careful records of their contacts. The block-level experiments produced mixed results, with Ann Arbor showing a slight decrease and Boulder showing a slight increase; neither effect was close to statistical significance due to the relatively small number of blocks in the study. Because of uncertainties about the contact rates, none of these experiments is used to calculate the weighted averages reported below.

Although the 1998 and 2000 studies showed convincingly that face-to-face canvassing could raise turnout among those contacted, they left many questions unanswered. Would canvassing work elsewhere? Would it work in competitive as well as uncompetitive municipal races? Would it work when academics were not crafting the messages or supervising

Table A-1. Results of Door-to-Door
Canvassing Experiments in Six Cities, 2001

Percent unless otherwise noted

Site	Control group		Treatment group		
	Turnout	Number of observations	Turnout	Number of observations	Contact rate
Bridgeport	9.9	911	13.9	895	28
Columbus	8.2	1,322	9.6	1,156	14
Detroit	43.3	2,482	45.7	2,472	31
Minneapolis	25.0	1,418	26.9	1,409	19
Raleigh	29.4	2,975	29.5	1,685	45
St. Paul	37.6	1,104	42.2	1,104	32

Source: The figures in this table were calculated based on the results in tables 1 and 2 in Donald P. Green, Alan S. Gerber, and David W. Nickerson, "Getting Out the Vote in Local Elections: Results from Six Door-to-Door Canvassing Experiments," *Journal of Politics,* vol. 65, no. 4 (2003), pp. 1083–096.

the teams of canvassers? A canvassing experiment that we conducted with David Nickerson in 2001 supplied answers to these questions for six cities; the answers were, for the most part, yes (see table A-1 for details of the results).[6] Analyzing the data for the six sites with a single regression model yielded an effect of 7.1 percentage points with a standard error of 2.2 percentage points.

In a study by David Nickerson in three of these sites (Columbus, Minneapolis, and St. Paul), canvassers randomly supplied a flyer providing information about the candidates to those who were contacted.[7] Looking only at those who were actually contacted ($N = 792$), he found that providing information had an effect of –0.7 percentage point (SE = 3.2). This result is not significantly different from zero.

Melissa Michelson's nonpartisan mobilization experiment extended previous work in three important directions.[8] First, her experiment shed light on how mobilization effects change when the contact rate is raised from 30 percent (the rate typical of most other studies) to a remarkable 75 percent. Second, it showed how mobilization works in a rural setting. The study took place in a low-turnout municipal election in a central California farming community. Third, it studied the effect of different messages by varying the campaign message between civic duty and ethnic solidarity.

Regardless of the message used, Michelson's team of Latino canvassers proved highly effective at mobilizing Latino voters, particularly Latinos registered as Democrats. For all Latinos, turnout increased from 13.8 percent ($N = 298$) to 18.5 percent ($N = 466$). For non-Latinos, turnout increased from 25.7 percent ($N = 758$) to 28.2 percent ($N = 1,243$). Canvassers contacted 73 percent of Latinos and 78 percent of non-Latinos. The scripts were not significantly different in terms of the effectiveness with which they mobilized voters. For purposes of maintaining consistency with other studies, we restrict the sample to the set of households whose members were all assigned to treatment or all assigned to control groups and include dummy variables for the number of voters in the household in order to take into account the fact that households with different numbers of voters had different probabilities of being assigned to the treatment group.

Again examining the effects of alternative messages in addition to the effects of Latino and non-Latino canvassers, Melissa Michelson and Herbert Villa focused on a sample of voters under the age of twenty-six, encouraging them to vote in the 2002 state and federal elections.[9] Turnout among Latino subjects rose from 7.2 percent ($N = 1,384$) to 9.3 percent ($N = 1,507$), and among non-Latino subjects it rose from 8.9 percent ($N = 1,438$) to 10.0 percent ($N = 1,455$). The contact rates were 51 and 39 percent, respectively. Again, Michelson and Villa found no evidence that the content of the canvassing script made any difference. To maintain consistency with other studies, we again restrict the sample to the set of households whose members were all assigned to treatment or all assigned to control groups and include dummy variables for the number of voters in the household in order to take into account the fact that households with different numbers of voters had different probabilities of being assigned to the treatment group. Michelson returned to Fresno in 2003, using students from her classes to conduct an experiment on the differential effects of partisan and nonpartisan appeals. Like the Bennion study, which also used students canvassing as part of a course assignment, this study found weak treatment effects. Overall, the control group ($N = 2,672$) turned out at a rate of 15.2 percent, compared to 14.9 percent in the treatment group ($N = 3,371$), which was contacted at a rate of 34 percent. Much more successful was a canvassing effort conducted by ACORN in Maricopa County, Arizona, in the week leading up to a municipal election. Michelson reports that this election featured a ballot measure to determine the future of the county hospital. ACORN conducted two rounds of canvassing, the first to identify voters sympathetic to the ballot measure and a second to urge supportive voters to vote. The canvassing effort targeted voters with Latino surnames who had voted in at least one of the previous four elections. ACORN made multiple attempts to contact voters (including making a small number of phone calls), the result being that 71 percent of those living in one-voter households were contacted at least once. This figure rose to 80 percent among two-voter households. This mobilization campaign had a powerful effect on turnout. Among one-person households, turnout rose from 7.4 percent in the control group (N = 473) to 15.9 percent in the treatment group (N = 2,666). Among two-person households, turnout rose from 6.9 percent in the control group (N = 72) to 21.0 percent in the treatment group (N = 2,550).

Recruiting student canvassers to deliver nonpartisan appeals to an area with a very competitive congressional election, Elizabeth Bennion found weak effects.[10] Turnout increased from 39.5 percent in the control group (N = 1,088) to 39.7 percent in the treatment group (N = 1,088), 41 percent of whom were reached by canvassers. Despite the closeness of the election, Bennion found that a civic duty appeal worked better than a close election appeal, although the difference is not statistically significant. To maintain consistency with other studies for purposes of meta analysis, we restrict the sample to the set of households whose members were all assigned to treatment or all assigned to control and include dummy variables for the number of voters in the household in order to take into account the fact that households with different numbers of voters had different probabilities of being assigned to the treatment group.

Unlike other studies of door-to-door canvassing, Nickerson used a placebo control design.[11] Half of those contacted were urged to recycle; the other half, to vote in the 2002 primary elections held in Denver and Minneapolis. Turnout increased from 47.7 percent (N = 279) to 56.3 percent (N = 283) among those urged to vote. Since by design the contact rate was 100 percent, the study had reasonable statistical power despite the small sample size. Perhaps the most interesting aspect of this experiment was Nickerson's demonstration that turnout among housemates of persons in the treatment group was significantly higher than turnout among housemates of those in the control group.

As part of a partisan get-out-the-vote campaign sponsored by the Michigan State Democratic Party before the 2002 general elections, David Nickerson, Ryan Friedrichs, and David King studied a small door-to-door canvassing experiment.[12] Because the campaign focused on eighteen- to thirty-five-year-olds outside of campus towns, subjects were geographically dispersed, and the contact rate was quite low, just 9 percent. Turnout increased from 43.9 percent (N = 2,458) to 45.3 percent (N = 4,854), suggesting a large effect, but subject to a great deal of uncertainty.

Andra Gillespie reports the results of three canvassing studies conducted in predominantly African American neighborhoods in 2002.[13] Two took place in Newark, New Jersey, during its May and June municipal elections. The May study involved large numbers of voters but lost statistical power on account of low contact rates. We focus here on those voters whose households were assigned to receive canvassing without other treatments. In May the control group (N = 703) voted at a rate of 50.9 percent, compared to the treatment group (N = 4,080), which voted at a rate of 49.4 percent; however, perhaps due to the inexperience of the student canvassers hired from outside of Newark, only 6 percent of the treatment group was actually reached. The June study used canvassers from Newark, many of whom were drawn from the campaign of a mayoral candidate. Both the control group (N = 376) and the treatment group (N = 1,776) voted at a rate of 17.6 percent. The contact rate for the treatment group was 30 percent. The St. Louis canvass was directed by the Youth Vote campaign at voters age eighteen to twenty-five before the 2002 general election. Turnout was 26.0 percent among the 4,129 voters assigned to the treatment group (38 percent of whom were contacted), compared to 25.9 percent among the 2,095 voters assigned to the control group.

Kevin Arceneaux reports the results of a 2003 experiment conducted in Kansas City in which ACORN canvassed extensively in predominantly African American precincts. The aim was to identify and mobilize those supportive of a ballot measure designed to preserve local bus service. Unlike most other canvassing experiments, this one was randomized at the level of the precinct, with fourteen assigned to the treatment group and fourteen to the control group. Among voters assigned to control precincts (N = 4,779), turnout was 29.1 percent, compared to 33.5 percent in the treatment group, 62.7 percent of whom were contacted.[14] Kevin Arceneaux conducted a pair of experiments in the context of a local primary election in New Mexico, again using random assignment at the level of the precinct.[15] Arceneaux collaborated with a Democratic candidate for county commissioner, who identified sixty potential precincts for canvassing. Eleven were randomly assigned to be canvassed by the candidate herself (comprising 3,227 voters); twenty-one were assigned to be canvassed by paid campaign workers (N = 5,623), and the remaining twenty-eight precincts were assigned to the control group (N = 8,325). Both canvassing efforts generated positive but statistically imprecise turnout effects.

In 2004 Carrie LeVan organized a nonpartisan canvassing campaign aimed at mobilizing voters in low-turnout, low-income, and largely Latino precincts in Bakersfield, California.[16] The study comprised 727 voters, 423 of whom lived in households that were assigned to the treatment group. The contact rate among those assigned to the treatment group was 50 percent. The study found strong canvassing effects. Among voters living in one-person households, for example, turnout was 41.0 percent in the control group and 54.5 percent in the treatment group. Gregg Murray and Richard Matland also conducted a canvassing study in a largely Latino area, Brownsville, Texas.[17] Turnout among the 3,844 individuals assigned to the control group was 33.3 percent, compared to 34.9 percent among the 7,580 assigned to the canvassing group, of whom 22 percent were actually contacted. Kevin Arceneaux collaborated with Strategic Concepts in Organizing and Policy Education (SCOPE) in Los Angeles, which canvassed in opposition to the "three strikes" statewide ballot measure.[18] Arceneaux found no turnout effect and, from a postelection survey, no evidence that canvassers persuaded voters to oppose the measure.

Finally, in 2004 an Election Day leafleting and canvassing experiment occurred in seven inner cities in battleground states.[19] The leaflets carried an "election protection" message. Canvassers and drivers were instructed to flush out voters from designated street blocks. Results were weakly positive or weakly negative, depending on the statistical method used to detect the effects. No contact rates are available, so this study is not used in the meta analysis.

Two large-scale canvassing experiments were conducted in Virginia in 2005. One was conducted by David Nickerson in collaboration with Young Democrats of America in the northern part of the state, targeting voters under thirty-six years of age; the other was conducted by a consulting firm in collaboration with pro-Democratic organizations. Both studies varied the timing and frequency of canvassing attempts. The Nickerson study is still undergoing analysis. The other Virginia study remains proprietary.

Julia Gray and Phillip Potter conducted a small canvassing experiment in connection with a Republican candidate running for local office in 2006.[20] The canvassing effort consisted of an appeal on behalf of the candidate and distribution of either a pencil or pen bearing the candidate's name. These campaign tokens were left with leaflets in the event that the target households were not contacted face-to-face, which biases upward to some (probably minor) extent the estimated effect of canvassing per se. Turnout in the treatment groups ($N = 680$) was 64 percent, compared to 63 percent in the control group ($N = 340$). The contact rate was 22 percent.

Melissa Michelson, Lisa García Bedolla, and Donald Green collaborated with several nonpartisan groups participating in the California Votes Initiative, which sought to mobilize low-propensity voters in 2006.[21] In the June 2006 primary and again before the November general election, SCOPE conducted a large-scale canvassing campaign in a predominantly African American and Latino section of Los Angeles. The Central American Resource Center (CARECEN) also conducted a canvassing campaign in both elections, focusing on a section of Los Angeles with a large Latino population, many of whom had emigrated from Central America. The Center for Community Action and Environmental Justice (CCAEJ), a group that focuses on community environmental issues, canvassed in both elections. Its June effort concentrated on Riverside County neighborhoods in which it has long been active; in November, CCAEJ canvassers branched out into a broader area of Riverside and San Bernardino counties. Both CARECEN and CCAEJ supplied voters with polling place information and encouraged voters to sign cards pledging to vote. Two other church-based organizations, neither of which had previously conducted a canvassing campaign, conducted canvassing in the November elections. A total of five sites were canvassed, each in areas nearby one or more churches affiliated with the organization. An overview of the twelve California canvassing experiments is provided in table A-2.

David Nickerson conducted a pair of canvassing experiments in 2006. The first was conducted in collaboration with the Clean Water Fund in ten low-income precincts in Grand Rapids, Michigan, before the 2006 general election.[22] Turnout among the 2,528 voters in the control group was 26.9 percent, compared to 26.8 percent among the 9,970 people in the treatment group, of whom 23 percent were contacted. ACCESS, a local social service provider to the Arab American community, conducted a door-to-door mobilization experiment in three predominantly Arab American zip codes in Dearborn, Michigan. Streets in each of the three zip codes were listed and randomly assigned to a treatment group: 147 streets containing 11,328 registered voters were assigned to the control group, and 295 streets containing 22,849 voters were assigned to the

Table A-2. Results of a Door-to-Door
Canvassing Experiment in Twelve California Sites, 2006

Percent unless otherwise noted

	Control group		Treatment group		
Site	Turnout	Number of observations	Turnout	Number of observations	Contact rate
CCAEJ (June)	11.1	350	19.6	1,431	19.7
CCAEJ (November)	47.1	2,377	48.1	7,209	23.5
SCOPE (June)	17.3	1,782	18.3	5,430	34.6
SCOPE (November)	33.7	3,578	36.7	11,789	45.3
CARECEN (June)					
No valid phone number	14.3	719	14.5	771	35.8
Valid phone number	21.7	1,694	22.0	1,933	44.2
CARECEN (November)	52.5	1,565	52.2	4,584	52.8
Church groups (all November)					
Los Angeles	42.4	5,803	41.0	632	13.3
Riverside/San Bernardino	35.7	12,221	35.9	1,762	23.1
Sacramento	35.3	218	39.7	234	32.9
Colusa	66.2	1,276	72.9	258	66.8
Orange County	37.3	542	34.2	863	47.6
Bakersfield	43.4	747	42.8	474	21.8

Source: The figures in this table were calculated based on data reported in Melissa R. Michelson, and Lisa García Bedolla, and Donald P. Green, *New Experiments in Minority Voter Mobilization: A Report on California Votes Initiative* (San Francisco: James Irvine Foundation, 2007).

treatment group. Turnout was 44.8 percent in the control group and 46.1 percent in the treatment group. Canvassers successfully contacted approximately 15 percent of voters on treatment streets.

The thirty-nine studies for which we have data on both vote outcomes and contact rates are used as the basis for a meta analysis. Each study is analyzed using bivariate probit. This technique uses a two-equation model, similar to two-stage least squares. In the first stage, random assignment to the treatment group predicts whether a person is actually contacted. In the second stage, contact by a canvasser predicts whether a person votes. We use probit rather than regression because several studies involve populations with very low base rates of turnout. The bivariate probit results are then subjected to a meta analysis. A Q-test reveals significant heterogeneity across experiments ($p < 0.001$), which

Figure A-1. Number of Contacts Needed to Produce One Vote

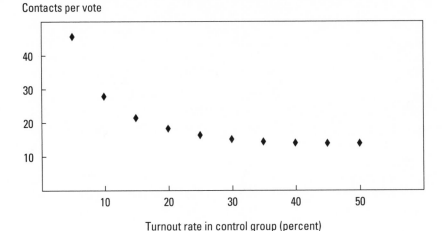

Contacts per vote

Turnout rate in control group (percent)

suggests that the average treatment effect should be estimated using a random-effects model. This model essentially allows each experimental site to add its idiosyncratic, random treatment effect (positive or negative) to the average effect of canvassing. The random effects model generates an average treatment effect of 0.175 probit, with a standard error of 0.032, which is almost identical to the meta analytic result presented in the first edition of this book.

Figure A-1 converts this result into more readily intelligible units. The X-axis is the expected voter turnout rate in the control group. The Y-axis is the number of contacts needed to produce one vote. (The reciprocal of this number reflects the number of votes per contact.) The figure suggests that it is typically harder to produce votes in very low-turnout elections or among subpopulations with very low voting rates. (The same point holds for subpopulations with very high voting rates.) When turnout is near 50 percent in the control group, as would be the case among registered voters facing a federal midterm election, votes are produced at a rate of one vote for fourteen contacts. This figure ignores the effect of spillover described in chapter 3. Although spillover is taken into account in our cost-per-vote estimate in chapter 10, we ignore spillover at various points throughout the book when illustrating the approximate number of door-to-door contacted that are needed to produce a certain number of votes.

Technical Results of Direct Mail Experiments

This technical appendix provides brief information on and results from each of the randomized experiments on direct mail. Throughout, we report experimental results estimated without covariates (except for those covariates that reflect the strata within which randomization was performed). This approach provides the most straightforward reading of the results, without danger of post hoc adjustment. We also restrict our attention to experimental contrasts between an untreated control group and an experimental group that received only mail.

Before 1998, the classic work on mobilization through direct mail was by Harold Gosnell.[1] Gosnell performed two experiments in Chicago, one before the presidential election of 1924 and another during the following year's mayoral election. Gosnell found an effect of 1 percentage point in 1924 and 9 percentage points in 1925. The study involved thousands of Chicago residents, who were enumerated by a census-like survey. The sole defect of this study is that it did not use random assignment; instead, Gosnell assigned alternating blocks to treatment and control groups.

The first randomized experiments were conducted by Samuel Eldersveld in 1956 and by Roy Miller, David Bositis, and Denise Baer in 1980.[2] See appendix A. These studies, however, were very small, involving just a few dozen subjects. We revisited the question of mail's effect on voter turnout in 1998.

During the final weeks leading up to the 1998 election, we conducted an experiment in which registered voters in New Haven received one, two, or three pieces of nonpartisan direct mail.[3] Each batch of mail reflected one of three themes: the need to do one's civic duty, the responsibility to stand up for one's neighborhood so that politicians will take an interest in its problems, or the importance of voting in a close election. Turnout in the control group, which was not assigned to receive mail, phone calls, or door-to-door canvassing, was 42.2 percent ($N = 11,596$). Among those assigned to be contacted solely by mail, turnout was 42.6 percent ($N = 2,550$) when receiving one mailer, 43.3 percent ($N = 2,699$) when receiving two, and 44.6 percent ($N = 2,527$) when receiving three. For the sample as a whole ($N = 31,098$), regression estimates that controlled for the effects of phone and door-to-door canvassing put the effects of each additional mailer at 0.5 percentage point (SE = 0.3), which was narrowly significant at the 0.05 level using a one-tailed test. As shown below, this finding foreshadowed later experiments with nonpartisan mailings.

The 1999 state legislative and municipal elections were the setting for a series of nonpartisan and partisan experiments that we conducted with Matthew Green.[4] In New Haven's mayoral election, nonpartisan mailings patterned after the civic duty and close election mailings used in an earlier study were sent to a random sample of the 1998 voter list. As noted in chapter 5, the blowout election offered an opportunity to see whether recipients were attending to the mailings' messages, in which case the close election appeal should have been ineffective. Results from these two experiments are summarized in table B-1. As predicted, the close election message had no effect, but the civic duty message performed as expected based on the 1998 results. The results suggest that returns from mailings begin to diminish after six mailings per household.

The partisan mail experiments involved a Democratic state legislative incumbent in New Jersey and a Connecticut mayoral challenger in the city of Milford.[5] As noted in chapter 5, the New Jersey experiments divided the target population into "prime" Democrats (those with a high propensity to vote), "nonprime" Democrats and Independents, and a random sample of the list of registered voters. The mailings boosted turnout among prime Democrats, but not among other Democrats. Turnout in the random sample rose with the number of mailings, but the effects were small given the number of mailings sent to each household. Combining all of the New Jersey samples suggests that mail did not significantly increase voter turnout. Some slight evidence for demobilization may be found in the negatively toned mayoral campaign, which sent nine mailings to each household.

Table B-1. Results of Nonpartisan and Partisan Experiments Involving Multiple Mailings, by Number of Mailings

Experiment	None	One	Two	Three	Four	Five	Six	Eight	Nine
1998 New Haven, nonpartisan									
Civic duty message									
Turnout rate	42.2[a]	41.7	46.3	44.8	...	...	...	...	...
Number of observations	11,596	935	984	902	...	...	...	...	...
Neighborhood solidarity message									
Turnout rate	42.2[a]	42.0	44.4	43.9	...	...	...	...	...
Number of observations	11,596	810	872	795	...	...	...	...	...
Close election message									
Turnout rate	42.2[a]	44.2	38.8	44.9	...	...	...	...	...
Number of observations	11,593	805	843	830	...	...	...	...	...
1999 New Haven, nonpartisan									
Civic duty message									
Turnout rate	38.9[b]	...	39.2	...	44.6	...	45.8	42.2	...
Number of observations	22,484	...	569	...	278	...	295	559	...
Close election message									
Turnout rate	38.9[b]	...	34.8	...	38.0	...	38.7	39.8	...
Number of observations	22,484	...	569	...	271	...	302	545	...
1999 New Jersey, partisan									
Prime Democrats									
Turnout rate	63.7	...	...	65.6	...	...	...	...	...
Number of observations	1,203	...	...	9,955	...	...	...	...	...
Other Democrats and Independents									
Turnout rate	54.2	...	...	...	...	54.2	...	...	
Number of observations	1,925	...	...	...	...	17,816	...	...	
Republicans and low-turnout Independents									
Turnout rate	23.1	...	...	...	23.5	...	24.1	...	...
Number of observations	1,863	...	...	...	990	...	1,447	...	...
1999 Connecticut mayoral, partisan with negative tone									
Turnout rate	56.1	...	...	...	...	...	...	55.0	
Number of observations	2,155	...	...	...	...	...	...	17,693	
2002 NALEO									
Los Angeles County (uncalled precincts)									
Turnout rate	22.6	...	...	21.9	...	...	...	...	
Number of observations	2,498	...	...	2,531	...	...	...	...	
Orange County (uncalled precincts)									
Turnout rate	18.8	17.3	...	...	...	...	...	...	
Number of observations	7,158	1,181	...	...	...	...	...	...	
Colorado (sample with phone numbers)									
Turnout rate	16.8	...	17.7	...	...	...	...	...	
Number of observations	21,486	...	20,707	...	...	...	...	...	
Colorado (sample without phone numbers)									
Turnout rate	3.2	...	3.2	...	...	...	...	...	
Number of observations	8,020	...	17,426	...	...	...	...	...	
Harris County									
Turnout rate	18.5	...	19.7	...	...	...	...	...	
Number of observations	3,615	...	13,899	...	...	...	...	...	
New Mexico									
Turnout rate	40.8	...	40.5	...	...	...	...	...	
Number of observations	10,002	...	25,769	...	...	...	...	...	

(continued)

Table B-1 (*continued*)

Experiment	None	One	Two	Three	Four	Five	Six	Eight	Nine
2002 Pennsylvania, partisan									
Other Republicans									
Turnout rate	63.6	...	65.1	...	...	...	...	...	...
Number of observations	1,306	...	9,301	...	...	...	...	...	...
Independents and Democrats									
Turnout rate	73.8	...	...	73.0	...	...	...	...	...
Number of observations	4,606	...	...	30,727	...	...	...	...	...
2002 gubernatorial primary									
(women's issues)									
Postelection survey									
Turnout rate	67.7	...	72.3	...	...	...	...	...	...
Number of observations	300	...	300	...	...	...	...	...	...
Validated vote									
Turnout rate	78.1		77.4	...	...	...	...	...	...
Number of observations	2,008		1,974	...	...	...	...	...	...
2004 Texas Republican legislator									
Chinese									
Turnout rate	25.0	33.3	32.8	42.7	38.9	40.0	...	...	...
Number of observations	12	12	61	307	653	508	...	...	...
Vietnamese									
Turnout rate	37.5	36.4	51.0	44.5	44.7	44.8	...	...	...
Number of observations	24	11	96	431	1,234	2,679	...	...	...
Negative mail in Florida									
municipal election									
Turnout rate	26.6	30.0	33.7	36.0	...	...	...	...	...
Number of observations	700	300	300	100	...	...	...	...	...

... Not applicable.
a. The control group is the same for all three New Haven experiments in 1998.
b. The control group is the same for both New Haven experiments in 1999.

In a field experiment conducted before the 2002 election, Janelle Wong classified Los Angeles County voters by last name into one of several Asian American groups: Chinese, Filipino, Indian, Japanese, and Korean.[6] Chinese Americans were sent one piece of bilingual nonpartisan direct mail encouraging them to vote. Other ethnic groups were sent one piece of direct mail in English. Among Chinese Americans, turnout in the control group was 29.0 percent (2,924); the treatment group turned out at a rate of 31.7 percent (1,137). Among other Asian groups, the control group voted at a rate of 38.5 percent ($N = 5,802$), compared with the treatment group rate of 39.4 percent ($N = 2,095$). See table B-2.

A report by Donald Green grew out of a randomized evaluation of the NAACP National Voter Fund's direct mail and phone bank efforts during the final weeks of the 2000 election campaign.[7] A small proportion of the target lists in Florida, Georgia, Michigan, Missouri, Ohio, Pennsylvania, New Jersey, New York, and Virginia was assigned to a control

Table B-2. Results of Nonpartisan and Partisan Experiments Involving a Single Mailing

Experiment	None	One
2002 Pennsylvania, partisan		
Prime Republicans		
Turnout rate	89.0	90.6
Number of observations	819	7,224
2002 Los Angeles County		
Asian Americans		
Turnout rate	35.4	36.7
Number of observations	8,726	3,232
2004 South Asians		
U.S. citizen appeal		
Turnout rate	52.2[a]	53.7
Number of observations	1,561	1,561
Person of color appeal		
Turnout rate	52.2[a]	54.2
Number of observations	1,561	1,561
Indian American appeal		
Turnout rate	52.2[a]	52.1
Number of observations	1,561	1,561
2004 Brownsville, Texas		
Turnout rate	33.3	36.3
Number of observations	7,580	3,794
2004 Northeast Republican legislator		
Turnout rate	26.4	26.3
Number of observations	7,999	48,078
2006 June APALC		
Chinese		
Turnout rate	8.0	8.2
Number of observations	12,076	3,408
Filipino		
Turnout rate	9.2	8.3
Number of observations	3,298	576
Korean		
Turnout rate	7.6	7.9
Number of observations	5,386	994
Vietnamese		
Turnout rate	8.2	7.8
Number of observations	3,829	1,294
2006 November APALC		
Cambodian		
Turnout rate	12.5	5.0
Number of observations	40	40

(continued)

Table B-2 (*continued*)

Experiment	*None*	*One*
Chinese (Chinese language)		
Turnout rate	25.8	29.6
Number of observations	4,524	2,069
Chinese (English language)		
Turnout rate	21.3	22.3
Number of observations	3,094	672
Filipino		
Turnout rate	32.9	33.2
Number of observations	1,520	596
Japanese		
Turnout rate	37.1	33.6
Number of observations	1,138	387
Korean (Korean language)		
Turnout rate	33.1	34.7
Number of observations	1,403	779
Korean (English language)		
Turnout rate	17.6	18.8
Number of observations	596	559
South Asian		
Turnout rate	29.9	40.2
Number of observations	271	276
Vietnamese (Vietnamese language)		
Turnout rate	26.6	29.6
Number of observations	1,089	862
Vietnamese (English language)		
Turnout rate	18.5	16.2
Number of observations	858	487
2006 November OCAPICA		
Chinese (Mandarin language)		
Turnout rate	32.7	35.0
Number of observations	1,809	1,385
Chinese (English language)		
Turnout rate	26.5	21.3
Number of observations	1,879	314
Korean (Korean language)		
Turnout rate	32.3	35.4
Number of observations	1,501	644
Korean (English language)		
Turnout rate	17.7	14.1
Number of observations	864	206
Vietnamese (Vietnamese language)		
Turnout rate	36.1	36.4
Number of observations	2,560	1,443
Vietnamese (English language)		
Turnout rate	24.5	20.9
Number of observations	4,927	345

Table B-2 (*continued*)

Experiment	*None*	*One*
2006 November church-related groups		
Fresno		
Turnout rate	36.5	30.7
Number of observations	211	251
Los Angeles, site 1		
Turnout rate	46.3	45.1
Number of observations	575	658
Los Angeles, site 2		
Turnout rate	47.7	46.4
Number of observations	550	621
Los Angeles, site 3		
Turnout rate	36.0	38.9
Number of observations	375	496
Los Angeles, site 4		
Turnout rate	54.0	47.9
Number of observations	565	685
Los Angeles, site 5		
Turnout rate	45.0	38.9
Number of observations	686	913
Los Angeles, site 6		
Turnout rate	49.9	46.2
Number of observations	515	964
Visalia		
Turnout rate	38.6	31.0
Number of observations	477	1,185
2006 Michigan primary		
Civic duty message		
Turnout rate	29.7[a]	31.5
Number of observations	191,243	38,218
2006 Florida: nonpartisan ballot awareness		
All Florida		
Turnout rate	37.1	36.3
Number of observations	8,532	5,982
Leon County		
Turnout rate	52.9	56.1
Number of observations	2,526	831
2006 Republican local candidate		
Cheap		
Turnout rate	63.0[a]	62.0
Number of observations	596	340
Costly		
Turnout rate	63.0[a]	58.0
Number of observations	596	340

a. Indicates that the control group is shared by more than one treatment group within the same study.

group. The target population varied from state to state but, on the whole, consisted of people living in neighborhoods with a high density of African Americans. Those with very high or very low propensities to vote were called; others were mailed and called. Although the sample was very large (for one-voter households: $N = 16,712$ for the control group and $N = 963,496$ for the treatment group), the experiment was marred by low contact rates. Many of those eligible to receive mail were never sent it. The two to three experimental mailings had no effect regardless of whether subjects had already received direct mail from the National Voter Fund ($\beta = -0.2$, SE $= 0.8$). Our meta analysis focuses on two states, New Jersey and New York, where mail was sent to groups that had identical rates of exposure to the National Voter Fund's phone-calling campaign.

Alan Gerber examined the turnout effects of direct mail sent by a Republican incumbent member of Congress in the course of a primary election campaign and a general election campaign.[8] The primary featured a credible challenger; the general election was won decisively. Randomization was performed at the precinct level. In the Republican primary election, 239 precincts were targeted for a two-piece direct mail campaign; five were placed in a control group that received no mail. Regression analysis that controlled for factors such as past history of turnout indicated that the mail increased turnout in the treatment precincts by 2.7 percentage points, with a standard error of 1.7 percentage points. The general election campaign excluded households in which all members were Democrats who voted in primaries. The remaining households were categorized as prime Republicans, nonprime Republicans, and others, depending on party registration and the number of times they had voted in primary elections. The three groups were sent one, two, and three mailings, respectively. Because randomization occurred at the precinct level, adjustments were made to the standard errors of each experimental comparison when combining the estimates with those of other partisan mail experiments.

An experiment presented by Emily Cardy tested the effect of advocacy mail from an abortion-rights interest group, which backed a pro-choice candidate in a gubernatorial primary campaign.[9] The group targeted strongly pro-choice voters who were previously identified by phone calls. The experiment consisted of three treatment groups: phone only, mail only, and phone plus mail. There were between 1,940 and 2,022 voters in each treatment group and the control group, totaling 9,980 voters. The five mailings were printed in full color on glossy paper and mailed between nineteen and six days before the election. David Niven conducted a field experiment in the context of a West Palm Beach mayoral election in 2003.[10] Up to three negative mailings about the incumbent were sent on behalf of the challenger, with 100 subjects in each treatment group. In 2004 a Republican state legislator in a northern state conducted a study of his direct mail reelection campaign. This experiment was set in motion before the Democratic challenger unleashed a wave of attacks linking the incumbent to the scandal-plagued Republican governor. Like the 2004 Texas experiment, which also involved an incumbent fighting off accusations of scandal, this one was conducted in the context of an unexpectedly close race. In 2006 Julia Gray and Philip Potter compared the effectiveness of high- and low-quality printing of mailings encouraging voter support for a Republican candidate for local office in Kentucky.[11] Of these candidate-related mailing experiments (and the advocacy mailings mentioned below), only the relatively small study by Niven found significant positive effects.

Ricardo Ramírez reports the results of a multisite, nonpartisan experiment in 2002 designed to mobilize Latino voters in low-voting precincts.[12] Large lists of registered voters with Latino surnames were obtained for Los Angeles County, Orange County (California), Houston, New Mexico, and Colorado. The treatments consisted of robo phone calls, direct mail, and (in Los Angeles and Orange counties only) live phone calls from local, volunteer phone banks. Each of these treatments was administered separately and in combinations, using a factorial design. The mailers all used bilingual text on multicolor, folding glossy paper. The number of mailers varied across sites from two to four. Despite the high quality of the printing and graphics, Ramírez's large-scale experiments showed them to have weak turnout effects.

Many other scholars have attempted to gauge whether ethnic communities can be mobilized using direct mail in 2004. Neema Trivedi tested alternative nonpartisan messages and graphic themes designed to mobilize Indian American voters living in New York City.[13] Her postcards conveyed ethnic, pan-ethnic, or civic duty appeals, but no message stood out as particularly effective. Richard Matland and Gregg Murray conducted a nonpartisan mail campaign in largely Latino Brownsville, Texas.[14] Households were randomly assigned a postcard with one of two messages. One emphasized greater power for Latinos if they became more politically active and voted. The other emphasized civic duty and the closeness of the election as the reasons recipients should go to the polls and vote. James Gimpel, Daron Shaw, and Wendy Tam Cho worked with a Republican state legislative campaign in a district with a large Asian American population.[15] The campaign created three groups of bilingual mailings: Korean, Vietnamese, and Chinese. They randomly assigned up to five pieces of mail encouraging support for the incumbent, an Anglo candidate running against a Vietnamese opponent. One mailing warned that not voting would hurt the neighborhood's interests. Two mailings emphasized that voting as an ethnic bloc would help to ensure that the group's interests would be considered—these mailings either were specific to the country of origin (targeting Vietnamese Americans, for instance) or mentioned Asian American interests. One mailing conveyed a civic duty message, and one encouraged voters to look out for their interests in health care, education, and other areas.

Several experiments have gauged the effects of direct mail sent by environmental 501(c)(3) and 501(c)(4) organizations. A proprietary study by Don Dresser examined the effects of mail to members of environmental groups and putatively pro-environmental voters in the context of the hotly contested 2004 presidential election in Minnesota. This study was replicated in 2006 by Donald Green in several western states and by Nicholas Reich in Maryland. These studies, which remain embargoed for the time being, assessed the effects of GOTV mail and mail designed to encourage voters to vote by mail. Two other proprietary studies of note were conducted in 2005 and 2006. A private consulting group in 2005 examined the effects of up to nine pieces of direct mail in the context of the Virginia gubernatorial election. Christopher Mann conducted an extraordinary series of large-scale experiments assessing the effects of appeals to register, vote by mail, and cast ballots. These studies were conducted on behalf of a women's interest group.[16]

The 2006 election was a watershed for direct mail experiments. Melissa Michelson, Lisa García Bedolla, and Donald Green collaborated with several California organizations in order to test the effects of various forms of nonpartisan direct mail on low-propensity voters from Asian American, Latino, and African American communities.[17] In the days leading up to the June primary, some organizations conducted tests of postcards reminding people to vote in the upcoming election. In some cases, these postcards were accompanied by hand-written notes encouraging the recipient to vote. Other organizations used bilingual mailings with more professional graphics and layout. These experiments were replicated in November, but this time many of the groups included a simplified voter guide (sometimes in the recipients' putative native language, if they were born outside the United States) designed to introduce them to

Table B-3. Testing the Effects of Postcards and Personalized Letters from Local Church-Related Groups, June 2006 Election

Site	Control	Postcard	Letter
Site 1			
Turnout rate	46.5	41.6	
Number of observations	467	517	
Site 2			
Turnout rate	39.8	42.8	38.1
Number of observations	314	488	223
Site 3			
Turnout rate	28.2	27.8	
Number of observations	804	1,600	
Site 4			
Turnout rate	15.4	18.2	17.2
Number of observations	117	170	134
Site 5			
Turnout rate	10.1	10.9	13.4
Number of observations	573	524	509
Site 6			
Turnout rate	14.4	15.3	13.4
Number of observations	458	393	434
Site 7			
Turnout rate	33.5	30.8	
Number of observations	505	1,044	
Site 8			
Turnout rate	30.5	36.8	
Number of observations	649	642	
Site 9			
Turnout rate	34.7	35.4	
Number of observations	1,010	2,008	

Source: Melissa R. Michelson, Lisa García Bedolla, and Donald P. Green, *New Experiments in Minority Voter Mobilization: A Report on the California Votes Initiative* (San Francisco: James Irvine Foundation, 2007).

the candidates and ballot measures. In all, dozens of experiments were conducted. Jason Barabas, Charles Barrilleaux, and Daniel Scheller conducted an innovative study designed to test which, if any, ballot measures in Florida might pique the interest of potential voters.[18] They sent a single mailing to samples of registered voters both across Florida and specifically in Leon County. Each mailing alerted voters to the importance of one ballot measure. The authors compared the mobilization effects of these mailings to those of a generic GOTV mailing. Like the California studies, the Florida results suggest relatively small differences in effects across different issues or appeals. See table B-3.

One of the most unusual mail experiments conducted in 2006 was inspired by Mark Grebner, a Michigan political consultant specializing in direct mail.[19] His idea was to shame people into voting by showing individuals their own and their neighbors' voting records in past elections. Mark Grebner not only developed the capacity to mass mail information about voters' participation; he also conducted some rather sophisticated experimental tests of his ideas. These tests were refined by a team of researchers including Alan Gerber, Donald Green, and Chris Larimer. In the days leading up to Michigan's August primary, Mark Grebner randomly distributed four kinds of direct mail: an appeal to civic duty, an appeal to civic duty combined with a message indicating that researchers would ascertain whether the recipient voted by looking at public records, an appeal to civic duty combined with a printout of whether each member of the household had voted in the past two elections, and an appeal to civic duty combined with a printout of whether each voter on the block had voted in the past two elections. For purposes of our meta analysis, we exclude the results of all but the civic duty message. However, the results for the other groups are striking. While 29.7 percent of the control group ($N = 191{,}243$) voted, turnout in the conditions where people were shown their own household's voting record jumped to 34.5 percent ($N = 38{,}218$). Among those shown their own and their neighbors' voting records, turnout was 37.8 percent ($N = 38{,}201$).

We perform a meta analysis on the seventy-five distinct experiments making up the twenty-eight distinct studies. The experiments in each study are first meta analyzed in order to come up with a summary result for that study. The input for this initial round of analysis is the linear effect of the number of mailings on voter turnout. This first round of meta analysis uses a fixed-effects specification because that specification is never convincingly rejected in favor of a random-effects model on the basis of a Q-test. Next we summarize the results across the twenty-eight studies by means of a meta analysis. This analysis is conducted first for all mail studies and then subdivided according to whether the mail was strictly nonpartisan or not. Overall, the studies show significant heterogeneity ($p < 0.001$), suggesting the use of a random-effects specification. The random-effects estimate for all twenty-eight studies is 0.197 percentage point, with a 95 percent confidence interval ranging from –0.025 to 0.419. Looking solely at the thirteen studies of strictly nonpartisan mail, we again see significant heterogeneity ($p < 0.001$), but the random-effects estimate is higher, 0.493, with a 95 percent confidence interval ranging from –0.010 to 0.995. This result implies that the overall average effect of nonpartisan mail is half a percentage point but, despite the enormous number of observations involved, still of borderline statistical significance. The results for partisan or advocacy mail suggest a much weaker effect. The Q-statistic is insignificant ($p = 0.841$), and the fixed effect and random effect specifications produce identical estimates and standard errors. The estimated average effect is 0.008 percentage point with a 95 percent confidence interval ranging from –0.101 to 0.117. Either way, partisan or advocacy mail is revealed to have a weak average effect, for even at the top of the 95 percent confidence interval, close to 1,000 people must be exposed in order to generate one vote.

Technical Results of
Phone-Calling Experiments

This technical appendix provides brief information on and results from each of the randomized experiments on phone calling. We report experimental results estimated without covariates (except for those covariates that reflect the strata within which randomization was performed). This approach provides the most straightforward reading of the results, without danger of post hoc adjustment. Most of the experiments discussed below present a simple comparison between a control group that received no campaign contact and a treatment group that was called (and in some cases reached) by a phone bank. Some experiments, however, involved comparisons between groups that received, for example, direct mail and groups that received direct mail and were also called. The latter type of experiment gauges the marginal effect of phone calls in a context where everyone is exposed to direct mail. As we note when discussing "synergy" in chapter 10, the two types of experiments tend to produce very similar estimates. Where possible, however, we report the results of studies comparing a phone-only treatment to an untreated control group.

Three early studies of the effects of phone canvassing were conducted by Samuel Eldersveld in 1956, Roy Miller, David Bositis, and Denise Baer in 1981, and William Adams and Dennis Smith in 1980.[1] As noted in appendix A, the first two studies involved very small samples. The first phone bank experiment to be performed on a scale large enough to produce informative results was conducted by Adams and Smith, who examined the consequences of a commercial phone bank campaign conducted on behalf of a candidate running in a Washington, D.C., special election. Using a postelection survey, Adams and Smith found the phone calls to have no effect on candidate preference. They did, however, report a large mobilization effect. Unfortunately, like Eldersveld, they lumped together the noncontacted members of the treatment group and the control group. Recalculating their estimates to correct this problem indicates that 23.8 percent of the control group voted ($N = 1,325$), compared with 29.6 percent of the treatment group ($N = 1,325$), 72 percent of whom were contacted. This pattern yields a treatment-on-the-treated effect of 8.1 percentage points (SE = 2.4), which is by far the largest effect to emerge from any commercial phone bank experiment.

During the weekend before the 1998 federal midterm election, we examined the effects of brief calls conducted by a commercial phone bank to New Haven residents living outside the ward containing the Yale University campus.[2] The calls were nonpartisan in nature. Each respondent received one of three scripts emphasizing civic duty, the importance of voting so that politicians have an incentive to listen to one's neighborhood, or the closeness of the election. None of the GOTV scripts increased turnout to a significant degree. The control group, which was excluded from all forms of attempted mobilization, voted at a rate of 42.2 percent ($N = 11,596$); those in the group slated for phone calls (and no other treatments) voted at a rate of 41.8 percent ($N = 846$), with 33 percent living in a household where at least one person was contacted. Phone calls also had no effect on those who were randomly assigned to be mobilized either by mail or by face-to-face canvassing. Those excluded from the phone treatment voted at a rate of 44.3 percent ($N = 12,506$), while those in the treatment group, 34 percent of whom lived in a household where at least one person was contacted, voted at a rate of 43.4 percent ($N = 6,150$). There were no significant differences among the three scripts in terms of the effectiveness with which they mobilized voters.

Another study conducted in 1998 was based on the same phone bank, scripts, and election as our New Haven study but drew its sample from the neighboring city of West Haven.[3] Phone canvassing was the sole treatment used to mobilize voters. Again, no differences were found in the mobilizing effects of alternative scripts. The estimated effects of GOTV calls were also weakly negative. The control group ($N = 7,137$) voted at a rate of 51.5 percent, compared with 51.1 percent among those assigned to receive a GOTV phone call ($N = 7,724$). Those assigned to receive a call asking them to donate blood ($N = 3,005$) voted at a rate of 50.9 percent.

Table C-1. Results of Nonpartisan Volunteer Phone Bank Experiments in Four Cities, 2000

Percent unless otherwise noted

	Control group		Treatment group		
List and site	Turnout	Number of obser- vations	Turnout	Number of obser- ations	Contact rate[a]
List of persons registered to vote by Youth Vote					
Albany	74.2	318	78.0	804	62
Stony Brook	70.6	279	78.8	680	89
Boulder	62.6	441	64.9	653	72
Eugene	61.2	497	61.7	705	74
Targeted list of registered voters eighteen to twenty-nine years of age[b]					
Boulder	28.0	1,175	28.2	1,143	35
Eugene	55.0	1,007	57.6	953	49

Source: David Nickerson, "Volunteer Phone Calls Can Increase Turnout," *American Politics Research* 15, no. 3 (2006): 271–92.

a. Counts messages left with roommates as contacts.

b. Supplied by a commercial vendor.

During the 2000 general election campaign, we conducted random-ized experiments designed to evaluate Youth Vote's volunteer phone bank efforts in Albany, Stony Brook, Boulder, and Eugene, all of which were aimed at young voters.[4] Volunteers in Albany and Stony Brook called only those people who had been registered to vote by Youth Vote earlier in the campaign. Volunteers in Boulder and Eugene called two lists of names: those people who were registered by Youth Vote and a random sample of registered voters eighteen to twenty-nine years of age (see table C-1 for detailed results). Given the conflicting results in Boul-der and Eugene, it does not appear that phone banks are more success-ful when mobilizing people who were registered by an affiliated campaign.

This study also reported the results of a small experiment conducted at Colorado State University, in which young voters were randomly called once or twice with GOTV messages alone or with GOTV messages and information about the location of their polling place. Compared with a single call, two calls did not increase turnout ($\beta = -0.4$, SE = 2.4).

Polling place information increased turnout, but not significantly (β = 3.1, SE = 3.1).

An early attempt to study the effects of advocacy phone calls may be found in Donald Green's randomized evaluation of the NAACP National Voter Fund's direct mail and phone bank efforts during the final weeks of the 2000 election campaign.[5] A small proportion of the target lists in Florida, Georgia, Michigan, Missouri, Ohio, Pennsylvania, New Jersey, New York, and Virginia was assigned to a control group. The target population varied from state to state but typically consisted of people living in neighborhoods with a high density of African Americans. Subjects in the phone treatment group were called twice in October by a commercial phone bank, twice during the weekend before the election with robo calls, and once on Election Day with a live reminder phone call. Those with very high or very low propensities to vote were called but did not receive mail; the rest of the population received mail and were called. Although the sample was very large (for one-voter households, N = 16,712 for the control group and N = 963,496 for the treatment group), the experiment was marred by low contact rates. Many of those eligible to be called were never called; some of those in the control group were called by mistake. Adjusting for these problems yielded estimates suggesting that assignment to the phone campaign raised turnout 2.3 percentage points with a standard error of 2.3 percentage points.

As part of the Youth Vote Coalition's 2001 GOTV campaign, which attempted to mobilize voters of all ages, David Nickerson conducted three phone bank studies.[6] Two live calling campaigns by volunteers were conducted in Boston and Seattle. The control group in Boston voted at a rate of 54.5 percent (N = 5,846), compared with 56.1 percent in the treatment group (N = 1,209). The treatment-on-the-treated effect was 2.9 percentage points (SE = 2.8). Seattle's calls appear to have had no effect, but the margin of error is large because less than 10 percent of the treatment group was reached. Turnout in the control group (N = 33,020) was the same as in the treatment group (N = 10,757), 64.7 percent. Some who were contacted were randomly supplied with polling information, which boosted their turnout 1.6 percentage points; however, the standard error of this coefficient was 2.9 percent. Seattle was also the site for a study of robo calls, in which the voting rate was 64.9 percent in the control group (N = 22,226) and 64.4 percent in the treatment group (N = 10,000).

An experiment presented by Emily Cardy tested the effect of advocacy mail from an abortion-rights interest group, which backed a pro-choice candidate in a 2002 gubernatorial primary campaign.[7] The group targeted strongly pro-choice voters who were previously identified by phone calls. Turnout in the control group was 78.1 percent ($N = 2,008$), compared to 77.7 percent among those who received two calls from a commercial phone bank ($N = 2,002$). The contact rate was approximately 50 percent.

In 2002 an enormous experiment targeted residents of Iowa and Michigan with working phone numbers.[8] The congressional districts of each state were divided into "competitive" and "uncompetitive" strata. Within each stratum, households containing one or two registered voters were randomly assigned to treatment and control groups. Only one type of treatment was used: GOTV phone calls, using a short "civic duty" script. Just one representative from each household was assigned to treatment or control; the other voter was ignored for purposes of calling and statistical analysis. A total of 60,000 individuals were assigned to be called by two commercial phone banks; the corresponding control group contained 1,846,885 individuals. The 2002 results turned out to be quite similar to the 1998 findings. The estimated effect of the treatment on the treated, controlling for the two design strata (state and competitiveness), was 0.36 percentage point. Due to the massive sample size, the standard error of this estimate was just 0.5 percentage point.

In a study conducted with David Nickerson, we examined the effects of several GOTV phone bank efforts designed to mobilize voters between eighteen and twenty-six years of age.[9] The largest experiment involved a national commercial phone bank that was paid a premium to deliver a longer script with greater supervision of the callers. Within more than a dozen metropolitan areas in the study, 27,142 people were assigned to the control group, and 54,804 were assigned to the treatment group. Over a four-week calling period, during which individuals were called between one and four times, the phone bank contacted at least once approximately 39 percent of the voters they sought to reach; during the last week, this rate was 26 percent. Calls during the first three weeks of the phone bank campaign had no apparent effect on turnout, but the last week's calls significantly increased voter participation: successful contact with voters increased turnout 5.1 percentage points (SE = 2.1). Since some of these calls were callbacks, this result may suggest the efficacy of follow-up calls with those previously contacted. A closely supervised local commercial phone bank in the Denver area, which used a lengthy script, also generated impressive results. In this experiment,

2,424 people were in the control group. Of the 4,849 people in the treatment group, 31 percent were successfully contacted. Its calls increased turnout 5.6 percentage points (SE = 3.0). By contrast, phone banks that relied on temps and other part-time workers produced relatively weak results. Despite contacting 46 percent of the 49,045 people in the treatment group (the control group numbered 27,142 people, the same as above), these phone banks increased turnout just 0.5 percentage point (SE = 0.6). When the sample is restricted to the subjects who were not also called by the commercial phone bank, this effect rose to 1.7 percentage points with a 0.9 percentage point standard error.

The study reported by David Nickerson, Ryan Friedrichs, and David King gauged the effectiveness of partisan calls before the 2002 election.[10] The sample consisted of voters eighteen to thirty-five years old who did not have a history of Republican voter registration and who resided in one of six state house districts. The calls were conducted by volunteers working for the Michigan Democratic Party. The control group consisted of 5,631 people; the treatment group consisted of 10,550, of whom 50 percent were contacted. The effect of the treatment on the treated was 3.2 percentage points, with a standard error of 1.7 percentage points.

John McNulty reports on a phone bank campaign conducted on behalf of the Coalition for San Francisco Neighborhoods in opposition to Proposition D, a municipal ballot issue that would have allowed the Public Utilities Commission to raise revenue bonds without voter approval.[11] A commercial phone bank targeted voters thought to be sympathetic to the "No on D" effort. Turnout in the control group was 57.4 percent (N = 1,485), as opposed to 57.6 percent in the treatment group (N = 28,479), of whom 50 percent were contacted.

A phone canvassing campaign conducted by Janelle Wong in 2002 used a mixture of English-speaking and bilingual callers to contact Los Angeles County voters classified by last name into one of several Asian American groups: Chinese, Filipino, Indian, Japanese, and Korean. Volunteer callers read a very brief script reminding listeners of the upcoming election.[12] Among Chinese Americans, turnout in the control group was 29.0 percent (N = 2,924), compared to 31.2 percent in the treatment group (N = 1,484), of whom 35 percent were contacted. Overall, however, the effects were weaker. For the entire sample, the estimated treatment-on-the-treated effect was 2.0 percentage points (SE = 2.4).

The effects of a multisite nonpartisan campaign designed to mobilize Latino voters in low-voting precincts were reported by Ricardo

Ramírez.[13] Lists of registered voters with Latino surnames were obtained for Los Angeles County, Orange County (California), Houston, New Mexico, and Colorado. The treatments consisted of robo phone calls, direct mail, and (in Los Angeles and Orange counties only) live phone calls from local, volunteer phone banks. Each of these treatments was administered separately and in combinations, using a factorial design. Those in the group receiving robo calls were called twice, each time in Spanish (except for Colorado residents, who received one call in English and another in Spanish). The results based on 368,844 observations indicate that contact by live phone banks had an effect of 4.6 percentage points (SE = 1.8), whereas a pair of robo calls had an effect of 0.04 percentage point (SE = 0.20). Excluding those observations that were assigned to multiple treatments in order to estimate the effect of each treatment in isolation yielded estimates that were statistically quite similar. Based on a sample size of 166,000, the regression analysis suggested that live calls had an effect of 4.5 percentage points (SE = 4.4), and a pair of robo calls had an effect of 0.08 percentage point (SE = 0.33).

Before the state's 2003 legislative elections, New Jersey's Public Interest Research Group conducted an experiment testing the effects of callbacks on young voters.[14] The experiment involved randomly assigning those who received the first call to a second round of Election Day phone calls. A control group of 1,399 voters was not called back; a treatment group of 1,418 was called on Election Day, and callers had direct conversations with 38 percent of those targeted. The control group voted at a rate of 13.2 percent, compared to 17.0 percent among the treatment group. Interestingly, the effects of the second round of calls were large, but only among those who in the first round of calls said that they intended to vote.

In 2004 a series of experiments examined the effects of phone calls of varying quality in the context of the November elections in North Carolina and Missouri.[15] The live calls were made by a commercial phone bank during the final week of the campaign. Three scripts were used: a standard brief GOTV script, a longer more interactive script, and a script that was long and also encouraged voters to mobilize their friends and neighbors. Our meta analysis focuses on those households whose members were assigned to only one condition. Among households with one registered voter, turnout rates were 57.9 percent in the control group (N = 95,803), 58.5 percent in the standard call group (N = 9,751), 59.3 percent in the interactive group (N = 9,598), and 59.0 percent in the group receiving requests to mobilize neighbors (N = 9,650). Contact rates for the three treatment groups were 34, 29, and 34 percent, respectively. During the final weekend of the 2004 presidential election campaign, two robotic messages from actress and recording artist Vanessa Williams were tested: either a GOTV message or an "election protection" message was sent robotically to large samples of black and white voters in North Carolina and Missouri, both non-battleground but somewhat competitive states. A total of 217,323 voters were in the treatment group and 1,902,436 in the control group. Neither message had any effect on either racial group in either state.

Another large-scale nonpartisan experiment in 2004 was conducted in Illinois.[16] A commercial phone bank made standard GOTV calls in the final days before the November election. Registered voters with known phone numbers were assigned to receive a standard GOTV call (N = 20,000) or to a control group (N = 3,434,055). Callers reached 47 percent of voters in the treatment group. Turnout rates were 63.8 and 62.9 percent, respectively.

An experiment measuring the effects of advocacy calls was conducted in a closely contested Democratic congressional primary in Pennsylvania in 2004.[17] The interest group's campaign targeted registered Democrats who had voted in at least one of the prior three elections. A control group of 4,007 was randomly excluded from a universe of 56,413 names. The treatment group was called once or twice. The first call was a voter identification survey designed to gauge whether voters planned to support the opposing candidate. Those who were not screened out on the first round of calls were called a second time and encouraged to support the candidate on the basis of issues they mentioned as important during the first interview. Approximately 7,800 people were contacted in the second round, implying a 15 percent contact rate. The control group voted at a rate of 53.1 percent, compared to 53.0 percent in the treatment group.

In 2005 Costas Panagopoulos conducted a pair of experiments in upstate New York in order to examine variations in the content and timing of phone calls from commercial phone banks. In Albany, lists of registered Democrats and Republicans were randomly assigned to receive either partisan calls encouraging them to vote in support of their party's mayoral candidate or nonpartisan calls encouraging them to vote. Turnout rates were 54.8 percent in the control group (N = 19,350), 54.4 percent in the partisan treatment group (N = 2,484, 59 percent of whom were contacted), and 55.3 percent in the nonpartisan treatment group

(N = 2,472, 60 percent of whom were contacted). In Rochester, nonpartisan calls were randomly slated for different weeks. Among those called four weeks before the election (N = 2,000), turnout was 51.6 percent; among those called during the two weeks before the election (N = 2,000), turnout was 51.3 percent; and among those called during the weekend before Election Day (N = 2,000), turnout was 51.3 percent. The control group (N = 19,000) turned out at a rate of 50.8 percent. Contact rates among the three treatment groups were 74, 74, and 52 percent, respectively.

A wide array of phone experiments took place in 2006. Jason Barabas, Charles Barrilleaux, and Daniel Scheller organized paid volunteers to call voters in Leon County, Florida.[18] The aim of the study was to test whether calling voters' attention to particular ballot measures increased their likelihood of voting. Turnout was 52.9 percent in the control group (N = 2,526), compared to 52.0 percent in the treatment group (N = 573), 52 percent of whom were reached by phone. Looking only at those contacted with different messages, variation in voting rates is not greater than one would expect by chance, suggesting that the issues mentioned did not have an effect.

The California Votes Initiative furnished an extensive set of nonpartisan experiments targeting low-propensity voters in 2006. Melissa Michelson, Lisa García Bedolla, and Donald Green report the results of several studies of robo calls and volunteer calls leading up to the June primary and November general election.[19] This extensive set of experiments is summarized in table C-2. The Asian Pacific American Legal Center (APALC) calls in June and November and the Orange County Asian Pacific Islander Community Alliance (OCAPICA) calls in November to Asian Americans were conducted by community volunteers and paid volunteers, some of whom were college students participating for credit. Many of the callers were bilingual, but to minimize language barriers, monolingual callers were assigned to call putative English speakers in November. CARECEN, NALEO, and Southwest Voter Registration and Education Project (SVREP) directed their calls to Latino voters, using bilingual callers. SVREP made a point of calling back voters who in an initial round of calls expressed an intention to vote. The Pacific Institute for Community Organization's (PICO's) church-affiliated groups conducted two types of phone campaigns. One set involved local pastors recording robo calls in English and Spanish. These calls were directed at low-propensity voters living in precincts near the churches. The other calls were live phone calls made by volunteers.

Table C-2. Results of Nonpartisan Volunteer Phone Bank Experiments in California, 2006

Study	Control group Turnout	Control group Number of observations	Treatment group Turnout	Treatment group Number of observations	Contact rate
2006 June APALC					
Chinese	8.0	12,076	8.2	3,408	19
Filipino	9.2	3,298	8.3	576	20
Korean	7.6	5,386	7.9	994	28
Vietnamese	8.2	3,829	7.8	1,294	14
2006 November APALC					
South Asian	29.9	271	33.0	542	36
Cambodian	12.5	40	17.4	242	27
Chinese (Mandarin language)	28.8	4,524	29.6	1,754	41
Chinese (English language)	21.3	3,094	22.1	1,135	28
Filipino	32.9	1,520	34.6	1,457	30
Japanese	37.1	1,138	35.4	804	34
Korean (Korean language)	33.1	1,403	33.8	1,086	50
Korean (English language)	17.6	596	18.2	435	17
Vietnamese (Vietnamese language)	26.6	1,089	24.5	196	46
Vietnamese (English language)	18.5	858	27.4	146	31
2006 June CARECEN					
Call only	21.7	1,694	22.4	657	28
2006 SVREP					
Calls to precincts not targeted for canvassing	34.3	6,435	36.5	20,124	23
2006 November NALEO					
Fresno County	20.8	2,667	23.1	5,324	41
Los Angeles County	49.4	1,471	47.0	9,789	26
Orange County	39.0	2,600	39.3	5,792	29
Riverside County	34.5	1,996	37.4	5,556	21
San Bernardino County	17.7	3,527	17.5	5,685	20
2006 November OCAPICA					
Korean (English)	17.7	864	15.2	33	38
Vietnamese (English)	24.5	4,927	29.8	312	30
2006 June PICO					
Fresno (robotic)	34.7	190	37.8	193	...
Los Angeles, site 2 (robotic)	46.5	467	41.6	517	...
Stockton, site 1 (live)	29.1	688	28.4	352	...
Sotckton, site 2 (live)	31.0	139	34.8	115	...
2006 November PICO[a]					
Stockton (live)	36.3	190	39.9	386	37
Colusa (live)	62.2	450	64.6	1,363	33

(continued)

Table C-2. (*continued*)

Study	Control group		Treatment group		
	Turnout	Number of observations	Turnout	Number of observations	Contact rate
Arbuckle (live)	40.4	245	46.9	520	47
Williams (live)	50.2	500	50.6	500	36
Fresno (robotic)	36.5	211	33.2	253	...
Los Angeles, site 1 (live)	46.3	575	44.1	672	23
Los Angeles, site 1 (robotic)	46.3	575	47.0	660	...
Los Angeles, site 2 (live)	47.1	550	48.1	615	26
Los Angeles, site 2 (robotic)	47.1	550	45.3	618	...
Los Angeles, site 3 (live)	36.0	375	42.2	500	21
Los Angeles, site 3 (robotic)	36.0	375	40.6	508	...
Los Angeles, site 4 (live)	54.0	565	49.0	789	17
Los Angeles, site 4 (robotic)	54.0	565	50.8	793	...
Los Angeles, site 5 (live)	45.0	686	38.5	919	23
Los Angeles, site 5 (robotic)	45.0	686	46.3	915	...
Los Angeles, site 6 (live)	51.8	357	48.6	650	23
Los Angeles, site 6 (robotic)	51.8	357	45.9	654	...
Los Angeles, site 7 (robotic)	49.9	515	52.8	956	...

a. The 2006 November PICO Los Angeles sites had the same control group for both robotic and live calls.

Several experiments in 2006 assessed the mobilizing effects of calls advocating candidates and issues. In a special congressional election in California, MoveOn directed its decentralized, web-based phone bank effort at voters who were identified as potential supporters of the Democratic candidate. Joel Middleton, who designed and analyzed the experiment, reports that turnout was 70.8 percent among the control group ($N = 2,203$), 72.6 percent among those urged to vote with a single call ($N = 2,215$, 75 percent of whom were reached), and 73.3 percent among those urged to vote with an additional follow-up call ($N = 2,206$, 48 percent of whom were reached a second time).[20] Proprietary reports on the effects of calls from commercial phone banks and robotic calls assessed the effects of phone calls from 501(c)(3) and 501(c)(4) organizations. Patterned after a study by Don Dresser, which examined the effects of commercial phone bank calls to members of environmental groups and putatively pro-environmental voters in the context of the hotly contested 2004 presidential election in Minnesota, experiments were conducted before the 2006 November election by Donald Green in several western states and by Nicholas Reich in Maryland. These studies assessed the effects of calls designed to encourage voting and calls designed to encourage voting by mail. Christopher Mann conducted an array of large-scale experiments assessing the effects of appeals to register, vote by mail, and cast ballots. One component of this study involved calls from a commercial phone bank. These studies were conducted on behalf of a women's interest group.[21]

An advocacy study that is currently in the public domain is a study of robotic calls made on behalf of a Texas Supreme Court incumbent running for reelection in a 2006 statewide primary.[22] Two calls recorded by the Republican governor on behalf of this candidate were delivered on the day before and day of the election. The experiment was conducted at two levels, targeting voters thought to be likely to vote in the primary and to support the governor. At the household level, 85,656 individuals were assigned to the treatment group and 85,271 to the control group. Turnout was 32.3 percent in both groups. In addition, precincts containing 144,942 voters were assigned to the control group, while precincts containing 147,660 voters were assigned to the treatment group. Turnout was 34.6 and 35.3 percent, respectively.

In order to synthesize the results of these studies, we divided them into three categories: robotic calls, live calls from commercial phone banks, and live calls from volunteer phone banks. A total of six studies of robotic calls, comprising eleven distinct experiments, were subjected to meta analysis. The results indicate that the average intent-to-treat effect of a robotic calling campaign (sometimes involving more than one call) is a 0.20 percentage point increase in turnout. The fixed effect model that generates this estimate cannot be rejected using a Q-test ($p = 0.805$), suggesting that robotic calls from different groups and speakers have similar treatment effects. The estimated average effect is not significantly greater than zero, and the 95 percent confidence interval ranges from –0.18 to 0.58. Adjusting for contact rates has little effect on these estimates, because more than 80 percent of the calls resulted in a successful contact, which in the world of robotic calls means either live contact or a message left via voice mail.

Commercial phone banks have been the subject of eleven studies comprising twenty-eight distinct experiments. Nine of those studies examine the effects of standard calls, one assesses high-quality calls, and one tests both types of calls. The average treatment-on-treated effect from a fixed-effects meta analysis is found to be 0.966 percentage point, compared to 1.000 from a random-effects meta analysis. The Q-statistic achieves statistical significance ($p = 0.016$), recommending the use of the random-effects model, which allows for the possibility of different treatment effects in different sites, calling houses, and target populations. A meta regression shows the two high-quality phone banks to have significantly greater effects than the standard phone banks ($p < 0.001$). The average effect among standard phone banks is estimated to be 0.553 percentage point, regardless of whether a fixed- or random-effects model is applied. The 95 percent confidence interval around this average effect spans from 0.073 to 1.034, indicating that commercial phone calls have a statistically significant but small effect on those who are reached. The two high-quality phone banks, by contrast, have an average effect of 2.862 percentage points, with a standard error of 0.527.

Finally, volunteer calls have been the subject of nineteen studies comprising forty-one distinct experiments. In light of significant heterogeneity across studies ($p = 0.018$), we use a random-effects meta analysis and find an average treatment-on-treated effect of 2.6, with a 95 percent confidence interval ranging from 1.4 to 3.7. Volunteer calls are found to have a statistically significant average effect that is more than four times larger than a standard call from a commercial phone bank.

Notes

Chapter One

1. This pattern is demonstrated in Stephen D. Ansolabehere, Alan Gerber, and James M. Snyder Jr., "Equal Votes, Equal Money: Court-Ordered Redistricting and Public Expenditures in the American States," *American Political Science Review,* vol. 96, no. 4 (2002): 767–78.

2. Daniel E. Bergan, Alan S. Gerber, Donald P. Green, and Costas Panagopoulos, "Grassroots Mobilization and Voter Turnout in 2004," *Public Opinion Quarterly,* vol. 69, no. 5 (2006): 760–77.

3. Alan Gerber, James G. Gimpel, Donald P. Green, and Daron R. Shaw, "The Influence of Television and Radio Advertising on Candidate Evaluations: Results from a Large-Scale Randomized Experiment," paper presented at the Annual Meeting of the Midwest Political Science Association, April 12–15, 2007.

4. Hal Malchow, *The New Political Marketing* (Washington: Campaigns & Elections Magazine, 2003), pp. 281–82.

Chapter Two

1. Democratic National Committee, *GOTV* (Washington, 1995), p. 28.

2. Republican National Committee, *State Legislative and Local Campaign Manual* (Washington, 2000), pp. 167, 189.

3. This advice was found at the Humboldt County California Green Party website: www.arcata.com/green [December 15, 2003].

4. Election protection messages are designed to encourage people to assert their right to vote, even in the face of challenges by poll workers claiming that they are ineligible. Groups seething over what they took to be fraud and intimidation in 2000 publicized hotlines in 2004 for voters to call in the event that they encountered problems.

Chapter Three

1. In the first edition of this book, we defined contact to include speaking to a voter's housemate. Thus, if a canvasser spoke to eight people at different addresses and each household contained an average of 1.5 voters, we counted that as twelve contacts. Because recent experiments have measured contact with the targeted individual (as opposed to household members), this edition speaks of direct contact (speaking with the targeted individual) and indirect contact (speaking with the target's housemate). Based on recent experiments, we also have reduced from eight to six the average number of contacted households that canvassers cover each hour.

2. On instructions to canvassers, see Ann Beaudry and Bob Schaeffer, *Winning Local and State Elections: The Guide to Organizing Your Campaign* (New York: Free Press, 1986); Catherine Shaw, *The Campaign Manager: Running and Winning Local Elections,* 2d ed. (Boulder, Colo.: Westview Press, 2000). Shaw (p. 132) advises, "When training canvassers, I tell them never to talk about the issues. That is for the candidate or the campaign team. No canvasser, I don't care how closely related to the campaign, can possibly know how a candidate stands on all the issues. So what do canvassers say when asked a question at the door? They can say, 'That is a good question. Why don't you give [the candidate] a call and ask him or her?' The only thing canvassers can truthfully say is why *they* are out working for the candidate."

3. Melissa R. Michelson, "Getting Out the Latino Vote: How Door-to-Door Canvassing Influences Voter Turnout in Rural Central California," *Political Behavior,* vol. 25, no. 3 (2003): 247–63.

4. Melissa R. Michelson, "Meeting the Challenge of Latino Voter Mobilization," *Annals of the American Academy of Political and Social Science,* vol. 601, no. 1 (2005): 85–101.

5. Alan S. Gerber and Donald P. Green, "The Effects of Canvassing, Direct Mail, and Telephone Contact on Voter Turnout: A Field Experiment," *American Political Science Review,* vol. 94, no. 3 (2000): 653–63; Alan S. Gerber and Donald P. Green, "Correction to Gerber and Green (2000), Replication of Disputed Findings, and Reply to Imai (2005)," *American Political Science Review,* vol. 99, no. 2 (2005): 301–13.

6. Elizabeth A. Bennion, "Caught in the Ground Wars: Mobilizing Voters during a Competitive Congressional Campaign," *Annals of the American Academy of Political and Social Science,* vol. 601, no. 1 (2005): 123–41.

7. Gregg R. Murray and Richard E. Matland, "Increasing Voter Turnout in the Hispanic Community: A Field Experiment on the Effects of Canvassing, Leafleting, Telephone Calls, and Direct Mail," paper presented at the Annual Meeting of the Midwest Political Science Association, Chicago, April 7–10, 2005.

8. Donald P. Green and Alan S. Gerber, "Getting Out the Youth Vote: Results from Randomized Field Experiments," unpublished manuscript (Yale University, Institution for Social and Policy Studies, 2001).

9. Kevin Arceneaux, "Using Cluster Randomized Field Experiments to Study Voting Behavior," *Annals of the American Academy of Political and Social Science,*

vol. 601, no. 1 (2005): 169–79; Donald P. Green and Melissa R. Michelson, "ACORN Experiments in Minority Voter Mobilization," in *The People Shall Rule: ACORN, Community Organizing, and the Struggle for Economic Justice,* edited by Robert Fisher (forthcoming).

10. Betsy Sinclair, Margaret A. McConnell, Melissa R. Michelson, and Lisa García Bedolla, "Strangers vs. Neighbors: The Efficacy of Grassroots Voter Mobilization," paper presented at the Annual Meeting of the American Political Science Association, Chicago, August 30–September 2, 2007.

11. Melissa R. Michelson, Margaret A. McConnell, and Lisa García Bedolla, "Heeding the Call: The Effect of Targeted Phone Banks on Voter Turnout," unpublished manuscript (California State University, East Bay, 2007).

12. Donald P. Green, Alan S. Gerber, and David W. Nickerson, "Getting Out the Vote in Local Elections: Results from Six Door-to-Door Canvassing Experiments," *Journal of Politics,* vol. 65, no. 4 (2003): 1083–96.

13. Green and Gerber, "Getting Out the Youth Vote."

14. Michelson, "Meeting the Challenge of Latino Voter Mobilization."

15. Melissa Michelson, Lisa García Bedolla, and Donald P. Green, *New Experiments in Minority Voter Mobilization: A Report on the California Votes Initiative* (San Francisco: James Irvine Foundation, 2007).

16. David W. Nickerson, Ryan D. Friedrichs, and David C. King, "Partisan Mobilization Campaigns in the Field: Results of a Statewide Turnout Experiment in Michigan," *Political Research Quarterly,* vol. 59, no. 1 (2006): 85–97.

17. Joel Middleton, "Are Canonical Findings Externally Valid? An Experimental Field Study of Canvassing in the 2004 Election," unpublished manuscript (Yale University, Institution for Social and Policy Studies, 2007).

18. David W. Nickerson, "Forget Me Not? The Importance of Timing and Frequency in Voter Mobilization," paper presented at the Annual Meeting of the American Political Science Association, Philadelphia, August 31–September 3, 2006.

19. Julia Gray and Philip Potter, "Does Signaling Matter in Elections? Evidence from a Field Experiment," paper presented at the Annual Meeting of the American Political Science Association, Chicago, August 30–September 2, 2007.

20. Kevin Arceneaux, "I'm Asking for Your Support: The Effects of Personally Delivered Campaign Messages on Voting Decisions and Opinion Formation," *Quarterly Journal of Political Science,* vol. 2, no. 1 (2007): 43–65.

21. Kevin Arceneaux and David W. Nickerson, "Who Is Mobilized to Vote? A Meta Analysis of Seven Randomized Field Experiments," paper presented at the Annual Meeting of the Midwest Political Science Association, Chicago, April 20–23, 2006.

22. Sinclair and others, "Strangers vs. Neighbors."

23. Kevin Arceneaux and David Nickerson, "Even if You Have Nothing Nice to Say, Go Ahead and Say It: Two Field Experiments Testing Negative Campaign Tactics," paper prepared for presentation at the Annual Meeting of the American Political Science Association, Washington, September 1–4, 2005.

24. David W. Nickerson, "Measuring Interpersonal Influence," Ph.D. dissertation, Yale University, Department of Political Science, 2004. An article-length version of this experiment is forthcoming in the *American Political Science Review.*

25. Beaudry and Schaeffer, *Winning Local and State Elections,* p. 91. This quotation is italicized in the original.

Chapter Four

1. For another take on conceptualizing and designing leaflets, see Ann Beaudry and Bob Schaeffer, *Winning Local and State Elections: The Guide to Organizing Your Campaign* (New York: Free Press, 1986); Catherine Shaw, *The Campaign Manager: Running and Winning Local Elections,* 2d ed. (Boulder, Colo.: Westview Press, 2000), p. 156. They advise, for instance, "When in doubt about leaflet design, keep it simple! Too many candidates fall into the trap of: 'I paid for this piece of paper, and I'm going to print on every square inch of it.'"

2. Alan S. Gerber and Donald P. Green, "The Effect of a Nonpartisan Get-Out-the-Vote Drive: An Experimental Study of Leafleting," *Journal of Politics,* vol. 62, no. 3 (2000): 846–57.

3. David W. Nickerson, Ryan D. Friedrichs, and David C. King, "Partisan Mobilization Campaigns in the Field: Results of a Statewide Turnout Experiment in Michigan," *Political Research Quarterly,* vol. 59, no. 1 (2006): 85–97.

4. Julia Azari and Ebonya Washington, "Results from a 2004 Leafleting Field Experiment in Miami-Dade and Duval Counties, Florida," unpublished manuscript (Yale University, Institution for Social and Policy Studies, 2006).

5. Valerie A. Frey and Santiago Suárez, "¡Movilización Efectiva de Votantes! Analyzing the Effects of Bilingual Mobilization and Notification of Bilingual Ballots on Latino Turnout," unpublished manuscript (Yale University, Institution for Social and Policy Studies, 2006).

6. Melissa Michelson, Lisa García Bedolla, and Donald P. Green, *New Experiments in Minority Voter Mobilization: A Report on the California Votes Initiative* (San Francisco: James Irvine Foundation, 2007).

Chapter Five

1. Because state laws are complex, varied, and subject to interpretation by local officials, direct mail firms make a point of investigating state and local laws before mail is sent out.

2. Microtargeting is a complex topic that warrants experimental evaluation in its own right. In brief, microtargeting databases usually are constructed by conducting an opinion survey with registered voters. The information on the voter file, augmented with consumer information, is used to forecast the survey responses. These forecasts are then imputed to other (nonsurveyed) people on the voter file. The predictive accuracy of these forecasts may be poor, which is why we use the word "ostensible" in the text to describe what microtargeters take to be groups of like-minded voters. A long-overdue experiment is one that tests whether individuals are more strongly influenced when they receive microtargeted rather than generic mail.

3. Donald P. Green, "Mobilizing African American Voters Using Direct Mail and Commercial Phone Banks: A Field Experiment," *Political Research Quarterly,* vol. 57, no. 2 (2004): 245–55.

4. Ricardo Ramírez, "Giving Voice to Latino Voters: A Field Experiment on the Effectiveness of a National Nonpartisan Mobilization Effort," *Annals of the American Academy of Political and Social Science,* vol. 601, no. 1 (2005): 66–84.

5. The U.S. Postal Service website (www.usps.gov) presents a complete rundown on mailing sizes and weights.

6. Catherine Shaw, *The Campaign Manager: Running and Winning Local Elections,* 2d ed. (Boulder, Colo.: Westview Press, 2000).

7. Lawrence Grey, *How to Win a Local Election* (New York: M. Evans and Company, 1999).

8. Grey, *How to Win a Local Election,* p. 163.

9. Harold F. Gosnell, *Getting-Out-the-Vote: An Experiment in the Stimulation of Voting* (University of Chicago Press, 1927).

10. Alan S. Gerber and Donald P. Green, "The Effects of Canvassing, Direct Mail, and Telephone Contact on Voter Turnout: A Field Experiment," *American Political Science Review,* vol. 94, no. 3 (2000): 653–63.

11. Alan S. Gerber, Donald P. Green, and Matthew N. Green, "Direct Mail and Voter Turnout: Results from Seven Randomized Field Experiments," unpublished manuscript (Yale University, Institution for Social and Policy Studies, 2000).

12. Alan S. Gerber, Donald P. Green, and Matthew N. Green, "The Effects of Partisan Direct Mail on Voter Turnout," *Electoral Studies,* vol. 22, no. 4 (December 2003): 563–79.

13. Gerber, Green, and Green, "The Effects of Partisan Direct Mail on Voter Turnout"; Alan S. Gerber, "Does Campaign Spending Work? Field Experiments Provide Evidence and Suggest New Theory," *American Behavioral Scientist,* vol. 47, no. 5 (2004): 541–74.

14. Donald P. Green, "Mobilizing African American Voters Using Direct Mail and Commercial Phone Banks: A Field Experiment," *Political Research Quarterly,* vol. 57, no. 2 (2004): 245–55.

15. Gerber, "Does Campaign Spending Work?" p. 550.

16. Janelle Wong, "Getting Out the Vote among Asian Americans in Los Angeles County: A Field Experiment," *Annals of the American Academy of Political and Social Science,* vol. 601, no. 1 (2005): 102–14.

17. Ramírez, "Giving Voice to Latino Voters," pp. 66–84.

18. Emily Arthur Cardy, "An Experimental Field Study of the GOTV and Persuasion Effects of Partisan Direct Mail and Phone Calls," *Annals of the American Academy of Political and Social Science,* vol. 601, no. 1 (2005): 28–40.

19. David Niven, "A Field Experiment on the Effects of Negative Campaign Mail on Voter Turnout in a Municipal Election," *Political Research Quarterly,* vol. 59, no. 2 (2006): 203–10.

20. Neema Trivedi, "The Effect of Identity-Based GOTV Direct Mail Appeals on the Turnout of Indian Americans," *Annals of the American Academy of Political and Social Science,* vol. 601, no. 1 (2005): 115–22.

21. Gregg R. Murray and Richard E. Matland, "Increasing Voter Turnout in the Hispanic Community: A Field Experiment on the Effects of Canvassing,

Leafleting, Telephone Calls, and Direct Mail," paper presented at the Annual Meeting of the Midwest Political Science Association, Chicago, April 7–10, 2005.

22. Wendy Tam Cho, James Gimpel, and Daron Shaw, "Turning Out the Vote in Texas," paper presented at the Annual Meeting of the American Political Science Association, Washington, September 1–4, 2005.

23. Melissa Michelson, Lisa García Bedolla, and Donald P. Green, *New Experiments in Minority Voter Mobilization: A Report on the California Votes Initiative* (San Francisco: James Irvine Foundation, 2007).

24. Jason Barabas, Charles Barrilleaux, and Daniel Scheller, "Issue Turnout: Field Experiments with Ballot Initiatives in Florida," paper presented at the Annual Meeting of the American Political Science Association, Chicago, August 30–September 2, 2007.

25. Alan S. Gerber, Donald P. Green, and Christopher W. Larimer, "Social Pressure and Voter Turnout: Evidence from a Large-Scale Field Experiment," *American Political Science Review* (February 2008, forthcoming).

26. Julia Gray and Philip Potter, "Does Signaling Matter in Elections? Evidence from a Field Experiment," paper presented at the Annual Meeting of the American Political Science Association, Chicago, August 30–September 2, 2007.

27. Christopher Mann, "Betting with Don Green: Comparing the Cost-Effectiveness of Absentee Ballot Recruitment and Canvassing for Voter Mobilization," paper presented at the American Politics Workshop, Yale University, February 22, 2006; Donald P. Green, "Report on the Effectiveness of Absentee Ballot Requests in Raising Voter Turnout," unpublished manuscript (Yale University, Institution for Social and Policy Studies, 2007).

28. Christopher Mann, "Field Experimentation in Political Communication for Mobilization," Ph.D. dissertation, Yale University, Department of Political Science, 2008.

29. Michelson, García Bedolla, and Green, *New Experiments in Minority Voter Mobilization.* The experiments in question found effects on the order of 1 percentage point, but they were based on just a few hundred voters.

Chapter Six

1. Lawrence Grey, in *How to Win a Local Election,* states, "Some people think using phone banks to call registered voters and solicit their votes is a good idea. We don't. While the phone banks might make it easier for the volunteers and may have had some success in the past, telemarketers have killed off the usefulness of this technique. People no longer want to get unsolicited phone calls trying to sell them something, even if the something is a political candidate." Lawrence Grey, *How to Win a Local Election* (New York: M. Evans and Company, 1999). For a much more optimistic assessment of the impact of phone calls, see Janet Grenzke and Mark Watts, "Hold the Phones: Taking Issue with a Get-Out-the-Vote Strategy," *Campaigns & Elections* (December/January 2005): 81–83.

2. This figure is somewhat different from that in the first edition, in which it was assumed the callers would complete eight calls to the intended targets and

leave another eight messages. We raise the average number of hourly contacts from eight to sixteen in light of contact-per-hour estimates furnished by recent volunteer phone bank efforts. Because the spillover effects of phone calls remain unknown, we focus solely on the effects of direct communication.

3. NALEO used a preliminary robo call a month before the fall 2006 elections to clean up its target lists of low-propensity Latino voters in five California counties. The call was subject to an experimental evaluation to see if it had an effect on turnout. The answer is no (β = –0.2; SE = 0.6; N = 61,422).

4. For other discussions of the goals and mechanics of GOTV phone calls, see, for example, Catherine Shaw, *The Campaign Manager: Running and Winning Local Elections,* 2d ed. (Boulder, Colo.: Westview Press, 2000); Grey, *How to Win a Local Election.*

5. David W. Nickerson, "Memo on the Effects of Phone-Banking Campaigns during the 2001 Election," unpublished manuscript (Yale University, Institution for Social and Policy Studies, 2002).

6. Ricardo Ramírez, "Giving Voice to Latino Voters: A Field Experiment on the Effectiveness of a National Nonpartisan Mobilization Effort," *Annals of the American Academy of Political and Social Science,* vol. 601, no. 1 (2005): 66–84.

7. Shang E. Ha and Dean S. Karlan, "Get-Out-the-Vote Phone Calls: Does Quality Matter?" unpublished manuscript (Yale University, Institution for Social and Policy Studies, 2007).

8. Melissa Michelson, Lisa García Bedolla, and Donald P. Green, *New Experiments in Minority Voter Mobilization: A Report on the California Votes Initiative* (San Francisco: James Irvine Foundation, 2007).

9. Alan S. Gerber and Donald P. Green, "The Effects of Canvassing, Direct Mail, and Telephone Contact on Voter Turnout: A Field Experiment," *American Political Science Review,* vol. 94, no. 3 (2000): 653–63; Alan S. Gerber and Donald P. Green, "Do Phone Calls Increase Voter Turnout? A Field Experiment," *Public Opinion Quarterly,* vol. 65, no. 1 (2001): 75–85; Alan S. Gerber and Donald P. Green, "Do Phone Calls Increase Turnout? An Update," *Annals of the American Academy of Political and Social Science,* vol. 601, no. 1 (2005): 142–54; Alan S. Gerber and Donald P. Green, "Correction to Gerber and Green (2000), Replication of Disputed Findings, and Reply to Imai (2005)," *American Political Science Review,* vol. 99, no. 2 (2005): 301–13.

10. Kevin Arceneaux, Alan S. Gerber, and Donald P. Green, "Comparing Experimental and Matching Methods Using a Large-Scale Voter Mobilization Experiment," *Political Analysis,* vol. 14, no. 1 (2006): 1–36.

11. Kevin Arceneaux, Alan S. Gerber, and Donald P. Green, "A Cautionary Note on the Use of Matching to Estimate Causal Effects: An Empirical Example Comparing Matching Estimates to an Experimental Benchmark," unpublished manuscript (Yale University, Institution for Social and Policy Studies, 2007).

12. Ha and Karlan, "Get-Out-the-Vote Phone Calls."

13. Grenzke and Watts, "Hold the Phones."

14. John E. McNulty, "Phone-Based GOTV: What's on the Line? Field Experiments with Varied Partisan Components, 2002–2003," *Annals of the American Academy of Political and Social Science,* vol. 601, no. 1 (2005): 41–65.

15. Christopher Mann, "Field Experimentation in Political Communication for Mobilization," Ph.D. dissertation, Yale University, Department of Political Science, 2008.

16. Emily Arthur Cardy, "An Experimental Field Study of the GOTV and Persuasion Effects of Partisan Direct Mail and Phone Calls," *Annals of the American Academy of Political and Social Science,* vol. 601, no. 1 (2005): 28–40.

17. Costas Panagopoulos, "Partisan and Nonpartisan Message Content and Voter Mobilization," unpublished manuscript (Fordham University, 2007).

18. David W. Nickerson, "Quality Is Job One: Professional and Volunteer Voter Mobilization Calls," *American Journal of Political Science,* vol. 51, no. 2 (2007): 269–82.

19. Costas Panagopoulos, "Timing Is Everything? Primacy and Recency Effects in Voter Mobilization Campaigns," unpublished manuscript (Fordham University, 2007).

20. Ha and Karlan, "Get-Out-the-Vote Phone Calls."

21. David Nickerson, "Volunteer Phone Calls Can Increase Turnout," *American Politics Research,* vol. 34, no. 3 (2006): 271–92.

22. David Nickerson, "Quality Is Job One."

23. David W. Nickerson, Ryan D. Friedrichs, and David C. King, "Partisan Mobilization Campaigns in the Field: Results from a Statewide Turnout Experiment in Michigan," *Political Research Quarterly,* vol. 59, no. 1 (2006): 85–97.

24. Ramírez, "Giving Voice to Latino Voters."

25. Janelle S. Wong, "Mobilizing Asian American Voters: A Field Experiment," *Annals of the American Academy of Political and Social Science,* vol. 601, no. 1 (2005): 102–14.

26. Preliminary evidence suggests that commercial phone banks do not appear to generate "spillover effects." In their study of phone calls in Illinois in 2004, Arceneux, Gerber, and Green found no evidence that people living in two-voter households were more likely to vote as a result of their housemate having been called. Similarly, Ha and Karlan's study of a commercial phone bank effort in North Carolina and Missouri in 2004 failed to find evidence of spillover within two-voter households. Arceneaux, Gerber, and Green, "A Cautionary Note on the Use of Matching to Estimate Causal Effects"; Ha and Karlan, "Get-Out-the-Vote Phone Calls."

Chapter Seven

1. Pew Internet and American Life Project, "The Internet News Audience Goes Ordinary," unpublished manuscript (Pew Research Center for People and the Press, 1999); Pew Internet and American Life Project, "Internet Activities," unpublished manuscript (Pew Research Center for People and the Press, 2007).

2. John Anthony Phillips, "Using E-Mail to Mobilize Young Voters: A Field Experiment," unpublished manuscript (Yale University, May 21, 2001).

3. David W. Nickerson, "Does E-mail Boost Turnout?" unpublished manuscript (University of Notre Dame, 2007).

4. Nickerson, "Does E-mail Boost Turnout?"

5. Alissa F. Stollwerk, "Does E-mail Affect Voter Turnout? An Experimental Study of the New York City 2005 Election," unpublished manuscript (Yale University, 2006).

6. While similar in many ways, 501(c)(4) organizations differ from 501(c)(3)s in their range of political activity. 501(c)(4)s can do an unlimited amount of lobbying, whereas 501(c)(3)s are more constrained. Only 501(c)(4)s are permitted to engage in political campaign activity, and that activity must be consistent with the organization's mission, but not be its primary purpose.

7. Note that 7.9 percent of the control group also recalled receiving this e-mail, which attests to the low reliability of survey-based measures of campaign exposure.

8. Tiffany C. Davenport, "Unsubscribe: New Evidence that E-mail Mobilization Can Be Effective after All; Results from a Randomized Field Experiment Comparing the Effects of Peer-to-Peer and Mass E-mail Messages on Voter Turnout," unpublished manuscript (Yale University, Institution for Social and Policy Studies, 2007).

9. Allison Dale and Aaron Strauss, "Text Messaging as a Youth Mobilization Tool: An Experiment with a Post-Treatment Survey," paper presented at the Annual Meeting of the American Political Science Association, Chicago, August 30–September 2, 2007.

10. Two prior text-messaging experiments were smaller in scope and generated less precise estimates. Ryan Friedrichs, "Young Voter Mobilization in 2004: Analysis of Outreach, Persuasion, and Turnout of 18–29-Year-Old Progressive Voters," unpublished manuscript (Skyline Public Works, 2006); Costas Panagopoulos, "The Impact of SMS Text Messages on Voter Turnout," unpublished manuscript (Fordham University, 2007).

Chapter Eight

1. Elizabeth M. Addonizio, Donald P. Green, and James M. Glaser, "Putting the Party Back into Politics: An Experiment Testing Whether Election Day Festivals Increase Voter Turnout," *PS: Political Science and Politics,* vol. 40, no. 3 (2007): 721–27.

2. "Parade in the Eighth Ward," *Hartford Daily Courant,* October 28, 1884, p. 3.

3. Addonizio, Green, and Glaser, "Putting the Party Back into Politics."

4. Adria Lawrence and Bethany Albertson, "How Does Television Change Us? An Analysis of Three Field Experiments," paper presented at the Annual Meeting of the American Association of Public Opinion Research, Miami, May 12–15, 2005.

5. Sendhil Mullainathan, Ebonya Washington, and Julia Azari, "The Impact of Electoral Debate on Public Opinions: An Experimental Investigation of the 2005 New York City Mayoral Election," unpublished manuscript (Yale University, Institution for Social and Policy Studies, 2007).

6. David W. Nickerson, "Results from the Spring 2006 *Candidates Gone Wild* Experiment," unpublished manuscript (Notre Dame University, Department of Political Science, 2007).

7. Elizabeth Addonizio, "Reducing Inequality in Political Participation: An Experiment to Measure the Effects of Voting Instruction on Youth Voter Turnout," paper presented at the Annual Meeting of the American Political Science Association, Chicago, September 2–5, 2004.

8. Several of the experiments were conducted in New Hampshire, a same-day registration state. Before conducting the First-Time Voter Program in New Hampshire, it was not clear what role registering the students to vote was having on the analysis. The New Hampshire studies helped to isolate the effects of the program not attributable to voter registration.

Chapter Nine

1. For one discussion of mass media and media consultants for smaller campaigns, see, for example, J. Sherie Strachan, *High-Tech Grass Roots: The Professionalization of Local Elections* (New York: Rowman and Littlefield, 2003). For a discussion of targeting and media, see, for example, Daniel M. Shea and Michael John Burton, *Campaign Craft: The Strategies, Tactics, and Art of Political Campaign Management* (Westport, Conn.: Praeger, 2001).

2. Jonathan Krasno and Donald Green, "Do Televised Presidential Ads Increase Voter Turnout? Evidence from a Natural Experiment," *Journal of Politics* (forthcoming, 2008).

3. Scott Ashworth and Joshua D. Clinton, "Does Advertising Exposure Affect Turnout?" *Quarterly Journal of Political Science,* vol. 2, no. 1 (2007): 27–41.

4. Joshua D. Clinton and John S. Lapinski, "'Targeted' Advertising and Voter Turnout: An Experimental Study of the 2000 Presidential Election," *Journal of Politics,* vol. 66, no. 1 (2004): 69–96.

5. Lynn Vavreck and Donald P. Green, "Do Public Service Announcements Increase Voter Turnout? Results from a Randomized Field Experiment," paper presented at the Annual Meeting of the American Political Science Association, Chicago, September 2–5, 2004.

6. Donald P. Green and Lynn Vavreck, "Analysis of Cluster-Randomized Experiments: A Comparison of Alternative Estimation Approaches," *Political Analysis* (forthcoming, December 2007).

7. Perhaps reflecting its putative effectiveness as a mobilizing tool, the "military draft" ad acquired some notoriety during the presidential campaign when the chairman of the Republican National Committee, Ed Gillespie, wrote a widely publicized letter to Rock the Vote's president demanding that the organization stop talking about the issue of the military draft. In his letter, Gillespie declared that the draft issue was an "urban myth" and that the ad and its campaign were being conducted with "reckless disregard for the truth." He also took Rock the Vote to task for calling themselves a nonpartisan 501(c)(3) group. Copies of the chairman's letter were also sent to the presidents of major networks, such as NBC, MTV, and HBO, whereupon Rock the Vote expanded the "carbon copy" list to include political humorists like Jon Stewart and David Letterman. Although the Rock the Vote ads became news in their own right, they

were aired relatively infrequently. Rock the Vote does not pay television stations to air its material; rather, it relies on its corporate partners to place its ads for free, as public service announcements. As a result, the ads were seldom shown in smaller media markets, where Rock the Vote's corporate partners had little control over television programming.

8. Costas Panagopoulos and Donald P. Green, "Field Experiments Testing the Impact of Radio Advertisements on Electoral Competition," *American Journal of Political Science* (forthcoming, 2008).

9. Costas Panagopoulos and Donald P. Green, "Preliminary Results from the 2006 Spanish-Language Radio Experiment," unpublished manuscript (Yale University, Institution for Social and Policy Studies, 2007).

10. Matthew Gentzkow, "Television and Voter Turnout," *Quarterly Journal of Economics,* vol. 121, no. 3 (2006): 931–72.

11. Alan Gerber, Dean S. Karlan, and Daniel Bergan, "Does the Media Matter? A Field Experiment Measuring the Effect of Newspapers on Voting Behavior and Political Opinions," Economic Applications and Policy Discussion Paper 12 (Yale University, February 15, 2006).

12. Panagopoulos and Green, "Field Experiments Testing the Impact of Radio Advertisements on Electoral Competition."

13. Steve Strauss, "TV as a Great Way to Get the Word Out—and Empty Your Wallet, too," *USA Today* (www.usatoday.com/money/smallbusiness/columnist/strauss/2003-08-25-tv_x.htm [August 25, 2003]).

Chapter Ten

1. Anthony G. Greenwald, Catherine G. Carnot, Rebecca Beach, and Barbara Young, "Increasing Voting Behavior by Asking People If They Expect to Vote," *Journal of Applied Psychology,* vol. 72 (May 1987): 315–18.

2. Roy E. Miller, David A. Bositis, and Denise L. Baer, "Stimulating Voter Turnout in a Primary: Field Experiment with a Precinct Committeeman," *International Political Science Review,* vol. 2, no. 4 (1981): table 1.

3. Jennifer K. Smith, Alan S. Gerber, and Anton Orlich, "Self-Prophecy Effects and Voter Turnout: An Experimental Replication," *Political Psychology,* vol. 24, no. 3 (2003): 594–604; Sendhil Mullainathan, Ebonya Washington, and Julia Azari, "The Impact of Electoral Debate on Public Opinions: An Experimental Investigation of the 2005 New York City Mayoral Election," unpublished manuscript (Yale University, Institution for Social and Policy Studies, 2007).

4. Christopher Mann, "Unintentional Voter Mobilization: Does Participation in Preelection Surveys Increase Voter Turnout?" *Annals of the American Academy of Political and Social Science,* vol. 601, no. 1 (2005): 155–68.

5. For further discussion and evidence on this point, see Alan S. Gerber, Donald P. Green, and David Nickerson, "Testing for Publication Bias in Political Science," *Political Analysis,* vol. 9, no. 4 (2001): 385–92.

6. (www.easyvoter.org/altruesite/files/evguide/Other/EVG%20casestudy.pdf).

7. Raymond E. Wolfinger, Benjamin Highton, and Megan Mullin, "How Postregistration Laws Affect the Turnout of Registrants," CIRCLE Working Paper 15 (University of Maryland, School of Public Policy, 2004).

8. Lisa García Bedolla and Melissa R. Michelson, "Do *Easy Voter Guides* Increase Turnout? Evidence from Asian American Voter Mobilization Experiments," unpublished manuscript (California State University, East Bay, 2007).

9. Alan S. Gerber, Donald P. Green, and Ron Shachar, "Voting May Be Habit Forming: Evidence from a Randomized Field Experiment," *American Journal of Political Science,* vol. 47, no. 3 (2003): 540–50.

10. Melissa R. Michelson, "Dos Palos Revisited: Testing the Lasting Effects of Voter Mobilization," paper presented at the Annual Meeting of the Midwest Political Science Association, April 3–6, 2003; David W. Nickerson, "Habit Formation from the 2001 Youth Vote Experiments," ISPS Working Paper (Yale University, Institution for Social and Policy Studies, December 15, 2003); David W. Nickerson, "Habit Formation from 2002 Placebo Controlled Experiments," ISPS Working Paper (Yale University, Institution for Social and Policy Studies, December 16, 2003). Taken together, these studies imply that each vote in the current election generates an additional 32.5 votes in the subsequent election (SE = 12.4). It is also true of the mail experiment revealing recipients' past voting record. The August intervention had significant effects the following November, although it remains to be seen whether these effects will persist through subsequent elections.

11. Donald Green, "Field Experiments Testing the Effects of Absentee Ballot Requests," unpublished manuscript (Yale University, Institution for Social and Policy Studies, 2007).

12. Julia Gray and Philip Potter, "Does Signaling Matter in Elections? Evidence from a Field Experiment," paper presented at the Annual Meeting of the American Political Science Association, Chicago, August 30–September 2, 2007.

13. Note that all the names you attempted to call belong in the treatment group, even those who could not be reached when called.

14. Kevin Arceneaux, Alan S. Gerber, and Donald P. Green, "A Cautionary Note on the Use of Matching to Estimate Causal Effects: An Empirical Example Comparing Matching Estimates to an Experimental Benchmark," unpublished manuscript (Yale University, Institution for Social and Policy Studies, 2007).

15. If you took out a set of observations before random assignment, you should note this.

16. Jeffrey A. Karp and Susan A. Banducci, "The Impact of Proportional Representation on Turnout: Evidence from New Zealand," *Australian Journal of Political Science,* vol. 34, no. 3 (1999): 363–77.

17. Mary Fitzgerald, "Greater Convenience but Not Greater Turnout," *American Politics Research,* vol. 33, no. 6 (2005): 842–67; Jan E. Leighley and Jonathan Nagler, "Electoral Laws and Turnout, 1972–2004," paper presented at the Annual Meeting of the American Political Science Association, Chicago, August 30–September 2, 2007. The introduction of Election Day registration in other states will shed further light on the effectiveness of this policy in raising turnout.

18. For reports that campaigns on both the right and left were attentive to experimental studies of GOTV tactics, see David Frum, "Bush's Secret Canadian Weapon," *National Post,* August 2, 2005, p. A12, and Matt Bai, "Who Lost Ohio," *New York Times Magazine,* November 21, 2004, p. 67.

19. The advantage of randomizing at the precinct level is that results can be gathered quickly, inexpensively, and without problems of attrition. The disadvantage is the cost of treating entire precincts or significant portions of them. The advantage of survey measures is the ability to measure effects within subgroups. The disadvantages are costs and problems of nonresponse. Nonresponse in particular may prevent one from being able to generalize beyond the population of people with a fairly high level of interest in politics.

Appendix A

1. The exceptions are a pair of canvassing experiments in which random assignment was performed at the precinct, rather than the household level. Extracting efficient estimates from this design requires one to control for past voting patterns. See Kevin Arceneaux, "Using Cluster Randomized Field Experiments to Study Voting Behavior," *Annals of the American Academy of Political and Social Science,* vol. 601, no. 1 (2005): 169–79.

2. Samuel J. Eldersveld, "Experimental Propaganda Techniques and Voting Behavior," *American Political Science Review,* vol. 50 (March 1956): 154–65; Roy E. Miller, David A. Bositis, and Denise L. Baer, "Stimulating Voter Turnout in a Primary: Field Experiment with a Precinct Committeeman," *International Political Science Review,* vol. 2, no. 4 (1981): 445–60.

3. Alan S. Gerber and Donald P. Green, "The Effects of Canvassing, Direct Mail, and Telephone Contact on Voter Turnout: A Field Experiment," *American Political Science Review,* vol. 94, no. 3 (2000): 653–63.

4. These results are slightly different from those reported in the article, given some post-publication corrections to the data. See Alan S. Gerber and Donald P. Green, "Correction to Gerber and Green (2000), Replication of Disputed Findings, and Reply to Imai (2005)," *American Political Science Review,* vol. 99, no. 2 (2005): 301–13.

5. Donald P. Green and Alan S. Gerber, "Getting Out the Youth Vote: Results from Randomized Field Experiments," unpublished manuscript (Yale University, Institution for Social and Policy Studies, 2001).

6. Donald P. Green, Alan S. Gerber, and David W. Nickerson, "Getting Out the Vote in Local Elections: Results from Six Door-to-Door Canvassing Experiments," *Journal of Politics,* vol. 65, no. 4 (2003): 1083–096.

7. David W. Nickerson, "Memo on the Effectiveness of Messages Used in Door-to-Door Canvassing Prior to the 2001 Elections," unpublished manuscript (Yale University, Institution for Social and Policy Studies, 2002).

8. Melissa R. Michelson, "Getting Out the Latino Vote: How Door-to-Door Canvassing Influences Voter Turnout in Rural Central California," *Political Behavior,* vol. 25, no. 3 (2003): 247–63.

9. Melissa R. Michelson and Herbert Villa Jr., "Mobilizing the Latino Youth Vote," paper presented at the Annual Meeting of the Western Political Science Association, Denver, Colo., March 27–29, 2003. This project, like Michelson's other experiments, is described in Melissa R. Michelson, "Meeting the Challenge of Latino Voter Mobilization," *Annals of the American Academy of Political and Social Science,* vol. 601, no. 1 (2005): 85–101.

10. Elizabeth A. Bennion, "Message, Context, and Turnout: A Voter Mobilization Field Experiment," paper presented at the Annual Meeting of the Midwest Political Science Association, Chicago, April 3–6, 2003.

11. David W. Nickerson, "Measuring Interpersonal Influence," Ph.D. dissertation, Yale University, Department of Political Science, 2004. An article-length version of this experiment is forthcoming in the *American Political Science Review.*

12. David W. Nickerson, Ryan D. Friedrichs, and David C. King, "Partisan Mobilization Campaigns in the Field: Results of a Statewide Turnout Experiment in Michigan," *Political Research Quarterly,* vol. 59, no. 1 (2006): 85–97.

13. Andra Nicole Gillespie, "Community, Coordination, and Context: A Black Politics Perspective on Voter Mobilization," Ph.D. dissertation, Yale University, Department of Political Science, 2005. The results for St. Louis reported here are based on a reanalysis that excludes those who were also exposed to a phone-calling campaign.

14. Arceneaux, "Using Cluster Randomized Field Experiments to Study Voting Behavior."

15. Kevin Arceneaux, "I'm Asking for Your Support: The Effects of Personally Delivered Campaign Messages on Voting Decisions and Opinion Formation," *Quarterly Journal of Political Science,* vol. 2, no. 1 (2007): 43–65. We are grateful to Kevin Arceneaux for providing a bivariate probit analysis for our meta analysis.

16. Carrie LeVan, "The Vicious Cycle and the Low-Propensity Voter," unpublished manuscript (California State University, Bakersfield, 2007).

17. Gregg R. Murray and Richard E. Matland, "Increasing Voter Turnout in the Hispanic Community: A Field Experiment on the Effects of Canvassing, Leafleting, Telephone Calls, and Direct Mail," paper presented at the Annual Meeting of the Midwest Political Science Association, Chicago, April 7–10, 2005.

18. Kevin Arceneaux and David W. Nickerson, "Even If You Have Nothing Nice to Say, Go Ahead and Say It: Two Field Experiments Testing Negative Campaign Tactics," unpublished manuscript (Temple University and University of Notre Dame, 2007).

19. Joel Middleton, "Are Canonical Findings in the Mobilization Literature Externally Valid? An Experimental Field Study of Canvassing in the 2004 Presidential Election," unpublished manuscript (Yale University, 2007).

20. Julia Gray and Philip Potter, "Does Signaling Matter in Elections? Evidence from a Field Experiment," paper presented at the Annual Meeting of the American Political Science Association, Chicago, August 30–September 2, 2007.

21. Melissa Michelson, Lisa García Bedolla, and Donald P. Green, *New Experiments in Minority Voter Mobilization: A Report on the California Votes Initiative*

(San Francisco: James Irvine Foundation, 2007). Our meta analysis incorporates results from all groups participating in the initiative, including one whose results are not included in the report. The results included in our meta analysis do not include covariates and do not weight or exclude subsamples.

22. David W. Nickerson, "Results from 2006 Clean Water Canvassing Experiment in Grand Rapids," report to the Michigan Center for Civic Participation, 2007.

Appendix B

1. Harold F. Gosnell, *Getting-Out-the-Vote: An Experiment in the Stimulation of Voting* (University of Chicago Press, 1927).

2. Samuel J. Eldersveld, "Experimental Propaganda Techniques and Voting Behavior," *American Political Science Review,* vol. 50 (March 1956): 154–65; Roy E. Miller, David A. Bositis, and Denise L. Baer, "Stimulating Voter Turnout in a Primary: Field Experiment with a Precinct Committeeman," *International Political Science Review,* vol. 2, no. 4 (1981): 445–60.

3. Alan S. Gerber and Donald P. Green, "The Effects of Canvassing, Direct Mail, and Telephone Contact on Voter Turnout: A Field Experiment," *American Political Science Review,* vol. 94, no. 3 (2000): 653–63. The results reported here are slightly different from those reported in the article, given some post-publication corrections to the data. See Alan S. Gerber and Donald P. Green, "Correction to Gerber and Green (2000), Replication of Disputed Findings, and Reply to Imai (2005)," *American Political Science Review,* vol. 99, no. 2 (2005): 301–13.

4. Alan S. Gerber, Donald P. Green, and Matthew N. Green, "Direct Mail and Voter Turnout: Results from Seven Randomized Field Experiments," unpublished manuscript (Yale University, Institution for Social and Policy Studies, 2000). The results here have been updated slightly from the first edition.

5. Alan S. Gerber, Donald P. Green, and Matthew N. Green, "The Effects of Partisan Direct Mail on Voter Turnout," *Electoral Studies,* vol. 22, no. 4 (2003): 563–79.

6. Janelle Wong, "Getting Out the Vote among Asian Americans in Los Angeles County: A Field Experiment," *Annals of the American Academy of Political and Social Science,* vol. 601, no. 1 (2005): 102–14.

7. Donald P. Green, "Mobilizing African American Voters Using Direct Mail and Commercial Phone Banks: A Field Experiment," *Political Research Quarterly,* vol. 57, no. 2 (2004): 245–55.

8. Alan S. Gerber, "Memo on the Effects of Partisan Direct Mail: Precinct-Level Experiments on Voter Turnout in a Congressional District," unpublished manuscript (Yale University, Institution for Social and Policy Studies, 2003).

9. Emily Arthur Cardy, "An Experimental Field Study of the GOTV and Persuasion Effects of Partisan Direct Mail and Phone Calls," *Annals of the American Academy of Political and Social Science,* vol. 601, no. 1 (2005): 28–40.

10. David Niven, "A Field Experiment on the Effects of Negative Campaign Mail on Voter Turnout in a Municipal Election," *Political Research Quarterly,* vol. 59, no. 2 (2006): 203–10.

11. Julia Gray and Philip Potter, "Does Signaling Matter in Elections? Evidence from a Field Experiment," paper presented at the Annual Meeting of the American Political Science Association, Chicago, August 30–September 2, 2007.

12. Ricardo Ramírez, "Giving Voice to Latino Voters: A Field Experiment on the Effectiveness of a National Nonpartisan Mobilization Effort," *Annals of the American Academy of Political and Social Science,* vol. 601, no. 1 (2005): 66–84.

13. Neema Trivedi, "The Effect of Identity-Based GOTV Direct Mail Appeals on the Turnout of Indian Americans," *Annals of the American Academy of Political and Social Science,* vol. 601, no. 1 (2005): 115–22.

14. Gregg R. Murray and Richard E. Matland, "Increasing Voter Turnout in the Hispanic Community: A Field Experiment on the Effects of Canvassing, Leafleting, Telephone Calls, and Direct Mail," paper presented at the Annual Meeting of the Midwest Political Science Association, Chicago, April 7–10, 2005.

15. Wendy Tam Cho, James Gimpel, and Daron Shaw, "Turning Out the Vote in Texas," paper presented at the Annual Meeting of the American Political Science Association, Washington, September 1–4, 2005. We are grateful to these authors for sharing with us their data on Chinese and Vietnamese Americans.

16. Christopher Mann, "Field Experimentation in Political Communication for Mobilization," Ph.D. dissertation, Yale University, Department of Political Science, 2008.

17. Melissa Michelson, Lisa García Bedolla, and Donald P. Green, *New Experiments in Minority Voter Mobilization: A Report on the James Irvine Foundation's California Votes Initiative* (San Francisco: James Irvine Foundation, 2007).

18. Jason Barabas, Charles Barrilleaux, and Daniel Scheller, "Issue Turnout: Field Experiments with Ballot Initiatives in Florida," paper presented at the Annual Meeting of the American Political Science Association, Chicago, August 30–September 2, 2007.

19. Alan S. Gerber, Donald P. Green, and Christopher W. Larimer. "Social Pressure and Voter Turnout: Evidence from a Large-Scale Field Experiment," *American Political Science Review* (forthcoming, February 2008).

Appendix C

1. Samuel J. Eldersveld, "Experimental Propaganda Techniques and Voting Behavior," *American Political Science Review,* vol. 50 (March 1956): 154–65; Roy E. Miller, David A. Bositis, and Denise L. Baer, "Stimulating Voter Turnout in a Primary: Field Experiment with a Precinct Committeeman," *International Political Science Review,* vol. 2, no. 4 (1981): 445–60; William C. Adams and Dennis J. Smith, "Effects of Telephone Canvassing on Turnout and Preferences: A Field Experiment," *Public Opinion Quarterly,* vol. 44 (Autumn 1980): 53–83.

2. Alan S. Gerber and Donald P. Green, "The Effects of Canvassing, Direct Mail, and Telephone Contact on Voter Turnout: A Field Experiment," *American Political Science Review,* vol. 94, no. 3 (2000): 653–63. These figures differ from the published results due to post-publication corrections to the data; see Alan S. Gerber and Donald P. Green, "Correction to Gerber and Green (2000),

Replication of Disputed Findings, and Reply to Imai (2005)," *American Political Science Review,* vol. 99, no. 2 (2005): 301–13.

3. Alan S. Gerber and Donald P. Green, "Do Phone Calls Increase Voter Turnout? A Field Experiment," *Public Opinion Quarterly,* vol. 65, no. 1 (2001): 75–85. These figures differ from the published results due to post-publication corrections to the data; see Alan S. Gerber and Donald P. Green, "Do Phone Calls Increase Turnout? An Update," *Annals of the American Academy of Political and Social Science,* vol. 601, no. 1 (2005): 142–54.

4. Donald P. Green and Alan S. Gerber, "Getting Out the Youth Vote: Results from Randomized Field Experiments," unpublished manuscript (Yale University, Institution for Social and Policy Studies, 2001). This work was subsequently published in David Nickerson, "Volunteer Phone Calls Can Increase Turnout," *American Politics Research,* vol. 34, no. 3 (2006): 271–92.

5. Donald P. Green, "Mobilizing African Americans Using Direct Mail and Commercial Phone Banks: A Field Experiment," *Political Research Quarterly,* vol. 57, no. 2 (2004): 245–55.

6. Nickerson, "Volunteer Phone Calls Can Increase Turnout."

7. Emily Arthur Cardy, "An Experimental Field Study of the GOTV and Persuasion Effects of Partisan Direct Mail and Phone Calls," *Annals of the American Academy of Political and Social Science,* vol. 601, no. 1 (2005): 28–40.

8. Kevin Arceneaux, Alan S. Gerber, and Donald P. Green, "Comparing Experimental and Matching Methods using a Large-Scale Voter Mobilization Experiment," *Political Analysis,* vol. 14, no. 1 (2006): 1–36.

9. Donald P. Green, Alan S. Gerber, and David W. Nickerson, "The Challenge of Bringing Voter Mobilization 'To Scale': An Evaluation of Youth Vote's 2002 Phone Banking Campaigns," unpublished manuscript (Yale University, Institution for Social and Policy Studies, 2003).

10. David W. Nickerson, Ryan D. Friedrichs, and David C. King, "Partisan Mobilization Campaigns in the Field: Results from a Statewide Turnout Experiment in Michigan," *Political Research Quarterly,* vol. 59, no. 1 (2006): 85–97.

11. John E. McNulty, "Phone-Based GOTV: What's on the Line? Field Experiments with Varied Partisan Components, 2002–2003," *Annals of the American Academy of Political and Social Science,* vol. 601, no. 1 (2005): 41–65.

12. Janelle S. Wong, "Mobilizing Asian American Voters: A Field Experiment," *Annals of the American Academy of Political and Social Science,* vol. 601, no. 1 (2005): 102–14.

13. Ricardo Ramírez, "Giving Voice to Latino Voters: A Field Experiment on the Effectiveness of a National Nonpartisan Mobilization Effort," *Annals of the American Academy of Political and Social Science,* vol. 601, no. 1 (2005): 66–84.

14. This study, which was conducted by Donald Green and Heather Smith, is described in Melissa R. Michelson, Lisa García Bedolla, and Margaret A. McConnell, "Heeding the Call: The Effect of Targeted Phone Banks on Voter Turnout," unpublished manuscript (California State University, East Bay, 2007).

15. Shang E. Ha and Dean S. Karlan, "Get-Out-the-Vote Phone Calls: Does Quality Matter?" unpublished manuscript (Yale University, Institution for Social and Policy Studies, 2007).

16. Kevin Arceneaux, Alan S. Gerber, and Donald P. Green, "A Cautionary Note on the Use of Matching to Estimate Causal Effects: An Empirical Example Comparing Matching Estimates to an Experimental Benchmark," unpublished manuscript (Yale University, Institution for Social and Policy Studies, 2007).

17. Donald P. Green, "A Study of an Advocacy Group's Voter Mobilization Efforts in a Democratic Congressional Primary," unpublished manuscript (Yale University, 2007).

18. Jason Barabas, Charles Barrilleaux, and Daniel Scheller, "Issue Turnout: Field Experiments with Ballot Initiatives in Florida," paper presented at the Annual Meeting of the American Political Science Association, Chicago, August 30–September 2, 2007.

19. Melissa Michelson, Lisa García Bedolla, and Donald P. Green, *New Experiments in Minority Voter Mobilization: A Report on the California Votes Initiative* (San Francisco: James Irvine Foundation, 2007).

20. Joel A. Middleton, "Relationship Management: Experimental Evaluation of MoveOn's Outreach in a Special Election in California's 50th District," unpublished manuscript (Yale University, 2007).

21. Christopher Mann, "Field Experimentation in Political Communication for Mobilization," Ph.D. dissertation, Yale University, Department of Political Science, 2008.

22. Donald P. Green and Daron R. Shaw, "Do Robo Calls from Credible Sources Affect Voting Behavior?" unpublished manuscript (Yale University, 2007).

Index